Speakers and the Speakership

Presiding Officers and the Management of Business from the
Middle Ages to the 21st Century

Edited by

Paul Seaward

Wiley-Blackwell

for

The Parliamentary History Yearbook Trust

This edition first published 2010
© 2010 Parliamentary Yearbook Trust

Blackwell Publishing was acquired by John Wiley & Sons in February 2007. Blackwell's publishing programme has been merged with Wiley's global Scientific, Technical, and Medical business to form Wiley-Blackwell.

Registered Office
John Wiley & Sons Ltd, The Atrium, Southern Gate, Chichester, West Sussex, PO19 8SQ, UK

Editorial Offices
350 Main Street, Malden, MA 02148-5020, USA
9600 Garsington Road, Oxford, OX4 2DQ, UK
The Atrium, Southern Gate, Chichester, West Sussex, PO19 8SQ, UK

For details of our global editorial offices, for customer services, and for information about how to apply for permission to re-use the copyright material in this book please see our website at http://www.wiley.com/wiley-blackwell.

The right of Paul Seaward to be identified as the editor of this work has been asserted in accordance with the Copyright, Designs and Patents Act 1988.

Wiley also publishes its books in a variety of electronic formats. Some content that appears in print may not be available in electronic books.

Designations used by companies to distinguish their products are often claimed as trademarks. All brand names and product names used in this book are trade names, service marks, trademarks or registered trademarks of their respective owners. The publisher is not associated with any product or vendor mentioned in this book. This publication is designed to provide accurate and authoritative information in regard to the subject matter covered. It is sold on the understanding that the publisher is not engaged in rendering professional services. If professional advice or other expert assistance is required, the services of a competent professional should be sought.

Library of Congress Cataloging-in-Publication Data
Speakers and the speakership : presiding officers and the management of business from the middle ages to the twenty-first century / edited by Paul Seaward.
    p. cm.
  Includes index.
  ISBN 978-1-4443-3289-6 (pbk. : alk. paper)   1. Great Britain. Parliament. House of Commons–Speakers.   2. Great Britain–Politics and government.   I. Seaward, Paul.
  JN678.S67 2010
  328.41′0762–dc22

                                                                                            2009044657

A catalogue record for this book is available from the British Library.

Set in 10/12 Pt Bembo by Toppan Best-set Premedia Limited
Printed and bound in Singapore
By Hó Printing Pte Ltd

1   2010

CONTENTS

List of Contributors   iv

PAUL SEAWARD, Introduction   1

ANNE CURRY, Speakers at War in the Late 14th and 15th Centuries   8

ALASDAIR HAWKYARD, The Tudor Speakers 1485–1601:
   Choosing, Status, Work   22

ALAN R. MACDONALD, Chancellors, Presidents and Speakers:
   Presiding Officers in the Scottish Parliament before the Restoration   49

COLEMAN A. DENNEHY, Speakers in the 17th-Century Irish Parliament   62

STEPHEN K. ROBERTS, The Reputation and Authority of the Speaker and
   the Speakership of the House of Commons, 1640–60   75

PAUL SEAWARD, The Speaker in the Age of Party, 1672–1715   90

RUTH PALEY, The Speakership of the House of Lords, 1660–1832   102

RICHARD W. DAVIS, Thurlow, Eldon and Lyndhurst and the Management
   of the House of Lords   118

SIR WILLIAM MCKAY, 'Nothing Could Exceed the Badness of
   His Character Even in This Bad Age'   129

THE RT HON. BARONESS BOOTHROYD, The Role of the Speaker in the
   20th Century   136

Index   145

LIST OF CONTRIBUTORS

The Rt Hon. Baroness Boothroyd, OM, PC was MP for West Bromwich and West Bromwich West from 1973 to 2000, deputy chairman of ways and means and deputy Speaker from 1987 to 1992 and Speaker of the house of commons from 1992 to 2000. Her autobiography was published in 2001. In 2005 she was appointed to the Order of Merit.

Anne Curry is professor of medieval history and head of the School of Humanities at the University of Southampton. She edited the 1422–53 section of the multi-volume *Parliament Rolls of Medieval England 1275–1504* (2005). She has published extensively on the Hundred Years War, especially on its 15th-century phase. She is the author of *Agincourt: A New History* (2005) and co-director of an Arts and Humanities Research Council-funded project 'The Soldier in Later Medieval England', which aims to create a searchable database of soldiers serving the English crown between 1369 and 1453. She is also president of the Historical Association (2008–11).

Richard W. Davis is emeritus professor of history at Washington University in St Louis. Educated at Amherst College, Columbia University and Cambridge University, he previously taught at the University of Rhode Island and the University of California, Riverside. Among his publications, the most recent is *A Political History of the House of Lords, 1811–1846: From the Regency to Corn Law Repeal* (Stanford, CA, 2008). Others include *Dissent in Politics, 1780–1830: The Political Life of William Smith, MP* (1971); *Political Change and Continuity, 1760–1885: A Buckinghamshire Study* (Newton Abbot, 1972); *Disraeli* (1976); *The English Rothschilds* (1983).

Coleman A. Dennehy teaches several courses at St Patrick's College, Maynooth in Ireland, mostly on early modern Ireland and also specifically on the Irish parliament (1200–1800). He has recently published, as editor, *Restoration Ireland: Always Settling and Never Settled* (Aldershot, 2008) and *History Matters* (Dublin, 2004). His research tends to focus on Irish parliamentary procedure in the 17th century.

Alasdair Hawkyard is a fellow of the Royal Historical Society. For 14 years he was co-editor and principal research assistant under S.T. Bindoff on the House of Commons 1509–58 section of the History of Parliament. He is currently completing the introductory survey to the volumes entitled *The History of Parliament: The House of Commons 1509–1558*, ed. S.T. Bindoff (3 vols, 1982).

Alan MacDonald is a lecturer in early modern Scottish history at the University of Dundee. His published works include *The Jacobean Kirk 1567–1625: Sovereignty, Polity and Liturgy* (1998); *The Burghs and Parliament in Scotland c.1550–1651* (2007) and a number of articles on ecclesiastical and parliamentary history.

Sir William McKay graduated from the University of Edinburgh in 1961. He joined the department of the clerk of the house of commons and served until 2002, being clerk of the House and chief executive of the House service from 1998 to 2002. He was honorary professor in the School of Law, University of Aberdeen (2003–7). He is observer, Council of the Law Society of Scotland (2006–present). He is author of *Clerks in the House of Commons 1383–1989: A Biographical List, Observations, Rules and Orders, an Early Procedural Collection* (1989) and (with Charles W. Johnson, formerly parliamentarian of the house of representatives) *Congress and Parliament Revisited* (forthcoming). He was editor of *Erskine May*, 23rd edn.

Ruth Paley is editor of the History of the House of Lords 1660–1832 section of the History of Parliament and was previously an assistant keeper at the Public Record Office. She is currently involved in the international *Blackstone Variorum* project which aims to produce an accessible modern scholarly text of the various editions of William Blackstone's *Commentaries on the Laws of England* that appeared during his lifetime. In collaboration with Elaine A. Reynolds, she is also preparing a monograph on the policing of London during the long 18th century. She is honorary editor of *Archives*, the journal of the British Records Association, a director of Archives for London and honorary treasurer of the British Association for Local History.

Stephen K. Roberts is editor of the House of Commons 1640–60 section of the History of Parliament. He is the author of a number of books and articles on mid-17th-century England and Wales, and has contributed to the *Oxford Dictionary of National Biography*. He is an editor of the journal *Midland History* and is general editor of the Worcestershire Historical Society.

Paul Seaward has been director of the History of Parliament since 2001. Previously he was a deputy principal clerk in the house of commons. His publications include *The Cavalier Parliament and the Reconstruction of the Old Regime, 1661–67* (1989), an edition of Thomas Hobbes, *Behemoth* (2009) and books and articles on 17th-century politics and political thought and on parliament in the 20th century. He is the general editor, with Martin Dzelzainis, of an edition of the works of Edward Hyde, earl of Clarendon.

Introduction

PAUL SEAWARD

The speakership of the house of commons is one of the oldest civil offices in the British state, certainly one of the oldest ones of any continuing significance, with origins in the late 14th century. The lord chancellorship is older still. Its connection with parliament dates back as far as the institution itself, although the office pre-dates what we would regard as a parliament, it had functions well beyond the simply parliamentary and its powers in the House were relatively weak. Moreover, since 2006 the link between the two positions has been formally broken, as the Lord Speaker has replaced the chancellor as chair of the House, bringing the role much closer to (but still quite distinct from) that of the Speaker in the Commons.

Prominent and ancient as they are, neither role as such has attracted much sustained academic attention, as opposed to walk-on parts in innumerable studies of Westminster politics. The most recent extended study of the history and functions of the Commons speakership remains the still essential 1964 book by Philip Laundy, then librarian of the Legislative Assembly of Southern Rhodesia.[1] More recent contributions have largely concerned the period after 1945, and have been connected with current controversies about the speakership.[2] There have been even fewer attempts to view the chancellorship in a broad historical perspective.[3] While much has been done since 1964 to amend and deepen our understanding of the history of parliament and politics from the middle ages onwards, little of this has had much impact on our understanding of the origins and operation of two of the most significant offices in the constitution of the United Kingdom. At a conference held in the Jubilee Room off Westminster Hall on 24 April 2008, the History of Parliament Trust and *Parliamentary History* invited a group of political historians to address the chair more directly and to reassess (within the periods of their expertise) the speakership of either House in the context of the advances in our knowledge of English and British political history since Laundy and his predecessors were writing. We also asked for comparative perspectives from Scotland and Ireland and the United States of America. The latter, provided by a former clerk of the house of commons, included reflections on the differential development of the office in two

---

[1] Philip Laundy, *The Office of Speaker* (1964): its predecessors were Michael MacDonagh, *The Speaker of the House* (1914) and Arthur Irwin Dasent, *The Speakers of the House of Commons* (1911). See also Laundy's contribution to S.A. Walkland, *The House of Commons in the Twentieth Century* (Oxford, 1978).

[2] A witness seminar organised by the Centre for Contemporary British History at the house of commons in 2002 covered 'The Role of the Speaker of the House of Commons' (available online at *http://www.ccbh.ac.uk* (accessed 7 September 2009). See also the notes by the Parliament and Constitution Centre of the House of Commons Library on the subject: *http://www.parliament.uk/commons/lib/research/briefings/snpc-05074.pdf*; *http://www.parliament.uk/commons/lib/research/briefings/snpc-04637.pdf*; and *http://www.parliament.uk/commons/lib/research/rp2001/rp01-030.pdf* (accessed 7 July 2009).

[3] John Campbell, *Lives of the Lord Chancellors* (8 vols, 1845–69).

jurisdictions which shared a common parliamentary culture. Finally, we invited one of the trustees of the History of Parliament, the former Speaker of the house of commons (1992–2000) Baroness Boothroyd, to give us her own account of what it was like to exercise the office.

Baroness Boothroyd described three roles of the chair in the Commons: the bringing of coherence and order to the proceedings of the House through the selection of Speakers and amendments; the administration of the House (as chair of the house of commons commission); and representing parliament abroad (and she has stressed else-where the extent of her activities in representing parliament to a wide range of audiences within the United Kingdom as well). Underlying her account, though, is a more informal political role, which might be characterised as parliamentary leadership, visible in her vocal defence of the rights of the House against a powerful government machine, and in her responses to the 'sleaze' scandal of the early 1990s.

Earlier Speakers might recognize this account in spirit, if not in detail. The adminis-trative function is the most obvious divergence from the past. Negligible before the House of Commons Offices Act 1812, and a small enough part of the Speaker's routine functions before the House of Commons (Administration) Act 1978, it is now a major preoccupation as the House has become, in spending terms, equivalent to a small government department, spending £478 million a year and employing nearly 3,000 staff – as well as handling budgets for each individual member, which are not only admin-istratively complex but also, as became painfully obvious in the course of 2009, politically misconceived. The speakership (so far as it is possible to tell) originated as a representative role, albeit as a spokesman for the Commons before the Lords and before the king, rather than as one who would promote the standing of the House before national or inter-national audiences. One might imagine, from the growing dominance of the post by lawyers from the 15th century (charted in Anne Curry's contribution to this volume), that the role of presiding officer and referee was, from relatively early on, part of the job, although the lack of any procedural record for the Commons before 1547 makes it impossible to establish. It is just as conceivable that the Speaker's early role was more akin to what many legislatures would refer to as a *rapporteur*.

Past lord chancellors might have more difficulty in assimilating Baroness Boo-throyd's description of her role into their own: chancellors have been members of the government and heads of a separate administrative structure, and in a House which regarded itself as effectively self-regulating, they have never possessed the same powers in respect of the maintenance of order and the facilitation of debate as has the Speaker of the Commons. The pre-union Scottish parliament offers, as Alan MacDonald reminds us, an alternative model for the management and direction of a legislature: the Scottish chancellor presided over a unicameral parliament, in which the presence of the monarch (and in the monarch's absence, the king's commissioner) made his own role rather less significant. Yet, as he also points out, the actual func-tions carried out in the chamber, in so far as they are possible to establish, were not dissimilar to those of the presiding officers at Westminster; the chancellor's subser-vience to the monarch was not qualitatively different from the role of the English chancellor, even if the circumstances in the chamber were different; and there is some evidence that the separate estates – like the two Houses at Westminster – did have their own presidents.

Central to the Westminster tradition of the speakership has been the principle of impartiality, and it is, in one way or another, the theme of many of the articles in this volume. 'Fairness and impartiality are the qualities which, above all, members expect to find in the Speaker and which will secure their support and respect', writes Baroness Boothroyd (see below, p. 136), and the same thing has been said by many Speakers and commentators on the subject, most recently by John Bercow on accepting the chair on 23 June 2009. We commonly regard this as a simple and unproblematic idea, obvious in its application to the function. But the link between the chair and the idea of impartiality is by no means a necessary one. As Sir William McKay points out in his comparison of the speakership in the house of commons and the house of representatives, a model of the office exists in which impartiality (at least with respect to political parties) plays no, or little part, in which the Speaker of the House is a national party figure. Furthermore, the notion of an impartial chair combines several different, not necessarily associated, impartialities, each with its own context and history. The general notion of a judicial lack of bias in any dispute between persons or parties perhaps reflects the House's early role in reviewing individual petitions and was reflected in the tendency for Speakers to go on to high legal or judicial office and in their adoption of a semi-judicial habit.[4] It is the most fundamental sense in which the Speaker has always been required to be impartial. But Speakers are expected, more specifically, to lack partiality towards any individual member or towards any political party, and to be independent of the crown, or the royal government. The history of the speakership in all of these respects is complicated.

The independence of the Speaker of, or his dependence on, the crown has fluctuated over the centuries. Speakers, as its spokesmen, were formally servants of the house of commons; but they were (and are) appointed with the approval of the crown and were frequently its own servants. Anne Curry's investigation of the relationship between the office of Speaker and the military activities of the crown in France in the late 14th and the first half of the 15th century shows how the appointment of a Speaker was a barometer of the relationship between the crown and the house of commons. A number of Speakers proposed in the Commons may possibly have been rejected by the crown. As Alasdair Hawkyard shows, under stronger Tudor government, Speakers were commonly royal councillors, generally proposed by the crown's own spokesmen in the Commons, the comptroller or treasurer of the household, and their appointment planned well in advance in government circles. This was still the practice in the mid 17th century, and a minute of the discussion on the appointment of a Speaker in 1672 indicates that it continued to be 30 years later, after the civil war (see below, p. 91). Coleman Dennehy's study of the Speakers of both Houses of the Irish parliament in the 17th century shows that crown nomination was also the rule there. But even if effectively appointed by the crown, Speakers were, nevertheless, officially the creation and mouth-piece of the Commons, and required frequently to convey unwelcome messages to the monarch. Since they were normally close colleagues of key figures in royal government, Speakers could often be considered to be part of its team of parliamentary managers, their most characteristic behind-the-scenes activity largely lost to us because it took place out of the reach of any written record. The office is best envisaged before the

---

[4] See the comment of Laundy, *The Office of Speaker*, 165. Since 1992 the costume has been abandoned, step by step: Baroness Boothroyd shed the wig and John Bercow has now given up the legal court dress.

construction of party government as a sort of go-between, a bridge between the crown and parliament, as much concerned with political negotiation as with the semi-judicial aspects of the job. Often, the bridge was not so much between the crown and parliament as between parliament and a dominant party or individual at the royal court. Pre-modern Speakers were often associates of powerful, even factional, figures within royal government. But the increasing significance of the Commons and preoccupation with the management of the Commons in the late 17th century meant that a Speaker might need to be a significant political figure in his own right, or through his command of the House might develop into one.

The political and constitutional changes set in train by the 1688 revolution would have a complicated effect on the office. On the one hand, the crown's grip on the post slipped markedly. The rejection of the king's candidate in 1679 was the first instance of a government nominee being refused in the House since the middle ages. Ministers could no longer assume that their candidate would be adopted unproblematically by the House. On the other hand, partisan considerations became much more prominent: the election of the Speaker at the beginning of a parliament became a trial of strength between the parties. In an era of party divisions a Speaker elected by the House would normally share the politics of the majority. At some points during the period between the revolution and the Hanoverian succession, it seemed possible that the speakership would become a key position within the party management of the House, maybe even the leadership of a dominant party – the model which later emerged in the United States, as described by Sir William McKay.

It is not easy to explain why this did not happen, and how the Westminster model of an impartial Speaker won out. For many years the office remained a protean one, its nature dependent on the ability and personality of its holder and the strength of a ministry, and also, no doubt, on how long it was held. With the long parliaments after the 1716 Septennial Act, speakerships became long, sometimes very long: Spencer Compton (13 years) was the first to have held the post for longer than five years since Sir Edward Turnor in the 1660s (12 years – itself a very unusual record, explained only by the peculiar longevity of the Cavalier Parliament); and was followed by Onslow (33 years); Cust (nine years); Norton (ten years); and Cornwall (nine years). There were five Speakers between 1700 and 1715; and five from 1715 to 1789. The long speakership of Arthur Onslow, from 1728 to 1761, has often been seen as creating a new model of impartial and independent Speakers. Certainly Onslow set great store by impartiality: 'I had, by my manner of acting in Parliament, some regard shewn to me from many of every denomination and they had reason to believe, I should be respectful and impartial to all.'[5] But as is now well established, Onslow's speakership exhibited many continuities with his predecessors. Peter Thomas has described the essentially reliable support that Onslow gave to the ministries of Walpole and Henry Pelham in his frequent interventions in committee, and his involvement on a number of occasions in high-level ministerial discussions. And the 'country' ideological baggage which Onslow carried had been packed by Paul Foley, Robert Harley and others of his predecessors in the 1690s and early 18th century (see below, pp. 100–1).

[5] P.D.G. Thomas, *The House of Commons in the Eighteenth Century* (Oxford, 1971), 299.

Perhaps the idea of impartiality became embedded, in part, because at critical points in the post's development, the intensity of the party divisions of the reign of queen Anne drained away. Onslow was already distinguished by his record of independent-minded and uncareerist whiggism before he stepped up to the chair, and he was presumably deliberately chosen for the role by a House which found it easier to agree on a Speaker with a less clear partisan identity. Perhaps it was also because Walpole's dominance of the Commons had been a catalyst for changes in the way the governments approached the management of the lower House. The establishment of a powerful premiership and the concept of a leader of the House left little room for another powerful political organiser. With roles more sharply defined than in the past, the mixed functions of the Speaker – between party leader and impartial chairman – were bound to be squeezed. The situation in the house of lords underlines the point. As Ruth Paley's article reveals, the role of Speaker of the Lords was a much more restricted one in a House which largely regulated itself. Yet politically, lord chancellors were usually far more significant figures than their Commons counterparts: men of the calibre and stature of Clarendon, Shaftesbury, Cowper, Hardwicke, Thurlow, Eldon and Brougham were front-rank politicians, and among their other duties were always deeply engaged in the process of securing reliable majorities in the House; they would also routinely intervene in debate in a way that was becoming very unusual in the Commons. But in the Lords as well as the Commons, the role was affected by the emergence of new and more specialised practices of political management. In the Lords, there was a sort of 'Leader of the House' who organised pre-sessional meetings on behalf of the government from around 1714, although the position only became more formally established in 1783. Before then, lord chancellors might easily dominate the Lords through ability and sheer force of personality, as Thurlow did. By the time covered by Richard Davis's contribution to this volume, the leader was a more formally established position, and although the relationship between the leader and the lord chancellor could be a source of strength (as Lord Grenville, the then leader, was hoping in 1792, and as was mostly true during the chancellorships of Eldon and Lyndhurst) it could also be a source of friction and weakness.

In the Commons, Onslow's speakership may have established impartiality in principle, but not in practice. The reference made by Abbot (Speaker 1802–17) to the Catholic Relief Bill in 1813 and the closeness of Manners Sutton (1817–35) to tory politics (he was certainly mooted as a candidate for the premiership in 1832) show that Speakers still regarded themselves as party politicians. The refusal of a suspicious whig house of commons to re-elect the tory, Manners Sutton, in 1835 was said by Laundy to have led to the recognition of the 'vital principles' on which the modern speakership is based including that a Speaker, once elected, should cease to have any connection with a political party. Certainly Shaw Lefevre (1839–57) had no ministerial career or pretensions, and he, Denison (1857–72), Brand (1872–84) and Peel (1884–95) consolidated a view of the office as of judicial authority and impartiality.

But if impartiality became firmly established as the guiding principle for the Speakers of both Houses, it was not always simple to exercise in practice, a point underlined by Baroness Boothroyd: 'When you have been committed all your adult life to the ideals and policies of one party, impartiality is a quality that you have to work at' (see below, p. 136). It was equally hard for other members to ignore a Speaker's past. Unionist outrage at the election of Gully in 1895, the sixth Liberal Speaker in a row, and the party's decision to oppose him at the general election coloured his tenure of the chair. Henry Fitzroy was opposed in his constituency by the Labour Party at the general election of 1935; Hylton Foster by Labour and Liberal Parties in his, at the general election of 1964. A minority of Speakers have been appointed from the ranks of significant politicians, and if anything, there was a revival of the practice after the Second World War. Lowther (1905–28), widely regarded as one of the best of Speakers, was briefly thought of as a possible leader of the Unionist Party on Balfour's resignation; the Conservative, William Shepherd Morrison (1951–59), who beat a Labour candidate in the first contested speakership election since 1895, had been chairman of the 1922 committee and held a number of cabinet positions in the 1930s and during the war; Hylton-Foster (1959–65) was solicitor general immediately before his election; Lloyd (1971–6) had filled the highest ministerial offices apart from the premiership, including service as foreign secretary during the Suez crisis, as chancellor of the exchequer and as leader of the House; Thomas (1976–83) held a series of ministerial positions in the 1966–70 Labour government, ending up in the cabinet as secretary of state for Wales. Arguably, impartiality has become more difficult within a more democratic politics in which constituents may expect more from their representative, whether or not he or she is Speaker. Harold Walker, a deputy Speaker, illustrated the dilemma when he spoke in 1984 on the miners' strike. He explained to the House the difficulty of his position 'as a Member in a constituency which is in the centre of the current controversy over coal closures; inevitably there are occasions on which it is impossible for me to keep silent as, in my capacity as a Deputy Speaker, I would wish to do'.[6]

Despite the premiership, and despite the existence in both Houses of a separate, government leader, the Speaker is naturally looked to to take on a sort of leadership of parliament as a whole. There have been times when Speakers, at least in formal terms, appeared as national leaders, as representatives of the representative body of the nation. Alan MacDonald explains how, after the covenanting revolution in Scotland, the Scottish parliament elected its own president who signified in his own name the decisions of the legislature (see below, pp. 55–8). Stephen Roberts describes how similarly during the Commonwealth, Speaker Lenthall (1640–53, etc.) formally represented the institution over which he presided. Indeed, he took on semi-royal status, regarded as 'the greatest man in England' by republicans. Although no longer the public face of a state, that aura of representative greatness lived on after the Restoration, and particularly after the revolution. From 1689 the Speaker of the house of commons was accorded formal precedence after the peers as the 'first commoner'; in 1919 he was promoted beyond most of the peers. Around the beginning of the 20th century the office could scarcely have been more prestigious. Edward Lummis, writing a short history of the speakership in 1900, claimed, albeit with a little exaggeration, that:

> The Speaker of the House of Commons has, in simple truth, many of the attributes of royalty. Within the precincts of the House he is invested with a rank superior to that of the Crown. . . . The Speaker lives in a Royal Palace. He has his own court, his own civil list, his own public household. He is approached and addressed with a

---

[6] Quoted in Barry Winetrobe's introduction to 'The Role of the Speaker of the House of Commons' (above, n. 2), 14.

ceremony and deference such as is shown to royalty. His person is girt with much of the divinity that doth hedge a king. He represents in his proper self the rights and privileges of all his subjects. In his own sphere his word is law, and, should that law be broken, he keeps his own officer to convey offenders to his own prison. His functions, multifarious as those of sovereignty itself, include many of a stately and ceremonial kind. He wears his own proper robes, which it is not lawful for other men to don. His sceptre is borne before him – the Mace of the most honourable House over which he rules: upon his head reposes his peculiar crown, the Speaker's Wig, and just where the throne stands in the House of Lords we find in the House of Commons the Speaker's Chair. Who shall deny that Mr Speaker is, in every sense in which it were not treason to call him so, a king?[7]

Important and respected as it is, it is very difficult to think of the office in quite the same terms today, perhaps because the house of commons itself does not occupy quite the same place in the life of the nation as it did in the days of the formidable Brand and Lowther; perhaps because a more democratic society is less susceptible to the mystique deployed by the 19th-century Speakers. Their successors have adapted. Horace Maybray King (1965–70), the first Labour Speaker, introduced a more demotic element to the speakership – among other things, turning on the Blackpool illuminations – and although his successors have not necessarily followed his lead, they have recognized the need for the Speaker to present a more accessible public face for the house of commons, as has the first holder of the office of Lord Speaker. But, as the most recent speakership contest has shown, there is still a demand for the Speaker to provide the sort of thoughtful leadership of a democratic institution that the politicians themselves, locked in the day-to-day party battle, cannot offer, even though the Speaker has precious few tools, other than the force of persuasion, to help him.

Sir William McKay observes that the neutrality of the Speaker at Westminster became 'one of the few means by which the iron grip of government on the legislature could be moderated' (see below, p. 135). Clearly the speakership has moved a long way since the days of Sir Edward Seymour or Sir Edward Coke; but as recent events have shown, maintaining not just impartiality, but the impression of impartiality, remains the critical test of the success of a Speaker. No volume of this kind can hope to provide any more than a few glimpses of the job of presiding officer over hundreds of years and hundreds of parliaments. But it can remind us that although the role in so protean an assembly as the British parliament is itself protean, there are continuities in the difficulties faced by those who exercise it, and that the way in which they exercise it, and the way in which they are viewed, can be closely related to the status and prestige of parliament itself.

[7] Edward Lummis, *The Speaker's Chair* (1900), 6.

Speakers at War in the Late 14th and 15th Centuries

ANNE CURRY

The significance of war in the development of the medieval English parliament is well known. The origins of the speakership are located in the context of the Hundred Years War, which began in 1337 and in which the English were still embroiled at the time of the Good Parliament of 1376. It was at this parliament that the Commons first chose a spokesperson, Sir Peter de la Mare, knight of the shire for Herefordshire. This article considers the military careers of de la Mare and his successors to the end of the Hundred Years War in 1453. Did the war have an impact on the choice of Speaker? Was a military man chosen for parliaments where military matters were to be discussed? We know the identity of the Speaker in 53 of the 64 parliaments between 1376 and 1453. Several served more than once, so that we are left with a group of 33 individuals to analyse. An overall trend is discernable. Up to 1407 all known Speakers were belted knights, and most had extensive military experience before they took up office. Only five of the 19 parliaments between 1422 and 1453 had Speakers of knightly rank: otherwise, Speakers with legal and administrative, rather than military, experience were chosen. In the years from 1407 to 1422 the speakership was occupied by a mixture of soldiers and administrators many of whom were closely connected to the royal duchy of Lancaster and to revival of English aggression towards France from 1415 onwards.

Keywords: Hundred Years War; Good Parliament; military service; warfare; Speaker; Richard II; Henry IV; Henry V; Henry VI; knight of the shire

The significance of war in the development of the medieval English parliament is well known. The first assembly to which two representatives from each shire and from a number of boroughs were summoned was occasioned in 1265 by a situation of civil war in England. The high level of military activity in the reign of Edward I, which caused that king to require equally high levels of extraordinary income, led not only to the increased frequency of meetings but also to the acceptance that the consent of the Commons was needed for direct taxation to be levied. The origins of the speakership are also fully located in the context of war, the Hundred Years War, which had begun in the late 1330s and in which the English were still embroiled at the time of the Good Parliament of 1376. The first phase of this war had seen great victories at Crécy and Poitiers, and the transfer of almost half of France to direct English rule in the treaty of Brétigny in 1360. The second phase, which began in 1369, had witnessed the swift loss of almost all the gains made earlier. The first half of the 1370s was characterised by a combination of ineffective English campaigns and inconclusive diplomatic negotiations under papal sponsorship. In the summer of 1375 an uneasy short truce had been agreed, but the English were playing a double game. Whilst they were ostensibly willing to participate in further negotiations at Bruges, they were also preparing for the reopening of hostilities.

The issue of writs of summons on 28 December 1375 for a parliament to meet at Westminster on 12 February 1376 was linked to this situation. On 20 January 1376 a postponement was ordered. The Good Parliament, as it soon became known, opened at Westminster on 28 April.[1] It was to witness much criticism of royal policies, or more precisely, the policies of John of Gaunt, duke of Lancaster, then in control of the government given the dotage of Edward III and the state of health of his eldest son, Edward of Woodstock (the Black Prince). Many of these criticisms related directly to the war. There was concern over the lack of defence of Calais as well as the problem of its funding. There was annoyance over the recent surrender to the French of St Sauveur-le-Vicomte in Normandy and of Bécherel in Brittany. Those stationed in Brittany were accused of extortion. The expeditionary army of 1372 was blamed for acts of pillage against the population of Hampshire as it assembled to cross to France. Heads had to roll. At the parliament, William, Lord Latimer and John, Lord Neville were impeached. Famously, a spokesperson of the Commons appeared for the first time – Sir Peter de la Mare, knight of the shire for Herefordshire, who was sitting in his first parliament.

It is impossible to know what were the personal talents which made him the Commons' choice. What we can know is that he was the steward of Edmund, earl of March (*d.* 1381). Not surprisingly, the earl was one of the peers requested by de la Mare on behalf of the Commons to 'consider those things in the realm which needed amendment'. Another was Guy, Lord Bryan (*d.* 1390). The choice of de la Mare is most likely a reflection of political factions – in this case comprising the nobility and their affinities – rather than of embryonic democratic constitutionalism. What Professor Roskell did not know when he published his magisterial study of the medieval speakers in 1965 was that Peter de la Mare, then esquire, had served as a soldier in the retinue of the earl of March, then aged 17 years, in the expedition to France in July 1369, the first campaign after the reopening of hostilities.[2] Guy, Lord Bryan was also on this campaign.[3] So too was William, Lord Latimer, then Sir William, steward of the household, who in 1376 was the object of attack by those who had previously been his comrades-in-arms.[4]

De la Mare's master, the earl of March, had every reason in 1376 to be annoyed with the foreign policy of the government since he had been a victim of it. In May 1375 he had led a royal army to Brittany and Normandy in the hope of rescuing Bécherel and St Sauveur-le-Vicomte. But a few weeks into the campaign, the government agreed to a truce with France, in the negotiation of which Lord Latimer and others were involved. An order was sent to the earl in Brittany telling him to retreat: 'desisting from all acts of

---

[1] *The Parliament Rolls of Medieval England 1275–1504*, ed. Chris Given-Wilson *et al.* (16 vols, Woodbridge, 2005) [hereafter cited as *PROME*], v: *Edward III, 1351–1377*, ed. Mark Ormrod, introduction, 289. For a fuller discussion, see G.A. Holmes, *The Good Parliament* (Oxford, 1975); C.C. Bayley, 'The Campaign of 1375 and the Good Parliament', *English Historical Review*, lv (1940).

[2] J.S. Roskell, *The Commons and their Speakers in English Parliaments 1376–1523* (Manchester, 1965). See also his 'Sir Peter de la Mare, Speaker for the Commons in Parliament in 1376 and 1377', *Nottingham Medieval Studies*, ii (1958), 24–37, reprinted in his *Parliament and Politics in Late Medieval England* (3 vols, 1981–3), ii, 1–14. The evidence for de la Mare's service under March in 1369 is that he took out letters of protection for one year on 30 July 1369 (TNA, C76/52, m. 7).

[3] TNA, E403/438, m. 36 (under 12 Sept. 1369, service of himself with 29 men-at-arms and 30 archers).

[4] TNA, E101/393/11, f. 76 (service of himself with 79 men-at-arms and 100 archers).

war, return with all your retinue into our kingdom of England so that you and the retinue shall be there with no default with the greatest possible haste'.[5]

The earl was not pleased. The crucial question is, of course, whether de la Mare was with him in France. If he was, then the origins of the speakership may lie in the desire of a disgruntled soldier who deliberately sought election to parliament to air his grievances, and those of the earl of March, Lord Bryan and others who had also been on the aborted campaign. So far, however, in the Arts and Humanities Research Council-funded project, 'The Soldier in Late Medieval England', we have not found evidence that de la Mare was present on the 1375 expedition. We know, however, that the earl of March's army contained 24 knights.[6] We also know that de la Mare not only served in the earl's retinue in 1369 but that he was active in raising troops in Herefordshire in 1373 for the earl's service in Ireland.[7] By the end of 1379, when March was appointed lieutenant of Ireland, de la Mare had been formally retained by the earl for service in peace and war, and crossed to Ireland to prepare for the earl's arrival there.[8] These connections are typical of 'career soldiers' in the late 14th and early 15th centuries.[9]

The aim of the 'Soldier' project is to create a database of all soldiers serving the English crown between 1369 and 1453. Save for short truces such as that of 1376, and for the period 1389–1415, this period experienced open war between England and France. In the late 14th century successes were limited despite considerable investment in men and money. Under Henry V, there was a return to the triumphs of the early phases of the Hundred Years War, with a famous victory at Agincourt and the conquest of Normandy. In 1420 Henry became heir to the throne of France, and the English occupied much of northern France. The English position remained strong until the late 1420s when the French managed to rescue Orleans and have Charles VII crowned at Reims. Even so, English control of much of Normandy persisted until 1450, and that of Gascony to 1453, and virtually every year from 1415 onwards expeditionary armies were sent from England. The period from 1369 to 1453 therefore sees a great intensity of military activity, funded essentially through taxation, and supporting not only the French war but also military activities in Ireland, Scotland, Wales, Spain, Portugal and the Low Countries. In this context, as in earlier centuries, parliament fulfilled a pivotal role in the granting (or reluctance to grant) taxation and also in the formulation of, and deliberation on, war policy. Biographical studies of MPs by Josiah Wedgwood and by the History of Parliament Trust have already shown that a number of the knights of the shire served in royal armies.

In this article, the focus is specifically on the military careers of those chosen as Speakers of the Commons between the first known nomination of de la Mare in 1376 and the end of the Hundred Years War in 1453. As we have said, this period saw almost constant military activity. The calling of parliament was very closely linked to war policy,

[5] TNA, E101/34/6, dated 20 July 1375, cited in Holmes, *Good Parliament*, 45.

[6] TNA, E403/451; E364/10, m. 4d. There is a muster roll for the expedition (TNA, E101/35/6) but it is damaged and contains only 423 of the 800 names of the soldiers known from the financial records to have been serving.

[7] *Calendar of Patent Rolls, 1370–4*, p. 353.

[8] TNA, E159/157.

[9] For examples, see the soldier profiles on the project website, *http://www.medievalsoldier.org* (accessed 7 September 2009).

since it was the taxation grants of the Commons which financed the crown's military ambitions, either directly or by providing security against which loans could be sought. We must ask whether this has any significance in terms of the men chosen as Speaker. There are two possible implications. First, was the choice of Speaker influenced by military considerations? Put baldly, was a military man chosen for parliaments where military matters were to be discussed? Do fluctuations in English military fortunes, or changes in the way war was fought, have any impact on this choice? Second, did a Speaker's own experience of warfare affect the conduct of his office during the parliament? On the whole we shall limit discussion to the military careers of Speakers before they were chosen for the office, since it was this past experience which may have influenced their selection and their performance of their office. Some of this ground has, of course, already been covered by Roskell but new information gleaned through the 'Soldier' project can be added.[10] With the many recent studies of English warfare in this period, we can also draw a greater sense of context. At base, however, a major dilemma remains. There is still some uncertainty over how a Speaker was chosen at the beginning of a parliament. Did their choice indicate what we might call 'the anticipatory mood' of the assembly?

Most Speakers had connections with the crown in one way or another, through officeholding, financial rewards, and service, of which military service was one example. Were they, therefore, truly independent? What role did the crown play in their selection? For the Tudor period there is little dispute on this matter: the Speakers were essentially crown nominees although they had to be acceptable to the Commons. For the period under consideration here, however, there is enough to suggest that at least on some occasions, the Commons made its own choices. The choice of de la Mare was hardly a 'government-friendly' move, and he found himself imprisoned in November 1376, five months after the parliament ended. In October 1399 the crown rejected the Commons' nominee, and in December 1420 there was a contested election between two nominees – both signs that the initiative lay with the Commons.[11] Each parliament was, of course, unique, and each has its own story to tell. Levels of 'independence of choice' could vary. We cannot go into detail here either on individual Speakers or parliaments but must instead emphasize some broad conclusions which are none the less important because they cover a period of almost 80 years of parliamentary history.

Between 1376 and 1453 there were 64 parliaments of varying lengths and frequency. For 11 of these (October 1383–January 1393) we do not know the name of the Speaker. For the remaining 53 we do, although there are some at the beginning of the period where the identification is not wholly secure.[12] These 53 parliaments saw 58 speaker-ships, since on five occasions there were two Speakers nominated. In 1399 the initial choice fell on Sir John Cheyne: he resigned almost immediately on the grounds of ill health but more probably he stood down because of the crown's rejection of him on religious grounds. The resignation of William Stourton in 1413 was also because of ill

[10] I am grateful to my co-investigator, Dr Adrian Bell of the University of Reading, and to the research assistants on the project, Dr Andy King and Dr David Simpkin, for information provided for this article.

[11] Roskell, *Speakers*, 136–7, 170.

[12] The suggestions of Roskell have been followed for the parliaments of 1379 (Sir James de Pickering); May 1382 and Oct. 1382 (Sir Richard de Waldegrave); Jan. 1395 (Sir John de Bussy).

health although there is, again, a possibility of royal rejection.[13] In 1437 the state of illness is undisputed since John Tyrell stood down midway through the parliament and died only a few months later.[14] The Speaker nominated in November 1449, Sir John Popham, was excused on the grounds of old age,[15] although we shall explore his choice more fully since it was highly significant in the context of the military position at this point in time. In 1454 there was a change of Speaker during the parliament because of a change of political regime, when, following the onset of the king's illness the dominance of the duke of Somerset gave way to that of the duke of York.[16] Again there is a link to foreign affairs, since York was keen to bring Somerset and his supporters to task for the loss of Normandy three years earlier.[17]

The 58 identifiable speakerships were held by 33 different men since several served more than once. Thomas Chaucer, son of the poet, held the largest number of nominations, serving as Speaker on five occasions between 1407 and 1421, including an unparalleled run of three parliaments in a row between 1407 and 1411.[18] Roger Flore and William Tresham were both chosen on four occasions, the former for another three parliaments in succession. A further four men served on three occasions, and seven on two.[19] Our sample can be broken down in other ways. Eighteen of the 33 individuals who held the speakership were belted (or dubbed) knights at the time they became Speaker.[20] John Tyrell was knighted soon after the second of his speakerships in 1431. In the context of this article, this is significant since it was at the point at which he crossed with a number of reinforcements to join the king in France, being shortly afterwards appointed treasurer of the household on 25 May. In times of royal campaigns, the treasurer of the household was also treasurer of wars. Tyrell, therefore, performed a key military function in the months following.[21]

An interesting contrast appears if we plot the distribution of knightly Speakers across the period. Of the 20 parliaments between 1376 and 1406 where we know the identity

---

[13] Roskell, *Speakers*, 154–5. Since Doreward's status as a lawyer is uncertain, Stourton is the first definite lawyer to have been nominated as Speaker.

[14] Roskell, *Speakers*, 216 n. 1.

[15] Roskell, *Speakers*, 237.

[16] Roskell, *Speakers*, 253–5.

[17] *PROME*, xii: *Henry VI, 1447–1460*, ed. A. Curry, introduction to the parliament of 1453, pp. 220–2.

[18] This might also have been achieved by Sir Richard Waldegrave and Sir John Bussy in the 1380s and 1390s respectively.

[19] Three occasions: Sir Richard de Waldegrave; Sir James de Pickering; Sir John de Bussy; John Tyrell. Two occasions: Sir Peter de la Mare; Sir John de Gildesburgh; Sir Arnold Savage; John Doreward; John Russell; Roger Hunt; William Burley.

[20] Roskell can be misleading here as he tends to use the description 'Sir' even when the Speakers were not formally belted knights, as in the case of John Doreward, Thomas Waweton, John Tyrell (before his dubbing in 1431).

[21] A. Curry, 'The "Coronation Expedition" and Henry VI's Court in France, 1430 to 1432', in *The Lancastrian Court*, ed. J. Stratford (Stamford, 2003), 43. Tyrell indented to serve with two men-at-arms and 12 archers (TNA, E404/47/173, 23 Apr.; E403/698, under 16 Mar. and 12 Apr. 1431). On 16 March he also received a reward of £100 for agreeing to serve the king in France (TNA, E403/696, under 16 March). See also *Proceedings and Ordinances of the Privy Council of England 1386–1542*, ed. H. Nicolas (7 vols, 1834–7), iv, 484. Parliament ended on 20 Mar. 1431. The exact date of his knighting is not certain. The military wage rate of 4s. per day suggests that he was deemed to hold the status of knight banneret. For his biography, see *The History of Parliament: The House of Commons, 1386–1421*, ed. J.S. Roskell, Linda Clark and Carole Rawcliffe (4 vols, Stroud, 1992) [hereafter cited as *HPC, 1386–1421*], iv, 683–6.

of the Speaker, all had a Speaker of knightly rank. The one exception was the first parliament of Henry IV but even that is only a partial exception since the first nominee, Sir John Cheyne, was a knight, who stood down to be replaced by an esquire (who was probably a lawyer), John Doreward. Of the 33 parliaments of the period from 1407 to 1453, however, only eight had a Speaker of knightly rank. The turning point seems to be the choice of Thomas Chaucer for the first of his speakerships in 1407, which ushered in four parliaments in a row where the Speaker was not a belted knight. From the middle of the reign of Henry V onwards, Speakers were most likely to be lawyers. Of the 33 parliaments between 1407 and 1453, 13 opened with a lawyer as Speaker. In 1437 the first Speaker, a knight, was replaced by a lawyer. Yet this was a period which saw intensive warfare with France between Henry V's reopening of the war in 1415 and the loss of Normandy in 1453.

It is the case, of course, that all of the Speakers of the period from 1376 to 1453 were knights of the shire and not burgess representatives. Furthermore, military activity was not the exclusive preserve of belted knights. Two of the Speakers of the rank of esquires – Thomas Chaucer and John Tyrell – had military experience before they took up office. Tyrell had served as a man-at-arms in the retinue of Humphrey, duke of Gloucester on the 1415 campaign, with a company of five men-at-arms and 16 archers, and again in the duke's company in 1417.[22] In both 1419 and 1420 he was listed as capable of military service, although he does not seem to have served again until he crossed with the reinforcements in 1431, in a capacity which should perhaps be seen as a military administrator rather than as a soldier. His knighting at that point may have been aimed at giving him status in his office as treasurer, as well as ensuring a greater financial incentive for his service. Arguably, therefore, his military service was limited. The same can be said for Thomas Chaucer. There is some suggestion he was with Gaunt in Spain in 1386, and he definitely served in the Welsh wars, although perhaps briefly.[23] He indented to go on the 1415 campaign but was not able to do so through illness. No further service is known. Indeed, both men seem to have preferred on the whole not to serve in armies. Yet that did not make them any less aware of the demands and context of war. Indeed, it is worth remembering that even the lawyers who served as Speakers, and for whom there is no evidence of military service, were often involved in aspects of military administration. John Doreward, for instance, was engaged in the Court of Chivalry as well as being used to report the state of the Welsh marches during the Glendower rebellion.[24] Thomas Waweton, like John Tyrell, was listed in 1419 as suitable for military service, although there is no evidence that he ever performed it.[25] Non-military Speakers were appointed from time to time as commissioners of array.[26] William

---

[22] TNA, E101/45/13, m. 3; E101/51/2, m. 11 (within the retinue of Sir Hugh Luttrell).

[23] He mustered as a man-at-arms in the force under John Beaufort, earl of Somerset, in 1403, detailed to the garrison of Camarthen and for the defence of Wales (TNA, E101/43/21, m. 4d). Sir John Tiptoft served in the same force (m. 4).

[24] *HPC, 1386–1421*, ii, 790–1.

[25] *HPC, 1386–1421*, iv, 791.

[26] For instance, William Burley in 1418 and 1421. He was also involved in 1415 in the payment of the Calais garrison (J.S. Roskell, 'William Burley of Boncroft', *Shropshire Archaeological Society*, lvi (1960), 263–72, reprinted in Roskell, *Parliament and Politics*, iii, 343–52).

Allington had extensive experience of military administration before he became Speaker in 1429 through his earlier roles as treasurer in Brest, Ireland and Normandy.[27]

Drawing a strict line between the military and non-military classes is exceptionally difficult in this period. For instance, John Doreward is known to have left armour in his will.[28] The biographies of non-military speakers produced by the History of Parliament Trust show them to have personal and official connections with men who were soldiers. William Stourton, for instance, had acted as receiver for the earl of Salisbury both for the latter's keepership of Carisbroke castle in 1384 and for service on the Scottish campaign in 1385.[29] None the less, the stark contrast between the periods before and after 1407 is so marked as to require further thought. It parallels the general decline in the number of belted knights in parliament, as already identified in the study of knights of the shire between 1376 and 1421.[30] Whilst this period opened with over 60% of belted knights sitting for the counties, it ended with 30% and on some occasions had fallen to even less. Strikingly, the lowest proportion of 13% coincided with the 1415 campaign. This suggests that warfare – and, in particular, Henry V's desire to raise as large an army as possible for his first invasion – could draw knights away from civil to military service. But this exceptional moment should not disguise the fact that there was an overall decline in the number of dubbed knights in 15th-century England, despite the war. This phenomenon has yet to be explored in more detail, but it may be that the state of war made the gaining of a knighthood more exclusive. There may even have been a financial concern on the part of the government since knights had to be paid twice the daily wage rate of an esquire. Within a parliamentary context, we can also suggest that increasing sophistication in the conduct of business, and the sheer bulk of it, made it preferable to have Speakers with legal rather than military expertise. Even by 1421, there was a rise in the number and proportion of lawyers as knights of the shire and burgesses.[31] Further work by the History of Parliament Trust will no doubt clarify the position for the remainder of the period, but a further decline in belted knights and a rise in lawyers are certain.

The changing nature of the type of person chosen as Speaker is all the more obvious if we look more closely at the men themselves. In the late 14th century, de la Mare's immediate successors were men with similar experience to himself. Indeed, many of them would have known each other because they served together in campaigns. Sir Richard Waldegrave and Sir John Gildesburgh, for instance, both served under Humphrey de Bohun, earl of Northampton, in the 1369 campaign.[32] Waldegrave had links with Guy, Lord Bryan, similar to those of de la Mare.[33] The year 1376 saw Waldegrave's

---

[27] *HPC, 1386–1421*, ii, 28–9.

[28] J.S. Roskell, 'Sir John Doreward of Bocking', *Essex Archaeology and History*, viii (1978 for 1976), reprinted in Roskell, *Parliament and Politics*, iii, 62.

[29] TNA, E403/502, m. 9; E403/508, m. 12, cited in J.S. Roskell, 'William Stourton of Stourton', *Proceedings of the Dorset Natural History and Archaeological Society*, lxxxii (1960), 155–66, reprinted in Roskell, *Parliament and Politics*, iii, 196.

[30] *HPC, 1386–1421*, i, Appendix B1.

[31] *HPC, 1386–1421*, i, Appendix B2.

[32] Waldegrave: TNA, C76/52, mm. 18, 22; Gildesburgh: TNA, C76/52, mm. 9, 12.

[33] J.S. Roskell, 'Sir Richard Waldgrave of Bures St Mary', *Proceedings of the Suffolk Institute of Archaeology*, xxvii (1957), pt 3, pp. 154–75, reprinted in Roskell, *Parliament and Politics*, iii, 32.

first parliament as it was de la Mare's, and it is tempting that he had sought election for similar reasons relating to the desire to criticize the recent failures in France. Gildesburgh, Sir John Bussy and Sir John Cheyne were all serving under John of Gaunt in the 1378 campaign which aimed to seize St Malo.[34] Gildesburgh and Cheyne were knighted during the campaign. Thomas Chaucer was also a retainer of Gaunt and may have served him in a military capacity in the Castilian campaign of 1386.[35] Waldegrave, Gildesburgh, Sir Arnold Savage and Sir Henry Retford all served on the Scottish expedition of 1385 in which Gaunt was a leading commander. Indeed, the links to particular peers is striking. In the early days of the speakership, as in 1376 itself, we might even suggest that the choice of Speaker reflected either royal or noble factionalism.

The Speakers of the late 14th century were men of considerable military experience. In the case of Sir John Gildesburgh, this dated back to the battle of Crécy where he was a page or esquire at the age of 15 years. He was also present at Poitiers in the retinue of Bartholemew, Lord Burghersh, in whose retinue he had served for some years. In 1359 he served on the Reims campaign.[36] He served again in the 1369 expedition, and in 1371 and 1372, under Humphrey de Bohun.[37] He was finally knighted on the 1378 campaign, and took up his first speakership two years later, also serving on Gaunt's Scottish campaign of 1380.[38] Sir John Pickering's service dated back to 1359, when he was still an esquire.[39] During the hiatus of the Anglo-French war following the treaty of Brétigny he served instead in Ireland with Lionel, duke of Clarence, continuing in service there from 1369 to 1372 under Sir William Windsor, husband of the king's mistress, Alice Perrrers. Waldegrave likewise had service dating back to 1359, when he served in the retinue of William de Bohun, earl of Northampton.[40] At the Scrope-Grosvenor case in the court of Chivalry he claimed to have been in arms for 25 years. Indeed, there is much in his career to suggest that he was the model for Chaucer's knight. In 1363 we find him assisting the Teutonic knights. Two years later he was in Turkey and then Alexandria, but in 1369 he joined with many of his knightly compatriots in serving on the expedition to France which followed the reopening of the war. We find him again in arms in 1371 and again in 1372 in expeditions under Humphrey de Bohun, the latter aimed at relieving La Rochelle after the disaster of the expedition under the earl of Pembroke. Whilst awaiting embarkation at Plymouth in 1371, he was

---

[34] For Bussy, *HPC, 1386–1421*, ii, 450–1. For Cheyne, TNA, E101/36/39, m. 1 (within retinue of Sir William de Beauchamp and Sir Lewis Clifford). Cheyne also served as a man-at-arms in the army of 1375 in the retinue of Edward, Lord Despenser (TNA, E101/34/5, m. 3), and on the expedition to Ireland in 1394 (J.S. Roskell, 'Sir John Cheyne of Beckford', *Transactions of the Bristol and Gloucestershire Archaeological Society*, lxxv (1956), 43–72, reprinted in Roskell, *Parliament and Politics*, ii, 65–94).

[35] J.S. Roskell, 'Thomas Chaucer of Ewelme', in Roskell, *Parliament and Politics*, iii, 153.

[36] TNA, C76/38, m. 11 (appointment of his attorneys, 23 Aug. 1359, no captain specified); C76/40, m. 10 (renewal of protection for service in the retinue of Sir Bartholemew Burghersh). He was an esquire at this point. I am grateful to Dr Andrew Ayton for these references.

[37] Roskell, *Speakers*, 125; *The Scrope and Grosvenor Controversy*, ed. N.H. Nicolas (2 vols, 1832), i, 217–8.

[38] TNA, C76/62, m. 2; *Scrope and Grosvenor*, ed. Nicolas, 218.

[39] TNA, C76/38, m. 16 (protection of 24 Aug. 1359 for service in the retinue of Henry of Grosmont, duke of Lancaster). I am grateful to Dr Andrew Ayton for this reference, which was not known to Professor Roskell. See J.S. Roskell, 'Sir James Pickering of Killington', *Transactions of the Cumberland and Westmorland Antiquarian and Archaeological Society*, new ser., lxi (1961), reprinted in Roskell, *Parliament and Politics*, iii, 1–26.

[40] *Scrope and Grosvenor*, ed. Nicolas, i, 165. Waldegrave had substantial military activity in the years following his speakerships.

involved in jousts, suggesting some degree of prowess in arms.[41] To date, no evidence has come to light that Sir Thomas Hungerford served abroad, but he was constable of the castles of Marlborough and Wallingford, a frequent commissioner of array, and was active in the diplomatic negotiations in Bruges in 1375 which led to the truce with France.[42]

Indeed, this involvement in the negotiation of a truce in 1375 stands in contrast to the militaristic preferences of Sir Peter de la Mare at the same point. It is, therefore, not coincidental that Hungerford, knighted as he set out with Gaunt for the negotiations at Bruges, was chosen as Speaker at the Bad Parliament of 1377 which sought to undo the work of its predecessor. Just as the earl of March and his party seem to have played a role in the nomination of de la Mare in 1376, so Gaunt was surely behind the choice of Hungerford in 1377. Behind these nominations lie a division between hawks and doves at this juncture of the Anglo-French wars. A military context can also be seen in the choice of Sir John Gildesburgh in January 1380. The Commons agreed a grant of one-and-a-half tenths and fifteenths but said that both this lay subsidy and the wool tax should be earmarked to pay for the army due to be sent to Brittany under Thomas of Woodstock. Gildesburgh was appointed receiver of the money for Woodstock. He was chosen as Speaker again at the parliament of November 1380 where the Commons petitioned that the new poll tax should be used to 'refresh' the leaders of the expedition to Brittany and to honour the covenants of Woodstock, and that it should not be used for any other purposes. Surely we see here the inclinations of 'a seasoned veteran of the French wars', keen to ensure secure continuation of, and support for, the English interests overseas.[43]

The Speakers of the early part of the reign of Henry IV follow the pattern already established in the previous decades. Sir Arnold Savage had military experience dating back to 1379 and on several fronts, including the garrisoning of Calais and naval activity in the 1380s.[44] Sir Henry Retford's experience also appears to stretch back to 1379: he, like Thomas Chaucer, was with Gaunt in Spain in 1386.[45] Sir William Sturmy saw service as an esquire in Thomas of Woodstock's expedition to France in 1380, and as a knight in the 1388 naval expedition under the earl of Arundel, as well as serving on the 1394 expedition to Ireland.[46] Sir John Tiptoft helped to put Bolingbroke on the throne,

---

[41] *HPC, 1386–1421*, iv, 736.

[42] J.S. Roskell, 'Sir Thomas Hungerford', *Wiltshire Archaeological and Natural History Magazine*, lvi (1956), 272–300, reprinted in Roskell, *Parliament and Politics*, ii, 15–44.

[43] As expressed by Roskell and Rawcliffe in *HPC, 1386–1421*, ii, 186.

[44] TNA, C76/64, m. 20 (1379, letters of protection for one year for service in France); C76/67, m. 14 (1383, Calais garrison under Sir John Devereux); C76/68, m. 11; C76/69, m. 14; C76/71, m. 14 (1384–6, Calais garrison, under Sir William Beauchamp). The last reference shows that he was knighted by August 1386. In 1387 he served under the earl of Arundel in the naval campaign (TNA, E101/40/33, mm. 6d, 13), and was similarly in the 1388 campaign (TNA, E101/41/5, m. 15d). He also served on the Scottish expedition of 1385, and had intended to serve on Gaunt's expedition to Spain in 1386 but had letters of protection revoked (*Calendar of Patent Rolls, 1385–9*, pp. 176, 189; J.S. Roskell, 'Sir Arnold Savage of Bobbing', *Archaeologia Cantiana*, lxx (1956), 63–83, reprinted in Roskell, *Parliament and Politics*, iii, 69).

[45] J.S. Roskell, 'Sir Henry de Retford', *Lincolnshire Architectural and Archaeological Society: Reports and Papers*, new ser., vii, pt 2 (1957–8), 117–25, reprinted in Roskell, *Parliament and Politics*, iii, 81–90. For his service in Brittany in 1379, see TNA, C76/64, m. 18.

[46] 1380: TNA, E101/39/9, m. 4 (in the company of Sir Hugh Calverley); 1388: TNA, E101/41/5, m. 5; 1394: TNA, E101/402/20, f. 34. The service in 1380 and 1388 was not known to Roskell. See J.S. Roskell, 'Sir William Sturmy', *Transactions of the Devonshire Association for the Advancement of Science, Literature and Art*, lxxxix (1957), 78–92, reprinted in Roskell, *Parliament and Politics*, iii, 91–106.

and also served in the Welsh wars.[47] His choice for one of the most difficult parliaments of Henry IV's reign in terms of financial problems may reflect royal interest in the need to attempt to control the Commons, not least as it was followed soon afterwards by his appointment as only the second layman to be treasurer.[48]

As we have seen, Thomas Chaucer, with relatively little military experience under his belt, appears to occupy a transitional point. That said, he was definitely a trusted associate of both Henry IV and Henry V, linked through marriage into the de Roet line to the royal family itself. He had been a retainer of Gaunt since at least 1389 and perhaps earlier. He also had extensive experience in diplomacy. It is also significant that his speakerships coincided with a period of little military action, although he was nominated in the parliament of November 1414 when a major campaign in France was decided upon. He was clearly a man to be trusted by both king and Commons. His predecessor in the previous parliament of May 1414, Sir Walter Hungerford, was a similarly trusted man from a similar Lancastrian stable, who had been knighted on the eve of Henry IV's coronation. There is little evidence of his military participation before he was nominated as Speaker but like Waldegrave before him, he had distinguished himself in jousting, this time at Calais in 1406.[49] What we see increasingly under Henry V is the dominance of men with experience in the duchy of Lancaster. Sir Walter Hungerford, as his father Thomas before him, held the chief stewardship of the estates south of Trent at the time of his speakership. Roger Hunt, Speaker in December 1420, was Hungerford's deputy in this post, at a time when Sir Walter was increasingly embroiled in the war in France, and had acted as agent for Tiptoft in 1415 when the latter was preparing to sail with a force to Gascony.[50] Roger Flore, a lawyer, was made steward of the duchy north of Trent shortly after his first of four speakerships at the parliament of October 1416.[51] Behind all this lay the significance of the duchy revenues for the crown's use at a time of exceptional military expenditure. Henry V's determination (or at least his need) to 'persuade' the Commons into support for his wars is reflected in the men who were nominated as Speakers.

This is surely the reign where royal influence appears at its strongest. Hungerford and Sir Walter Beauchamp were close associates of the king. The latter may have been with Henry as prince at the battle of Shrewsbury.[52] He had been knighted during the early stages of the Agincourt campaign, although invalided home.[53] He was an ideal go-between in March 1416 in the light of the king's desire to emphasize the need to keep up the war effort for the defence of Harfleur, and he served with the king again

---

[47] His service under John Beaufort, earl of Somerset in the garrison of Camarthen and defence of Wales in 1403 was not known to Roskell (TNA, E101/43/21, m. 4). Tiptoft was also seneschal of Landes and held custody of the castle of Dax but there is no proof that he ever served in Gascony in person before 1415.

[48] J.S. Roskell, 'Sir John Tiptoft', in Roskell, *Parliament and Politics*, iii, 107–50; *HPC, 1386–1421*, iv, 62.

[49] *HPC, 1386–1421*, iii, 448.

[50] *HPC, 1386–1421*, iii, 456.

[51] J.S. Roskell, 'Roger Flore', *Transactions of the Leicestershire Archaeological and Historical Society*, xxxiii (1957), 36–44, reprinted in Roskell, *Parliament and Politics*, iii, 255–64.

[52] J.S. Roskell, 'Sir Walter Beauchamp', *Wiltshire Archaeological and Natural History Magazine*, lvi (1956), 342–58, reprinted in Roskell, *Parliament and Politics*, iii, 237–54.

[53] TNA, E101/44/30, no. 1, m. 2.

in the army raised in the following months to save the town.[54] The impact of the king's absence with so many of the military classes both in 1415 and later is reflected in the choice of Speaker. At the parliament of November 1415, which followed the victory at Agincourt but which was held whilst the king and his army were still in France, there was a notably low participation rate of dubbed knights as knights of the shire, since so many were with the king. The Speaker chosen, Sir Richard Redmayne, was an elderly man, probably born in the 1350s.[55] He had been knighted by 1376, and had substantial military experience under his belt, including service in the 1378 naval campaign, the garrison at Roxburgh which his father had commanded, and on the 1394 and 1399 campaigns to Ireland.[56] He, too, had shown prowess in the joust. As a veteran soldier, he was in a good position to mediate the king's victory. There was also a personal investment since his second son, Thomas, was serving as an archer on the French campaign in the retinue of Sir Richard's step-son, Sir Brian Stapleton.[57] Sir Richard's northern roots (he was knight of the shire for Westmorland) also stood him in good stead, since there were ongoing anxieties about the Anglo-Scottish frontier. Furthermore, John, duke of Bedford, keeper of the realm in his brother's absence, held the earldom of Kendal, creating a personal territorial link.

The parliament of December 1420, however, reveals that the king could not take parliament for granted. It is not a coincidence that this parliament, the first to be held since the sealing of the treaty of Troyes in May, saw a disputed election for the speakership between Roger Hunt and John Russell which went to a vote. Hunt was the most experienced lawyer to date to hold the office, and had already sat in seven parliaments by 1420.[58] He also had extensive links with Sir Walter Hungerford, who had made him his deputy in the duchy of Lancaster during the 1415 invasion, and with Sir John Tiptoft. It is not impossible that the disputed election had something to do with reservations about the treaty. The parliament expressed concern at the king's continuing absence and at the nature of the Troyes settlement, requesting a reissue of the 1340 statute that England would never be subordinate to France. There was also no tax grant made. It is difficult to know, however, which 'parties' the two contestants represented. Hunt's patrons, Hungerford and Tiptoft, were heavily involved in Henry V's endeavours in France. He may, therefore, have been seen as likely to control the Commons in the king's favour. That said, he was chosen as Speaker again in 1433 when the financing of the war was a major issue. This could suggest that he was seen by the Commons as a man of independent and equitable views. Indeed, it is significant that Humphrey, duke of Gloucester closed the 1420 parliament after only two weeks, postponing real discussion of the treaty and of the financial needs of the king until Henry himself returned in the following year and attended the May 1421 parliament in person. For that parliament the

[54] TNA, E101/48/10/103; E403/624, m. 4.

[55] J.S. Roskell, 'Sir Richard Redmayne of Levens', *Transactions of the Cumberland and Westmorland Antiquarian and Archaeological Society*, new ser., lxii (1962), 113–44, reprinted in Roskell, *Parliament and Politics*, iii, 205–36.

[56] In addition to the information provided by Roskell, he took out a protection for naval service in 1378 under Sir John Devereux (TNA, C76/61, m. 7), and was a man-at-arms under the captaincy of his father at Roxburgh in 1381–2 (E101/531/29, mm. 2, 6).

[57] TNA, E101/45/4, m. 11.

[58] Overall he sat in 17 out of 21 parliaments between 1413 and 1433 (*HPC, 1386–1421*, iii, 457).

veteran Lancastrian, Thomas Chaucer, was chosen as Speaker. The Commons was correspondingly more co-operative.

The reign of Henry VI sees the speakership dominated by non-knights. Between 1422 and 1453, there were 19 parliaments but only five of them had Speakers of knightly rank. Furthermore, two of these were exonerated (Tyrell in 1437 and Popham in November 1449) and replaced by esquires, and one, Sir Thomas Charleton, was a knightly replacement in 1454 for the initially-nominated Speaker, Thomas Thorpe esquire. Sir Thomas Waweton seems not to have had a military career, and Sir Richard Vernon had next to none.[59] The majority of the Speakers of the reign were men with substantial legal and administrative experience who had no military experience whatsoever.[60] This reflects the way parliamentary business was moving but also the way the war with France was developing. The treaty of Troyes made it possible for the English to draw on French revenues to finance the war. Indeed, this is what they did, with the result that between 1422 and 1428 no grants of the lay subsidy were requested of the English parliament. This contributed to a growing divide between the English in France and the English in England, which was further fanned by the needs of an occupation. The campaigns of the late 14th century had been time-limited, and had generated a constant need to reassess strategy, sometimes in the face of differing views within the military and political community. In other words, the war remained a major subject for discussion. Under Henry IV, the French front subsided only to be replaced by wars closer to home which cost money but were generally less divisive. The successes of Henry V, and his premature death, created a need for occupation and hence the development of a separate English regime in France. Increasingly, there was a divide between Lancastrian England and Lancastrian France. This is exemplified by the decreasing numbers of members of the Commons with military experience at the same time that soldiers based in France developed lengthy careers, but based largely overseas.

What is striking, however, is that in moments of crisis, Speakers with military links were preferred.[61] In the face of the raising of the siege of Orleans and the losses of the summer of 1429 which led to the coronation of Charles VII at Reims, parliament was called in order to gain taxation to fund a major expedition with which the young king, crowned at Westminster during the parliament, would cross to his French kingdom. The Speaker chosen was William Allington, who had served as receiver of Brest in 1397, treasurer of Calais in 1398, treasurer of Ireland in 1403 and of Normandy between 1419 and 1422.[62] Who better for both the crown and the Commons than the medieval

---

[59] Waweton was listed as one of the Bedfordshire gentry qualified to perform military service but there is no evidence that he ever did so (*HPC, 1386–1421*, iv, 789–93). Vernon served on the 1416 expedition (J.S. Roskell, 'Sir Richard Vernon of Haddon', *Derbyshire Archaeological Journal*, lxxxii (1962), 43–54, reprinted in Roskell, *Parliament and Politics*, iii, 265–76). He may also have served as a man-at-arms under the earl marshal in the 1417 expedition but this identification is uncertain (TNA, E101/51/2, m. 27).

[60] Richard Baynard, brother-in-law of John Doreward and a close friend of John Tyrell, was amongst those in Essex seen in January 1420 as qualified for military service but there is no evidence he ever served (*HPC, 1386–1421*, ii, 150–2).

[61] This was not the case in 1435, however, when John Bowes was chosen as Speaker for reasons unknown (J.S. Roskell, 'John Bowes of Costock', *Transactions of the Thoroton Society of Nottinghamshire*, lx (1956), 8–19, reprinted in Roskell, *Parliament and Politics*, iii, 331–42).

[62] J.S. Roskell, 'William Allington', *Proceedings of the Cambridgeshire Antiquarian Society*, xxx, reprinted in Roskell, *Parliament and Politics*, iii, 317–30.

equivalent of an old colonial administrator to know what was needed and also what was possible, and to persuade all towards a common goal? Not only was the Commons generous but also a large army was recruited in the months which followed the parliament. The choice of Sir John Popham in November 1449 points to a different response to crisis. By this time, the English position was much diminished, and on the point of diminishing further now that Charles VII had invaded the duchy and, by the time the parliament met, had taken Rouen. On this occasion Sir John Popham, probably the only surviving veteran of Agincourt present at the parliament, was chosen, even though this was only his second parliament.[63] It is tempting to think that he was selected by the Commons as a rebuke to the government – a symbol of past successes which they had ruined by mismanagement. This was, after all, the parliament in which the duke of Suffolk, whose father and brother had died on the Agincourt campaign, was impeached largely for war failure. It is possible that Popham had had himself elected in order to complain: his only other parliament was that of 1439 in which the contentious release of the duke of Orleans had been agreed. Popham had, after all, been in the retinue of the duke of York at the battle of Agincourt. He had seen York, as well as Suffolk's elder brother, die there. He had served almost continuously in military and diplomatic activity in France from 1417 to 1442.

That the choice of Popham was a symbolic act is further suggested by the fact that he immediately expressed his wish to stand down. No doubt the government, still effectively headed by Suffolk, was pleased to let him to do so, and to accept the replacement Speaker, William Tresham. Indeed, the government may have 'facilitated' the replacement. Tresham, a lawyer, was a dutiful royal servant who had most recently served as Speaker at the parliament at Bury St Edmunds in February 1447, the parliament linked to the demise of Humphrey, duke of Gloucester.[64] That said, the Commons got its way in bringing Suffolk to trial in the third session of the November 1449 parliament. As Roskell concluded: 'Tresham's own allegiances are likely to have been in a state of flux and confusion at this time of national calamity and threatening strife.'[65]

Calamity and strife continued to colour English politics at the next parliament which opened in November 1450. By this time, Normandy was lost and Gascony was under threat. Yet Henry VI had continued to show confidence in Edmund Beaufort, duke of Somerset, the erstwhile lieutenant-general in France, appointing him constable of England and captain of Calais after his enforced evacuation from Normandy. Not surprisingly, the parliament was to see criticism of Somerset and of others considered responsible for the recent defeats. There is strong suspicion that Richard, duke of York was behind this. It is, therefore, extremely significant that the man chosen as Speaker was Sir William Oldhall. Not only was he a veteran of the wars, with service dating back at

[63] J.S. Roskell, 'Sir John Popham, Knight-Banneret, of Charford', *Proceedings of the Hampshire Field Club and Archaeological Society*, lii (1959), 43–55, reprinted in Roskell, *Parliament and Politics*, iii, 353–82; A. Curry, 'Popham, Sir John (c.1395–1463)', *ODNB*, Oxford University Press, 2008 [*http://www.oxforddnb.com/view/article/22542* (accessed 19 Dec. 2008)].

[64] Significantly, John Say, Speaker in the Feb. 1449 parliament, for which he was richly rewarded by the crown, and closely linked to the duke of Suffolk, first sat in the 1447 parliament where Suffolk's influence was substantial (J.S. Roskell, 'Sir John Say of Broxbourne', *East Herts Archaeological Society*, xiv (1959), 20–41, reprinted in Roskell, *Parliament and Politics*, ii, 153–74).

[65] J.S. Roskell, 'William Tresham of Sywell', *Northamptonshire Past and Present*, ii, no. 4 (1957), 189–203, reprinted in Roskell, *Parliament and Politics*, ii, 137–52 (quote at 146).

least to 1416, but he had developed strong links with York in France in the 1440s. He had himself lost lands and revenues in Normandy as a result of the defeats. Therefore he had ample reason to wish to bring to task those responsible, setting aside any notion that he might have been encouraged to do so by York. Furthermore, Oldhall had never previously sought election as an MP. We have a significant parallel with de la Mare. Both men were Speakers in their first parliament. Both were chosen because of issues concerning military policy. Both found themselves indicted after the parliament. De la Mare was arrested, Oldhall managed to enter sanctuary at St Martin-le-Grand. In the next parliament which met from 6 March 1453 there were further actions against Oldhall, including a full attainder and outlawry.[66] The political triumph of Somerset over York was symbolised by the choice of Thomas Thorpe as Speaker. As noted earlier, however, the king's illness led to York's appointment as protector. The tables were now turned. Thorpe was arrested and replaced by Sir Thomas Charleton, and Oldhall secured a writ of error, although it was not until the eve of the 1455 parliament, which followed the Yorkist victory at St Albans, that he was able to leave sanctuary and to be fully acquitted.

The events of 1449–54 show clearly how politicised the choice of Speaker had become within the context of the war in France, and also how politicised the individual remained even after he had held office. Not only can this be seen in the case of Oldhall, but also in what happened to William Tresham after his service as Speaker in the troubled parliament of November 1449. On York's return to England in September 1450, the duke wrote to Tresham to arrange a meeting with him *en route* to London. We can only speculate what the duke wanted to discuss. Writs of summons and election had been issued on 5 September. Was the duke assuming that Tresham might once again be chosen as Speaker? Since Tresham had co-operated in the impeachment of Suffolk, was York wishing to discuss with him the possible impeachment of Somerset? These suggestions gain extra credence by the fact that Tresham was murdered on his way to meet the duke. Rumours circulated that those who ambushed him were the men of Lord Grey of Ruthin, a member of the Lancastrian, pro-Somerset party.[67] We have, therefore, come full circle from 1376. There can be no doubt that the war with France had a significant influence on the parliaments of the period, whether in support or in criticism of government policy, in celebration of success or in recriminations for failure. Within this context, it is not surprising that the choice of Speaker was important for both crown and Commons, and that at particular junctures, the selection of a man with military experience was preferred by one side, or both.

[66] J.S. Roskell, 'Sir William Oldhall', *Nottingham Medieval Studies*, vii (1963), 79–105, reprinted in Roskell, *Parliament and Politics*, ii, 193–4; A. Curry, 'Oldhall, Sir William (*d.* 1460)', *ODNB*, Oxford University Press, 2008 [*http://www.oxforddnb.com/view/article/20684* (accessed 19 Dec. 2008)].

[67] According to the annals ascribed to William of Worcester, cited in Roskell, 'William Tresham', 150.

The Tudor Speakers 1485–1601: Choosing, Status, Work*

ALASDAIR HAWKYARD

During the Tudor period the Speaker was nominated by the crown. The house of commons acquiesced with the crown's nomination, but not entirely passively. There is a body of evidence suggesting that the crown's nominee became the focus of disapprobation once his name became known. What hostility there was to the Speaker-designate from the mid 16th century was displayed to better effect outside the House than within.

Keywords: treasurer of the household; comptroller of the household; vice-chamberlain of the household; privy council; Speaker-designate; shires; urban counties; cathedral cities; shire towns; boroughs

1

The election of the Speaker was the first item of business undertaken by the house of commons following the opening of parliament. There were 32 men who held the speakership in 33 parliaments between the accession of Henry VII in 1485 and the death of Elizabeth I in 1603.[1] Of these, Thomas Englefield, Sir John Baker, John Pollard and John Puckering served as Speaker in two parliaments,[2] and Humphrey Wingfield, Richard Onslow and John Popham were replacements respectively for Sir Thomas

---

* This article originated as an expansion of the analysis first advanced in A. Hawkyard, *The House of Commons 1509–1558: Introductory Survey* (forthcoming) to see if in a greater context it still held. The article has benefited from the advice and comments of Caroline Baron, Paul Cavil, Linda Clark, Clyve Jones, Hannes Kleineke and John Murphy. The graphs were prepared by Peter Berrie. The map was drawn by Phillip Judge.

[1] Thomas Lovell (1485), John Mordaunt (1487), Sir Thomas Fitzwilliam (1489), Richard Empson (1491), Robert Drury (1495), (Sir) Thomas Englefield (1497, 1510), Edmund Dudley (1504), Sir Robert Sheffield (1512), Thomas Neville (1515), Sir Thomas More (1523), Thomas Audley (1529), Humphrey Wingfield (Feb. 1553 *vice* Audley appointed chancellor), Richard Rich (1536), Nicholas Hare (1539), Thomas Moyle (1542), Sir John Baker (1545, 1547), James Dyer (Mar. 1553), John Pollard (Oct. 1553, 1555), Robert Broke (Apr. 1554), Clement Heigham (Nov. 1554), William Cordell (1558), Sir Thomas Gargrave (1559), Thomas Williams (1563), Richard Onslow (Sept./Oct. 1566 *vice* Williams deceased), Christopher Wray (1571), Robert Bell (1572), John Popham (Jan. 1581 *vice* Bell deceased), John Puckering (1584, 1586), Thomas Snagge (1589), Edward Coke (1593), Christopher Yelverton (1597) and John Croke (1601). For brief lives of these men and entries on their constituencies see J.S. Roskell, *The Commons and their Speakers in English Parliaments 1376–1523* (Manchester, 1965); *History of Parliament. Biographies of the Members of the Commons House 1439–1509*, ed. J.C. Wedgwood with A.D. Holt (1936); *The House of Commons 1509–1558*, ed. S.T. Bindoff (3 vols, 1982); *The House of Commons 1558–1603*, ed. P.W. Hasler (3 vols, 1980). These sources provide the material not otherwise cited here.

[2] The establishment of a link between 'no more than two successive Parliaments through a re-elected Speaker' from 1376 onwards was noted by Roskell in *Speakers*, 335–6. Roskell observed that it was 'on the whole quite an infrequent occurrence'. However, he found only one example (Sir John Baker) 'under the Tudors' before Sir John Puckering's two speakerships, thus overlooking those of Thomas Englefield and John Pollard.

Audley, on his appointment as lord chancellor, and for Thomas Williams and Robert Bell, both of whom died while serving as Speaker.[3]

With the single exception of Thomas Lovell in 1485, all the Speakers at the time of their election were men with distinguished records of public service. Lovell, however, was an attainted traitor. For his part in the rising against Richard III in 1483 he had been attainted in the parliament of 1484; he fought with Henry Tudor at the battle of Bosworth in August 1485. Chief Justice Sir William Hussey to whom Henry VII referred the matter, concluded that, like the king himself, his attainder needed no reversal.[4]

The practice originating under Richard II, and spasmodically followed over the next 80 years, of opting for a king's councillor, who was a substantial commoner (or emerging as one), continued.[5] At least 11 (that is one-third of the 32) belonged to this category,[6] and in addition John Pollard, Richard Onslow, John Puckering and John Croke were members of the council in the marches, and Sir Thomas Gargrave a member of the council in the north. William Cordell was master of the rolls. Richard Onslow, John Popham and Edward Coke were solicitors general.[7] Of the remainder, all but John Mordaunt, Robert Broke, Thomas Williams and Robert Bell were employed in branches of the royal administration. Richard Empson, Thomas Audley, Humphrey Wingfield, Richard Rich, James Dyer, John Pollard, Robert Broke and Christopher Wray worked for the duchy of Lancaster.[8] Richard Rich was also chancellor of the court of augmentations, and Thomas Moyle was general surveyor of the more ancient court of general surveyors of the king's lands.[9]

With the exception of Thomas Neville in 1515, all the Speakers were distinguished lawyers.[10] As recorders of London, Sir Thomas Fitzwilliam, Robert Broke and John Croke held one of the most prestigious legal appointments in the kingdom, and three others (Sir Robert Sheffield, Richard Onslow and Edward Coke) had held the office previously. While it is possible that the uneven survival of documents from the inns of court may explain why no evidence has been found for any legal training for Neville,

---

[3] Bell's appointment as chief baron of the exchequer six months before his death in July 1577 would have necessitated his replacement had he not then died before the re-assembly of parliament.

[4] Sir William Hussey referred to the case 14 years earlier of Sir Thomas Tresham '*qui fuit intend que il sera Speaker de le Parlement*', *History of Parliament, Register of the Ministers and of the Members of Both Houses 1439–1509*, ed J.C. Wedgwood (1938), 384 n. 1; Roskell, *Speakers*, 74, 298; S.J. Gunn, 'Sir Thomas Lovell (c. 1459–1524): A New Man in a New Monarchy?', in *The End of the Middle Ages? England in the Fifteenth and Sixteenth Centuries*, ed. J.L. Watts (Stroud, 1998), 117–53; *ODNB*, xxxiv, 531.

[5] Roskell, *Speakers*, 336–7. The nine (or possibly ten) serving as Speaker in 13 parliaments out of 55 were Sir John Bussy (1394, 1395, Jan. 1397, Sept. 1397), ?Sir John Cheyne (1399), John Doreward (1399), Sir Arnold Savage (Jan. 1404), Sir William Sturmy (Oct. 1404), William Allington (1429), Sir John Tyrell (1437), Thomas Thorpe (1453), Sir John Say (1463, 1467) and William Catesby (1484).

[6] Sir John Baker, William Cordell, Robert Drury, Sir Thomas Englefield, Nicholas Hare, Clement Heigham, Thomas Lovell, Sir Thomas More, Thomas Neville, Richard Rich and Sir Robert Sheffield.

[7] Richard Rich had ceased to be solicitor general two weeks before the summoning of the parliament of 1536 and William Cordell two months before the assembly of the parliament of 1558.

[8] This trio followed in a tradition inaugurated in 1377 whereby the duchy had provided a string of Speakers to successive parliaments: see Roskell, *Speakers*, 338–40.

[9] As with the duchy of Lancaster nominees after 1399, the Commons, in accepting Rich and Moyle as Speaker, was choosing 'a royal servant of a special sort': see Roskell, *Speakers*, 339.

[10] L.W. Abbott, *Law Reporting in England 1485–1585* (1973), 57, 153. In the period 1394–1484, 14 of the 35 Speakers were lawyers, they presided over 25 of the 55 parliaments. See also S.J. Payling, 'The Rise of the Lawyers in the Lower House, 1395–1536', *Parliamentary History*, xxiii (2004), 108–9.

he differed significantly from all the other occupiers of the speakership during the century. He, alone, was of noble birth, being a younger brother of the 5th Lord Bergavenny. He was married to the daughter of a minor northern peer. Neville's origins and background were sufficiently unusual for a Speaker to merit comment in the account in the *Lords Journal* of his formal presentation to Henry VIII where he was described as '*ex nobili domo et familia procreatus, germanus frater Domini Burgevenney*'.[11] Lord Bergavenny enjoyed a fluctuating relationship with Henry VIII, one moment close, another estranged.[12] The delay in Thomas Neville's election may reflect this as much as his apparent lack of legal experience.[13]

2

In 1485 the two representatives for Colchester described how the house of commons chose Thomas Lovell as Speaker:

> The vijth day of November, be ix of the clokke, so for to procede un to a (leccion for) . . . a Speker. So the lection gave his voyse unto Thomas Lovel, a (gen tilman) . . . Lyncolnes Inne. That doon, it pleased the Knyghts there there [*sic.*] present (for to rise from) their sets and to for to goo to that plase where the Speker stode and . . . set hym in his sete. That don, there he thanked all the maisters of the plase. (Than) . . . the Recorder of London [Thomas Fitzwilliam] for to shewe the custume of the place. This was his seying: . . . Speker, and all my maisters, ther hath ben an ordir to this place in tymes (passed that) ye shuld commaunde a certeyn of Knyghts and other gentilmen, such as it pleaseth (yow) . . . to the nombre of xxiiij, and they to goo togedir un to my Lord Chaunceler, (and there) to show unto his lordship that they have doon the Kyngs commaundement in (the chosyn) of our Speker, desyring his his [*sic.*] lordship if that he wold shew it un to the Kyngs (grace. And) . . . whan it plesith the Kyng to commaunde us when we shall present hym upon the ix day of Novembre. (That) same day, at x of the cloke, sembled Maister Speker and all the Knyghts, sitteners and burgeyses in the parlament house, and so departed in to the parliament chambir (be fore) the Kyngis grace and all his lords spiritual and temporal and all his Jugs, (and so) presented our Speker before the Kyngs grace and all his lords spiritual and temporal.[14]

Their account broadly holds true over the century of interest to us. Later references expand upon their succinct summary, and indicate, as in so many of its procedures, the members, in choosing the Speaker, followed long-established conventions but deviated from these whenever it suited them, or perhaps more simply they forgot. A single reference suggests that, as described above, the recorder of London, in the absence of anyone else to preside over the assembly, ensured its propriety. In 1584 William

[11] *LJ*, i, 20.
[12] *ODNB*, xl, 495–7.
[13] *LJ*, i, 19. See below, p. 00.
[14] *Parliamentary Texts of the Later Middle Ages*, ed. N. Pronay and J. Taylor (Oxford, 1980), 185–6.

Fleetwood had to remind Sir Francis Knollys and Sir James Croft of the correct procedure although the pair should have been familiar with it.[15]

From a diversity of sources the complexity of the process in the late Tudor period can be pieced together. Towards the end of the formal opening of parliament, the lord chancellor or the lord keeper instructed the members who had come to witness the ceremony to return to their own premises. Once there they were to elect one of their number to be 'the mouth of them all, and to speake for and in the name of them'.[16] There is no clue in the records if they did so at once, or if, like others participating in the formal opening, they went off to dinner,[17] before returning. The men who had attended the ceremony were only a token delegation of the whole House. It is clear that on their re-entering the chamber they did not rejoin the whole complement of their fellow-members. Ostensibly all those returned had presented their credentials and taken their oaths in the course of the morning but, whatever the expectation, not everyone arrived in time for the assembly. Also, it is a reasonable inference that during the protracted ritual of the formal opening some of the members left behind in the house of commons had not bothered to await the reappearance of their colleagues there. Others may not have come back after their meal. One of the reasons for the delay in starting proceedings may have been a hope that more would arrive. Patience paid off in November 1584 when it was recorded: 'the number appearing upon the view not to be less than the whole', that is somewhere approaching the full complement of 486.[18] Nothing like this figure was achieved when Richard Onslow replaced Thomas Williams and John Popham replaced Robert Bell. In September 1566 there were only 152 present, that is a third of the entire House.[19] Fifteen years later the under-clerk noted: 'the Number . . . was not great'.[20]

For whatever reason, maybe for no more than a symbolic gesture of defiance over complying with its instructions to elect a Speaker, the House made no haste to do so. In October 1597 Hayward Townshend described how for a while the members 'all satt silent'.[21] Another man, probably the under-clerk, recalled how everyone had sat 'some space of time very silent'.[22] After a while one of the privy councillors present rose. He 'usually first breaketh the silence and putteth the rest in minde of the speech made in the Upper House touching the chosing of a Speaker'.[23] The man was almost invariably the treasurer of the household,[24] the leading privy councillor in the house of commons,

---

[15] *The Proceedings in the Parliaments of Elizabeth I*, ed. T.E. Hartley (3 vols, Leicester, 1981, 1995) [hereafter cited as *Proceedings*], ii, 65.

[16] Sir Thomas Smith, *De Republica Anglorum*, ed. M. Dewar (Cambridge, 1982), 80.

[17] *A Chronicle of England during the Reigns of the Tudors by Charles Wriothesley, Windsor Herald*, ed. W.D. Hamilton (Camden Society, 2nd ser., xi, 1875), 47, 94.

[18] Sir Symond D'Ewes, *The Journals of All the Parliaments during the Reign of Queen Elizabeth* (1682), 333.

[19] *CJ*, i, 73.

[20] *CJ*, i, 115.

[21] *Proceedings*, iii, 226.

[22] D'Ewes, *Journals*, 548.

[23] *Proceedings*, iii, 282; D'Ewes, *Journals*, 621.

[24] Sir Thomas Cheyne (Mar. and Oct. 1553: *CJ*, i, 24, 27); Sir Francis Knollys (1571, 1572, 1583, 1584, 1593: *CJ*, i, 82; *Proceedings*, i, 197, 336; D'Ewes, *Journals*, 392, 548); Sir William Knollys (1597, 1601: *Proceedings*, iii, 208, 300).

and one of the trio of household officials who managed the crown's interest there, sometimes in conjunction with a minister (Thomas Cromwell, Sir William Cecil and Sir Robert Cecil), sometimes not. In the absence of the treasurer, as for instance in 1555 when Sir Thomas Cheyne was sick, another of the trio, the comptroller stood in.[25] No evidence has been found of the third member of the trio, the vice-chamberlain, nominating a member for the speakership, perhaps because it was he upon whose shoulders ultimately fell the responsibility of ensuring the election of the crown's chosen man. It was either the treasurer or the comptroller who recommended the candidate. They put up the name of only a single man. As a matter of courtesy, or maybe only when they sensed a measure of hostility towards their candidate, they allowed, as they did in 1581, anyone 'without Prejudice to the Residue of the House, to name whom they would, or thought good'.[26] In 1584 when the nominee was John Puckering, 'none was heard to disallow or speak against the said choice';[27] another eye-witness recalled how his nomination was approved 'by some other voices, the rest saying nothing which was taken for a consent'.[28] The reception accorded Christopher Yelverton's nomination in October 1597 was even less warm. The members 'hawked [that is cleared their throats] and spat'. 'The Howse murmured like a still confused noyse a good while.' Yelverton was taken aback. He 'blushed and putt of his hatt, and after satt bareheaded'.[29] Thomas Neville's nomination in 1515,[30] Humphrey Wingfield's in 1533[31] and Richard Rich's in 1536[32] may have provoked even more unfavourable reactions.

There was an expectancy on the part of the treasurer and the comptroller that their nominee would be approved without opposition. This was at variance with the generally received notion that the members had the freedom of choice as to who was to be their Speaker. William Lambarde, one of the representatives for Aldborough in the parliament of 1563, noted the discrepancy.[33] What is clear is that the crown expected to designate the Speaker and to have its nominee chosen. A measure of the complexity of the process whereby the crown decided on the person whom it wanted can be gained from what happened in 1497. Whether the financially careful Henry VII added a further twist to the discussion and bartering is impossible to say. The king initially accepted Lord Chamberlain Daubeny's proposal of Robert Sheffield as Speaker, and in gratitude Daubeny offered him 'the fee of the Speaker' which presumably amounted to £100. He changed his mind in response to pressure from another councillor, Sir Reynold Bray, then chancellor of the duchy of Lancaster, and instead backed Thomas Englefield. When the

---

[25] Sir Edward Roger (1563: D'Ewes, *Journals*, 79); Sir William Knollys (1598: *Proceedings*, iii, 226; D'Ewes, *Journals*, 548).

[26] *CJ*, i, 117; D'Ewes, *Journals*, 281.

[27] D'Ewes, *Journals*, 333.

[28] *Proceedings*, i, 524.

[29] *Proceedings*, iii, 227, 328.

[30] *LJ*, i, 19. See below, p. 00.

[31] Vienna, Haus-, Hof-, und Staatsarchiv, England Hofkorrespondenz, Berichte an Karl V, no. 11 calendared *CSP Spanish 1531–3*, pp. 593–4 and *Letters and Papers Henry VIII* [hereafter cited as *LP Hen. VIII*], vi, 62–3.

[32] *LJ*, i, 85. See below, p. 00.

[33] *William Lambarde's Notes on the Proceedings of the House of Commons (1584)*, ed. P.L. Ward (House of Commons Document No. 10, nd), 56–7.

king remunerated Speaker Englefield, he did so on the understanding that Englefield would return £50 once he had received the sum from Bray.[34]

Two other later sources provide an insight into what actually took place. In his biographical notes on his father-in-law, Sir Thomas More, William Roper described a meeting at York Place between Cardinal Wolsey and More shortly after the end of the parliament of 1523. Wolsey evidently attributed much of the difficulty experienced by him in handling the parliament to More's management of the Commons. He said: 'Would to God, you had been at Rome, Mr More, when I made you Speaker.' To which More replied: 'Your Grace not offended, so would I too, my lord.'[35] Thirty years later, on 14 January 1553, with over six weeks to go to the opening of parliament, the duke of Northumberland returned certain papers to Lord Chamberlain Darcy together with a covering letter which he concluded with a postscript on parliamentary matters. He wrote: 'It was time the King's pleasure were known for the Speaker of the House that he might have secret warning as usual, the better to prepare for his preposition.'[36] There is nothing in either of these references to suggest either Wolsey or Northumberland was deviating from customary practice. In 1584 Queen Elizabeth reminded Speaker Puckering on his drawing her attention to matters then of concern to the house of commons that he 'was your [that is the Commons'] mouth by her allowance'.[37] In 1601 she alluded more directly to the same dependence: 'Mr Speaker [John Croke], whome we did constitute the mouthe of the Lower House'.[38]

Yet more illuminating is a note by Edward Coke preserved among his papers how on 28 January 1593, Elizabeth I and the privy council, then at Hampton Court, decided upon him as Speaker-designate. This agreement occurred midway between the summoning of parliament on the previous 4 January and its assembly on the following 19 February. Coke was thus speaking from personal experience when in his *Institutes* he remarked how the monarch 'doth name a discreet and learned man whom the Commons elect'.[39] Among the privy councillors present at the meeting approving the choice of Coke was the 1st Lord Hunsdon, the queen's cousin and her lord chamberlain. Bearing in mind the part played by two of Hunsdon's predecessors in the crown's choice of Speaker-designate it is tempting to conclude that his selection was a task performed by successive lord chamberlains.

Once the name of the Speaker-designate had been announced to the members he went through the form of trying to excuse himself from the task and to suggest that

---

[34] TNA, E101/414/6, ff. 128, 129; M.M. Condon, 'Ruling Elites in the Reign of Henry VII', in *Patronage, Pedigree and Power in Later Medieval England*, ed. C. Ross (Gloucester, 1979), 132. Steven Gunn has postulated that in the autumn of 1503 Edmund Dudley declined appointment as a serjeant-at-law in the knowledge that Henry VII intended him for the speakership in the forthcoming parliament. Dudley received his discharge on 1 Nov. 1503, i.e., long before the decision to hold a parliament had been taken, and probably two months before the king turned his mind to the choice (*ODNB*, xvii, 67; J.H. Baker, *The Order of Serjeants at Law* (Selden Society, suppl. ser., v, 1984), 166, 265–6).

[35] *The Lyfe of Sir Thomas Moore Knighte, Written by William Roper, Esquire*, ed. E.V. Hitchcock (Early English Texts Society, cxcvii, 1935), 19.

[36] TNA, SP10/18, no. 5, calendared *CSPD*, 1547–53, p. 288.

[37] BL, Harleian MS 6853, f. 285.

[38] *Proceedings*, iii, 292.

[39] HMC, *Rep.* ix (2), 373a: *Acts of the Privy Council*, xxiv, 28; E. Coke, *The Fourth Part of the Institutes of the Laws of England* (1671), 8.

others were more suited to it. He spoke from the floor of the House. In 1597 Christopher Yelverton argued:

> he that suplieth this place [that is the speakership] ought to be a man bigg and comely, stately and well spoken, his carriage Majestical, his Nature haughty and his Purse plentiful and heavy: but contrarily, the stature of my body is small, my self not so well-spoken, my voice low, my carriage Lawyer-like and of the common fashion, my Nature soft and bashful, my Purse thin, light and never plentiful.[40]

This exercise in self-deprecation perhaps tells us more about Yelverton's personal appearance and characteristics than the qualities commonly expected in a Speaker. His reference to his relative poverty, however, hints that the speakership could be a drain on its holder's resources.

Approval of the Speaker-designate was almost invariably by acclamation,[41] the members sometimes crying out the Speaker's name, rather than simply 'Aye'.[42] The known descriptions of the acclamations are terse, yet informative about the extent of the enthusiasm shown by the members when endorsing the regime's choice. In April 1554 Robert Broke was chosen 'with one Voice'.[43] This was also the experience of Sir Thomas Gargrave in 1559, Thomas Williams in 1563 and Christopher Wray in 1576.[44] In 1584 silence followed Sir Francis Knollys's nomination of John Puckering[45] until William Fleetwood, the recorder of London, who was sitting beside him on the lower row spoke to others around them 'Cry Puckering'. 'And then they and I beginning the rest did the same.'[46] In 1598 'all the Howse gave a lowde cry'.[47] However, another observer recalled perhaps more accurately 'none was heard to disallow or speak against the said choice'.[48] When a year previously the members expressed their unhappiness at Yelverton's nomination once he had made a speech intimating his unworthiness, Sir William Knollys as comptroller browbeat the assembly: 'If you doe not approve of my opynion, and accept Mr Seriant Yelverton's answere then we must proceed to the nominacion of some other, but if you please to impose it on him then say "I".'[49]

Occasionally the house of commons did proceed to the nomination of some other. This had occurred in 1420 when the names of Roger Hunt and John Russell were put forward. As the support for the pair was evenly balanced, the matter was put to a scrutiny or test (*examinacio*), Hunt winning narrowly by four voices ('*voces*'), '*etc.*'. What happened following the nomination of Thomas Neville in 1515, Humphrey Wingfield in 1533 and

---

[40] D'Ewes, *Journals*, 687.

[41] *CJ*, i, 47; *Proceedings*, iii, 282.

[42] *CJ*, i, 62; *Proceedings*, iii, 65.

[43] *CJ*, i, 33.

[44] *CJ*, i, 53, 62.

[45] This silence may have reflected the members' awareness that as a burgess for Bedford, Puckering did not meet a (possible) expectation of theirs that the Speaker should be a knight of the shire.

[46] *Proceedings*, iii, 65.

[47] *Proceedings*, iii, 228. Knollys's preparedness to accept an alternative nominee was perhaps a tacit recognition on his part that Yelverton as a burgess for Northampton was not, as ostensibly preferred by the members, a knight of the shire.

[48] D'Ewes, *Journals*, 388.

[49] *Proceedings*, iii, 228.

Richard Rich in 1536 is less clear. All that is certain is that their elections did not go smoothly. Contrary to the custom whereby the Speaker's presentation took place on the third working day of a parliament,[50] Neville's occurred on the fourth, no explanation for the delay being given.[51] Wingfield's presentation was also a day late.[52] With Rich, the house of commons had to ask for an extra day to make its decision. In the event, this turned out to be unnecessary as he was presented on the third working day.[53]

If one accepts the version given in the *Commons Journal* for January 1581, John Popham's election was 'with full Consent of Voices' but an account preserved in a copy made for Sir Simonds D'Ewes suggests otherwise. The (unknown) writer of this account noted how George Bromley, until recently attorney general of the duchy of Lancaster, was nominated to stand against Popham. Bromley was a knight for Shropshire. His nomination was put forward or supported by a member whose name is not recorded. This man compared the two candidates:

> In zeale to religeon, in settled minde, to holde the religeon sett forth by lawe, without alteracon, in skill of the lawes of England, in honestie and discretion, they both be Equall, In all other learninges, Mr Bromley is farre superior, and his deliverance in speech, shallbe founde verie good, Again he is alreadie advaunced in good place of her majestie soe as her majestie may better burden him with such service.

> Againe he is nowe a small pracitezer, otherwise than attendinge his office, soe that it shalnot be hurtefull to him, as to Mr Popham for losinges of Clientese, nor soe hurtefull to poore Clientes for lackinge theire Counsellor. I put these reasons the rather because I knowe there wilbe difficultie to perswade him to like of the place, which Mr Onlsowe fled ever with the losse of his Lyfe, comonlie the fittest men doe least seeke for offices, though they weare gainefull.[54]

In an aside he observed: 'If his brother [Sir Thomas, then lord chancellor] were of the house he were incomparably fitt.'[55] At the division Bromley lost by 12 votes to Popham's 82.[56] This was close. Even so, the outcome was probably a foregone conclusion once the vice-chamberlain and the ushers of the chamber had marshalled the household contingent, as they must have, on behalf of Popham.[57]

---

[50] M. McKisack, *Representation of English Boroughs in the Middle Ages* (Oxford, 1931), 142; Roskell, *Speakers*, 63–4; *The History of Parliament: The House of Commons, 1386–1421*, ed. J.S. Roskell, Linda Clark and Carole Rawcliffe (4 vols, Stroud, 1992) [hereafter cited as *HPC, 1386–1421*], i, 53; ii, 456; iv, 247.

[51] V.F. Snow, *Parliament in Elizabethan England: John Hooker's Order and Usage* (1977), 165; *LJ*, i, 19.

[52] Vienna, Haus-, Hof-, und Staatsarchiv, England Hofkorrespondenz, Berichte an Karl V, no. 11 calendared *CSP Spanish* 1531–3, p. 594 and *LP Hen. VIII*, vi, 63.

[53] *LJ*, i, 85–6.

[54] BL, Harleian MS 253, ff. 33–33v.

[55] BL, Harleian MS 253, f. 33.

[56] BL, Harleian MS 253, f. 33v. The total present was 152 which accords with the under-clerk's observation of the number of members present two days not being 'great' (*CJ*, i, 115). The under-clerk interestingly mentions that the members were invited 'to name whom they would' (*CJ*, i, 117). This evidence when evaluated with other pointers suggests that something may have gone awry here in the journal's composition.

[57] For evidence how the regime customarily procured its wishes and objectives see Alasdair Hawkyard, *The History of Parliament. The House of Commons 1509–1558* (survey volume, forthcoming).

Had George Bromley won the division, then his younger brother Sir Thomas would have directed the upper House and he the lower, a remarkable fraternal combination. This prompts me to wonder if this scenario had not actually been the vision of Chancellor Bromley, the merits of which he failed to commend to his colleagues on the privy council, but which then one of his associates tried to induce the house of commons to accept.

In 1598, once the House had approved Speaker Yelverton's election, Comptroller Knollys made 'a lowe reverence' and sat down.[58] The man chosen then customarily asked to be excused from accepting the post for the members to chose someone more suitable.[59] In 1563 the secretary of state, Sir William Cecil, welcomed the members' choice and insisted upon Speaker Williams accepting his election.[60] After a brief pause the comptroller then stood up together with another privy councillor and went down to where the Speaker was sitting on the lower row in order to formally conduct him to the Speaker's chair.[61] In 1601 John Croke recorded how they 'came up to the place where I sate and tooke me by each hand'.[62] Customarily the comptroller stood on his left hand and the treasurer on the right.[63] The combination of officials who conducted the Speaker to the chair varied: in March 1553, November 1554, January 1563, April 1571 and January 1581 it was the comptroller and, by implication, the treasurer;[64] in September 1566 and in October 1601 the comptroller and the vice-chamberlain;[65] and in October 1597 the comptroller and Sir Robert Cecil, then principal secretary.[66] On being placed in his chair, the Speaker-elect immediately stood up and made 'a short and honest excuse why hee should not bee chosen'.[67] If he had actually done this before being led to the chair, he instead thanked those who had elected him, as in 1597 Speaker Yelverton duly did.[68]

The appointment of Speaker Audley first as lord keeper, then as lord chancellor, while the parliament of 1529 stood prorogued meant that a replacement had to be found for him for the remainder of the parliament.[69] His replacement from 1533 was Humphrey Wingfield, who had been returned at the outset of the parliament for Great Yarmouth. This has led historians to conclude that Speaker Wingfield was 'the first burgess to be

---

[58] *Proceedings*, iii, 228.

[59] *CJ*, i, 82.

[60] *CJ*, i, 62.

[61] *CJ*, i, 62, 73; D'Ewes, *Journals*, 333, 469.

[62] *Proceedings*, iii, 284.

[63] *Proceedings*, i, 269.

[64] *CJ*, i, 24, 37, 62; *Proceedings*, i, 269.

[65] *CJ*, i, 73; *Proceedings*, iii, 284.

[66] *Proceedings*, iii, 228. But according to notes compiled for Speaker Yelverton, it was Sir John Fortescue, the chancellor of the exchequer, and not Secretary Cecil (*Proceedings*, iii, 210).

[67] *Proceedings*, i, 197.

[68] *Proceedings*, iii, 210.

[69] There were precedents from the 15th century for replacing Speakers during the course of a parliament. During the parliament of May 1413 William Stourton was superseded by John Doreward, in 1437 Sir John Tyrrell by William Burley, and in the parliament of 1453 Thomas Thorpe by Sir Thomas Charlton (Roskell, *Speakers*, 27, 70, 71, 84, 92, 216, 253–4; *HPC, 1386–1421*, iii, 498–9).

named Speaker',[70] 'all the previous Speakers having been knights of the shire'.[71] This may have been the case, but the sense of hierarchy innate at the time suggests otherwise. Although there is no direct evidence that he moved to a more prestigious seat, there exists a pointer that he did.[72]

Little is known about how Humphrey Wingfield became Speaker. Henry VIII, who under normal circumstances did not attend the opening of sessions after the initial assembly, came in February 1533, presumably to hear Chancellor Audley instruct the house of commons to elect a replacement for himself. Wingfield's election may have proved problematic as his presentation to the monarch took place a day later than was customary.[73] More is known about the replacements of Thomas Williams and of Robert Bell, two Speakers later in the century who died while parliament stood prorogued. The two men nominated as their replacements by the Elizabethan regime, Richard Onslow and John Popham, were, at the time of nomination, solicitor general, and, as such, the recipients of writs of assistance to attend the house of lords. In 1566, at the opening of the second session of the parliament of 1563, Sir Edward Rogers announced Speaker Williams's death. He advised the members to refer the matter to the house of lords and to ask their lordships to be suitors, together with four privy councillors from the Commons, to Queen Elizabeth: 'that shee should graunte them free election for a newe Speaker'. She consented to this proposition, issuing letters patent addressed to the lord keeper to that effect.[74] The same procedure was followed in 1581 at the opening of the third session of the parliament of 1572.[75] On this occasion the House consulted a 'Book of notes' kept by the under-clerk giving precise details about what had happened in 1566. The under-clerk read these out aloud to the assembly.[76] Two days later a delegation of members returned to the upper House to hear the commission to the lord chancellor to allow the lower House 'to proceed to the choice of a Speaker'. Later that same day another delegation went to the Lords to notify it that 'Mr Popham, being her Majestie's Solliciter General, was a member of our Howse, and that [we] were desirous to have him ioyne us in the election of our Speaker'. Popham 'shortly came downe accordingly'. Before the election proceeded a member identified simply as 'Mr Lewknor'[77] moved that, 'considering prayer was necessary to be used in all such action, that we might all ioyne in prayer to God to directe us in our doyings'. He offered a prayer 'for that purpose' which the under-clerk then read aloud. The whole House then said the Lord's Prayer. After that it elected Popham.[78]

[70] S.E. Lehmberg, *The Reformation Parliament* (Cambridge, 1970), 171; J. Loach, *Parliament under the Tudors* (Oxford, 1991), 46.

[71] Roskell, *Speakers*, vii.

[72] Hawkyard, *The House of Commons 1509–1558* (forthcoming).

[73] Vienna, Haus-, Hof-, und Staatsarchiv, England Hofkorrespondenz, Berichte an Karl V, no. 11 calendared *CSP Spanish* 1531–3, pp. 593–4 and *LP Hen. VIII*, vi, 62–3.

[74] *CJ*, i, 73; *LJ*, i, 625; *Proceedings*, i, 122.

[75] *LJ*, ii, 20.

[76] D'Ewes, *Journals*, 278–81; *CJ*, i, 116.

[77] Either Edward Lewknor, one of the burgesses for New Shoreham, whose puritanical persuasion suggests that it was he, or his kinsman Richard, a citizen for Chichester.

[78] *Proceedings*, i, 524.

On the day following the Speaker's election the treasurer and the comptroller accompanied by a delegation of members informed the lord chancellor or the lord keeper of the outcome. In 1495 Sir Richard Guildford as comptroller made the announcement together with Reynold Bray and Richard Empson, respectively chancellor and attorney general of the duchy of Lancaster.[79] The official records sometimes only mention one of the pair. In 1497 Sir Thomas Lovell as treasurer is said to have headed the delegation alone,[80] and in 1512 Sir Edward Poynings as comptroller.[81] In 1510 neither of the pair are mentioned when Sir Robert Drury, one of the councillors, did so.[82] It was customary, at least until 1512, for the pair to withhold the name of the person (*non nominando personam*) chosen.[83] The purpose of the delegation was to let it be known that the house of commons had complied with its instructions to elect a Speaker, not to announce the name of its choice which awaited until his presentation. By 1584 this practice had changed. In that year Sir Thomas Bromley also told the house of commons to let the privy council know of its decision so that it 'should expect what the Queenes pleasure and aunswere was concerning him so chosen'.[84] A day was fixed for the presentation which was almost invariably the third working day of the assembly.

On the morning of the presentation the members assembled at ten o'clock.[85] They had to await the arrival of the monarch, or when the ceremony was in Whitehall to go there once the monarch was ready. In March 1553, April 1554 and January 1558 it took place not in the Parliament Chamber but in the Waiting Chamber at Whitehall.[86] In 1553 the presentation was in the early afternoon, in March at one o'clock and seven months later at two o'clock.[87] In 1584 it was 'aboute three'.[88] The Speaker-elect was then conducted to the Parliament Chamber by the treasurer on his right-hand side and the comptroller on his left (Fig. 1).[89] In 1597 Speaker Yelverton was led there by Comptroller Knollys and Sir John Fortescue, a privy councillor, who was then chancellor of the exchequer,[90] and four years later Speaker Croke was led by the same pair.[91] The trio were accompanied by a select number of members to witness the ceremony on behalf of the

---

[79] *The Parliament Rolls of Medieval England*, ed. Chris Given-Wilson *et al.* (16 vols, Woodbridge, 2005) [hereafter cited as *PROME*], xvi, 136; *Rotuli Parliamentorum* (6 vols, 1767–77) [hereafter cited as *Rot. Parl.*], vi, 458.

[80] *PROME*, xvi, 285; *Rot. Parl.*, vi, 510.

[81] *LJ*, i, 23.

[82] *LJ*, i, 4.

[83] *PROME*, xv, 92, 339; xvi, 10, 93, 136, 285, 322; *Rot. Parl.*, vi, 268, 388, 410, 458, 510, 521; *LJ*, i, 11. The custom had originated following William Catesby's election in 1484 (*PROME*, xv, 9, 83). Previously the name of the man chosen was announced at the same time as the chancellor was informed about the successful outcome of the election.

[84] R. Glover, 'Of Nobiity Political and Civill', in T. Milles, *The Catalogue of Honor or Tresury of True Nobility Peculiar and Proper to the Isle of Great Britaine . . . Translated out of Latyne into English* (1610), 67.

[85] *PROME*, xvi, 285.

[86] *CJ*, i, 24, 34; *LJ*, i, 54–5.

[87] *CJ*, i, 24, 27.

[88] Glover, 'Of Nobility', 68.

[89] *CJ*, i, 53; D'Ewes, *Journals*, 40, 79; *Proceedings*, i, 269.

[90] *LJ*, ii, 193.

[91] *LJ*, ii, 229.

Figure 1: *The Presentation of the Speaker*
The presentation of the Speaker in 1584 from Robert Glover, *Nobilitas politica vel civilis* (1608). This shows from behind the Speaker standing on his specially provided platform and making his oration. On either side of him stand the treasurer of the household and the comptroller of the household. They wear red gowns and hold their white staves of office. BM, Department of Prints and Drawings – 1867,0403.674 (PRN: PPA166833). Reproduced with permission of the trustees of the British Museum.

rest of their colleagues: in 1584 these consisted of knights of the shire and citizens ('Burgesses of the Citties'),[92] and in 1597 there were 15 'deputies of the shires'.[93] Beside the bar there was, at least from 1584, 'a small platform' which the Speaker alone mounted.[94] After making three 'most low' obeisances to the monarch he asked to be released from the speakership and another more fit than he chosen.[95] When the monarch indicated satisfaction with him, he proceeded to make an oration. According to Henry Elsynge, the clerk of the parliaments (1621–35), Thomas Neville made a speech in 1515 not outshone until Sir Thomas Crewe's in 1624.[96] He concluded his oration with four requests: for freedom of access to the monarch; for forgiveness in advance of any unintended provocation; for the liberty of speech; and for privilege from arrest.[97] Neither the oration nor the petitions are recorded with any regularity. The entry in the parliament roll is formulaic.[98] The details given in the journals of both the upper and lower Houses are brief, if they exist at all. This reflects the purposes of these records which was fundamentally to note the passage of legislation, where what we know is mentioned only incidentally whenever the clerk saw fit to deviate from the basic entry and to add a sprinkling of details normally omitted. This has led some historians to conclude either they were not always requested or the first extant reference is evidence of an innovation.[99] By far the least is known about the petition for forgiveness in advance, even though it is clearly summarized in the formulaic entry repeated by successive clerks of the parliament together with the protestation.[100] In 1536 Richard Rich asked to be excused for misleading reporting. From 1559 it is known to have been made regularly.[101] The same procedure of an oration followed by petitions was adopted in October 1566 and January 1581 when Richard Onslow and John Popham were replacement Speakers.[102]

[92] Glover, 'Of Nobility', 68.

[93] *De Moisse: A Journal of All that was Accomplished by Monsieur de Moisse Ambassador in England from King Henri to Queen Elizabeth Anno Domini 1597*, ed. G.B. Harrison and R.A. Jones (1931), 30.

[94] *De Moisse*, ed. Harrison and Jones, 30.

[95] Roskell, *Speakers*, ch. 2; 21–2, 24–30; Glover, 'Of Nobility', 68. The text of what is probably Edmund Dudley's protestation in 1504 survives (*Parliamentary Texts of the Later Middle Ages*, ed. Pronay and Taylor, 197–200).

[96] H. Elsynge, *The Ancient Method and Manner of Holding Parliaments in England* (3rd edn, 1675), 165.

[97] That there were four is clear from D'Ewes (*Proceedings*, 165) and Smith (*De Republica Anglorum*, 80–1). John Hooker, however, in his parliamentary diary for 1571 ('Hooker's Journal of the House of Commons in 1571', ed. J.B. Davidson, *Transactions of the Devonshire Association*, xi (1879), 473–5) and his *Notes and Usages* of 1572 (Snow, *Parliament*, 165–6), states there were only three. What Hooker did, as V.F. Snow noted in 1977, was to indicate three 'but then goes on to list four' (Snow, *Parliament*, 165 n. 54). Hooker seems to have noticed that something was amiss in his journal entry, and then went on to correct mistakes there only to compound them in his revised version. See also, *Proceedings*, i, 269, 337, 338, 525–6; ii, 64, 65, 206, 257–62, 300–4; iii, 65; Glover, 'Of Nobiity', 68. For details of this at greater depth see Roskell, *Speakers*, ch. 2; 21, 39–40, 253–4; Hawkyard, *The House of Commons 1509–1558* (forthcoming); J.E. Neale, *The Elizabethan House of Commons* (1949), 358–63.

[98] E.g., *PROME*, xv, 92.

[99] G.R. Elton, in his discussion of Speaker More's oration in 1523 is perhaps the classic example of this method of reasoning, *The Tudor Constitution: Documents and Commentary* (Cambridge, 1960), 254–5.

[100] Roskell, *Speakers*, 33–7, 39; *PROME*, xv, 92–3, 779; vi, 10, 93, 143, 285, 322.

[101] *LJ*, i, 85; G.R. Elton, *The Parliament of England 1559–1581* (Cambridge, 1986), 331–2.

[102] *Proceedings*, i, 125–8, 525–6.

On her way out of the Parliament Chamber to the Queen's Bridge to return to Whitehall at the conclusion of the ceremony in 1597, Elizabeth I honoured Speaker Yelverton with a highly personal and singular sign of favour: 'her Majetie passing by me pulled of her glove, and gave me her hand to kisse: and said, "You sir, you are welcome to the butts, sir", and laid both her handes about my neck, and staied a good space; and so most gratiously departed. And in her privie chamber after, amongst her ladies, said she was sorry, she knewe me noe sooner.'[103] The reason for this conspicuous display of favour and the circulation not long afterwards of words spoken in the private apartments at Whitehall was twofold, to indicate to Yelverton, notwithstanding the hostile reception to his nomination, that he had royal backing and to remind the members of his being the queen's chosen man. In 1601, less ostentatiously, and perhaps ill, the queen simply offered her hand to Speaker Croke who kissed it, 'but not one word she spake unto him'.[104]

3

Of the Speaker, William Lambarde noted: 'He . . . must be a knight or burgess returned.'[105] Lambarde's phraseology is curious. A 'knight or burgess returned' simply means a person duly chosen at a parliamentary election, in other words an elected member. Bearing in mind Lambarde's evident dependence on records kept by the under-clerk which no longer survive, two explanations come to mind. First, there had been an attempt sometime before 1563, for which no other evidence is known, to impose on the house of commons a person who was not a member of it. Second, there had been an order earlier that the Speaker could only be a knight of the shire but this had been amended during the 1540s when in 1542, Thomas Moyle may have entered the House as one of the citizens for Rochester or in 1545, when Sir John Baker entered it as a burgess for Lancaster.

Lambarde's terse remark disguises, or takes for granted, two apparent contemporary expectations, that preferably the Speaker should be of knightly rank and that ideally he should enter the House as one of the knights of the shire. Only six of the Speakers met the expectation of being knights in their own right when nominated and approved.[106] In the case of six others, this omission was promptly rectified by the monarch, at the opening ceremony or on presentation (or within days of these two occasions).[107] The knighting of Thomas Moyle at the opening of the parliament of 1542 formed part of the celebrations to mark the arrival of Welsh members. It looks as though the Speaker in March 1553, James Dyer, was likewise honoured early on in the parliament. Three others were knighted shortly after the prorogation or dissolution, either while still Speaker or at the conclusion of their term of office.[108] John Mordaunt's experience had

---

[103] *Proceedings*, iii, 206–7.

[104] *Proceedings*, iii, 306.

[105] *William Lambarde's Notes*, ed. Ward, 56.

[106] Sir Thomas Fitzwilliam, Sir Robert Drury, Sir Robert Sheffield, Sir Thomas More, Sir John Baker and Sir Thomas Gargrave.

[107] Thomas Neville, Humphrey Wingfield, Richard Rich, Nicholas Hare, Thomas Moyle and William Cordell.

[108] Thomas Audley, Robert Broke and Clement Heigham.

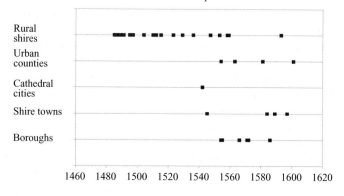

Each point is a Speaker. His position on the lower horizontal axis is the year when
he became Speaker. His position on the left vertical axis is on one of five bands
depending on the status of his constituency on being chosen.

Figure 2: *Type of Constituency*

been very different. Seventeen years elapsed between his speakership and his knighthood
in 1504 on the occasion of Prince Henry's creation as prince of Wales.[109] A dozen had
passed for Richard Empson when he was knighted at the same occasion.[110] Robert Bell
was knighted on 4 January 1577 while the parliament of 1572 was in recess and shortly
before his appointment as a baron of the exchequer. Elizabeth I's reluctance to ennoble
her principal subjects is often commented on but her similar indisposition to bestow
knighthoods has passed almost unobserved. The Speakers in the late 16th century were
among the casualties of this. Both John Popham and John Puckering waited until 28
May 1592 when Popham was made chief justice of the king's bench and Puckering lord
keeper.[111] Edward Coke, Christopher Yelverton and John Croke had to wait until the
arrival of James I after his accession in 1603.

The evidence as to their expected status as knights of the shire is perhaps less clear
cut. Deficiencies in the surviving returns mean that the names of the constituencies
for 11 of the 32 Speakers cannot be identified with certainty (Fig. 2).[112] Of the
remainder, nine were elected for rural shires,[113] and four for urban counties.[114] Another
six were returned for shires towns and boroughs.[115] Humphrey Wingfield, who
replaced Sir Thomas Audley as Speaker during the course of the parliament of 1529,

[109] W.A. Shaw, *The Knights of England* (2 vols, 1906), ii, 34; *ODNB*, xviii, 425.

[110] Shaw, *The Knights of England*, ii, 34; *ODNB*, xviii, 425.

[111] E. Foss, *The Judges of England* (9 vols, 1851–64), v, 533; *ODNB*, xlv, 425.

[112] Thomas Lovell, John Mordaunt, Richard Empson, Sir Thomas Englefield, Edmund Dudley, Sir Robert
Sheffield, Thomas Neville, Sir Thomas More, Richard Rich, Nicholas Hare and Thomas Moyle.

[113] Thomas Fitzwilliam, Thomas Audley, Sir John Baker (1547), James Dyer, John Pollard (Oct. 1553),
Robert Broke, William Cordell, Sir Thomas Gargrave and Edward Coke.

[114] Robert Broke, Thomas Williams, John Popham and John Croke.

[115] Sir John Baker (1545), Clement Heigham, John Pollard (1555), John Puckering, Thomas Snagge and
Christopher Yelverton.

had been elected as a member for Great Yarmouth but there are reasons for believing that he transferred to a more prestigious seat on becoming Speaker.[116] However, neither of the two other replacement-Speakers later in the period, Richard Onslow in 1566 and John Popham in 1581, seem to have been expected to transfer to seats for shires, Onslow remaining as member for the modest Sussex borough of Steyning and Popham for the urban county and cathedral city of Bristol. This may have been because, unlike in 1532–3, there were no vacancies available in the shires where a Speaker might have been accommodated.

The nine men known to have been Speakers who were knights of the shire, with the single exception of Sir John Baker in 1547, invariably sat for the counties where they lived (Fig. 3). This accorded with the expectation in the act of 1413 that knights of the shire should be resident in the shire that they represented.[117] This compliance with statute persisted generally well into the 16th century and beyond. This enables us to infer that at least ten of the Speakers whose constituencies are unknown entered the parliament concerned as elected knights for the shire.[118] It was, however, put to the test late in Henry VIII's reign, and after that it was not always met. After that date Speakers sometimes represented urban counties,[119] where they had links. This seems to have been deemed to meet the residential qualification. However, this compromise solution was not always possible. In 1542 Thomas Moyle may have been returned for Rochester where he was to be chosen repeatedly for a decade: the members for Rochester occupied places on the lower row in the House, and thus ranked amongst the highest persons there. The constituency returning Nicholas Hare in 1539 defies identification unless he procured election for Lancashire or one of the three adjoining shires in the Scottish marches where, as an East Anglian, he had no clout. However, his dependence upon the 3rd duke of Norfolk, then commander in the north, who assured the government of a compliant membership from the area, suggests the means whereby this was achieved. Hare is almost certainly to be counted with the Speakers-designate whose elections to parliament did not go smoothly.[120] He seems to have been the first of this category. Sir John Baker in 1545 was evidently the second. He entered the last Henrician parliament as the senior burgess for Lancaster, presumably on a duchy of Lancaster ticket, although by that time his earlier links with the duchy had long been severed. There is no evidence that anyone argued that a person not a knight of the shire should be disqualified from nomination for the speakership. This apparent silence may reflect gaps in records from the period. However, non-compliance with statute may throw light on the cool reception given in the house of commons to several of the nominees.

The meagre evidence for elections where the Speaker-designate failed to obtain election for the county where he lived merits close attention. The privy council

---

[116] Hawkyard, *The House of Commons 1509–1558* (forthcoming).

[117] 1 Hen. V, c. 1.

[118] Thomas Lovell, John Mordaunt, Richard Empson, Robert Drury, (Sir) Thomas Englefield, Edmund Dudley, Sir Robert Sheffield, Thomas Neville, Sir Thomas More and Richard Rich.

[119] Of the cities, towns and boroughs represented in parliament, a select number enjoyed county status. These were the urban counties. They had sheriffs of their own to whom the writs for election were addressed, who held the elections in accordance with the electoral law for the shires, and who made the returns. The elections were often said to have been 'in full county court', and the men chosen often called knights of the shire.

[120] See below, pp. 37–41.

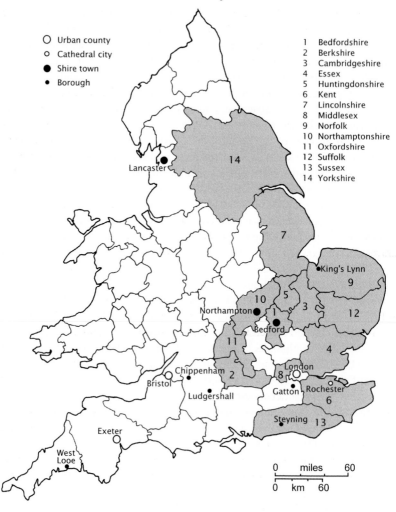

Figure 3: *Speakers and their Constituencies*

sometimes expressed support for candidates at elections. In August 1547 and January 1553 it did so on behalf of Speakers-designate, in Kent for Sir John Baker and in Cambridgeshire for James Dyer. When the freeholders in Kent got wind of the privy council's manœuvring they objected vociferously, and it was forced to appease them. This was to no avail as Baker had to turn for a seat in Huntingdonshire (where he had no property). The experience of John Pollard late in 1555 was even more fraught. For the previous three parliaments he had been able to count on a seat for Oxfordshire but in that year the county preferred two others, neither of whom cut much of a figure there. Following this, he presented himself to the electors at Gloucester, where he held the recordership and which was an urban county as well as a cathedral city. The election was disorderly, and the civic enquiry into it, held afterwards, established that he had angered the citizens by demanding the seat customarily allotted to the recorder. Ostensibly he got in as the junior burgess for Chippenham two days before the opening but, as his name was inserted in a different hand on the election indenture,[121] it looks as though he was jobbed in without the townsmen's knowledge, and maybe even after the indenture's arrival in London. Pollard's misfortunes presumably cast light on Nicholas Hare's fate in 1539, Sir John Baker's in 1545 and 1547, and Clement Heigham's in 1554. The county of Suffolk seems to have displayed a remarkable degree of independence. In 1539 it elected Sir Anthony Wingfield, the vice-chamberlain of the household, together with Sir Arthur Hopton, a gentleman of modest stature, upon whose parliamentary career Thomas Cromwell, the crown's electoral manager, had earlier shown favour.[122] It is highly likely that Nicholas Hare found a place for a northern shire.[123] The situation in late 1554 was strikingly similar as the two knights chosen were privy councillors and stalwarts of the Marian regime, and Heigham had to look further afield to West Looe in Cornwall where a lien between the borough and Lincoln's Inn seems to have operated in his favour. The electors in Kent seem to have snubbed Baker in much the same way as Oxfordshire men did Pollard, as in 1545 they chose the comparatively unknown George Harper to sit with Sir Thomas Cheyne, and in 1547 the equally inexperienced Sir Thomas Wyatt with him.

No evidence has been found to suggest that in 1563 Thomas Williams put his name forward to sit for Devon. The two knights chosen had both repeatedly represented the shire.[124] Instead, he was returned for Exeter, an urban county and a cathedral city, where he was a familiar figure and which retained him as legal counsel. His fellow-member was the city's recorder, Geoffrey Tothill. Two points deserve comment. First, the city rejected two nominees of the 2nd earl of Bedford to whom at other times it listened more sympathetically. Second, Williams took precedence over Tothill who otherwise might have expected to have been entitled to the senior place, as he was to be on two subsequent occasions. In 1601 John Croke, recorder of London, was one of the capital's four members. London was another urban county.

Similarly there is no evidence that in 1571 Christopher Wray tried to secure election for Lincolnshire. He enjoyed the support of the 6th earl of Westmorland whom he advised on legal matters. Yet it was Sir Henry Clinton, a son of the 1st earl of Lincoln, and Thomas Heneage, a courtier high in Elizabeth I's favour, who were chosen knights. Wray got in for the Wiltshire borough of Ludgershall which had a reputation as a haven of last resort for those wanting a place in the house of commons. A year later the county election for Norfolk was contested, with two dependants of Lord Keeper Bacon obtaining their return.[125] Bell who as recorder had represented King's Lynn in the previous two parliaments was re-elected there again. The circumstances are not entirely clear. The town had originally

---

[121] TNA, C219/24/188.

[122] If this premise is correct, Suffolk appears to have displayed a remarkable degree of electoral independence from outside pressure. In 1545 Wingfield also seems to have fallen victim to it, and with the help of the 3rd duke of Norfolk he had obtained a place for one of the duke's boroughs in Sussex.

[123] See above, p. 37.

[124] Sir John Chichester and Sir Gawain Carew.

[125] Henry Woodhouse and Francis Wyndham, one the son-in-law of Bacon, and the other shortly to become another.

envisaged returning two townsmen. This was perhaps on the presumption that Bell would be one of the knights for the shire, but in the week leading up to the opening it replaced one of the pair with Bell.

In 1584 and 1586 John Puckering, a Yorkshireman born but a migrant to Hertfordshire, had little chance of obtaining election in his adopted county where Sir Ralph Sadler repeatedly procured the senior seat until his death. The election there in 1584 was contested (but whether Puckering was one of the contestants is unknown) and two years later the two knights from the previous parliament were re-elected. On the earlier occasion Puckering as a member of the council in the marches of Wales found a place for Carmarthen Boroughs which, in the event, he declined on being returned for the more prestigious English county town of Bedford. Had he sat for Carmarthen Boroughs he would have been the first Speaker to have represented a Welsh constituency.[126] Bedford did not re-elect him in 1586. Like John Pollard 30 years before at Chippenham, he was put in at the last moment for an undistinguished borough in Surrey. Gatton belonged to the Copley family but during the minority of the young heir the patronage there was exercised by Lord Burghley as master of the court of wards. The indenture for the election just over two weeks before the opening of parliament was delivered to Burghley with a blank space left for the name of the senior burgess. Burghley then personally inserted Puckering's name.[127]

Bedford, which had provided John Puckering with a seat earlier, was to do so again in 1589 for Thomas Snagge. Snagge was a Bedfordshire man who had married a local coheiress. He had been returned as knight for the county twice before 1589 when two kinsmen of the local nobility got in. In a period when the evidence for the activities of members in the House is increasingly substantial, Oliver St John and Edward Radcliffe are unusual for leaving no trace. Snagge seems to have turned from a place for the county to the county town where he held the recordership. His election there was evidently not without incident as on 18 December 1588, not long after the election, the municipal authorities discussed a ban on canvassing before any future elections. Canvassing, it should be remembered, was one of the grounds on which, in 1555, Gloucester had registered a complaint against John Pollard.

Like John Puckering, Christopher Yelverton was a migrant, settling in Northamptonshire only after his marriage. In 1593 he had sat with Lord Burghley's son, Sir Thomas Cecil. Four years later Cecil was re-elected with another Northamptonshire man with considerable experience in county management.[128] On 8 October 1597, just two weeks before the opening, Yelverton, in his capacity as recorder of the county town, was elected at Northampton, together with his son Henry. In this instance the evidence is too slight to argue with any certainty that Yelverton had tried for the county and been rejected. But in the light of the reception of the announcement of his nomination as Speaker, it is tempting to add him to the list of

---

[126] This distinction went four centuries later in 1976 to Thomas George Thomas, later Viscount Tonypandy. The first Welshman to be Speaker was Sir William Williams (21 Oct. 1680–28 Mar. 1681), but he sat for the English urban county of Chester.

[127] TNA, C219/30/100.

[128] Sir Richard Knightley.

Speakers-designate who failed at the first hurdle, only to succeed on a second or third attempt.

John Puckering was not alone in obtaining his return for a borough as a precaution against failure at the shire election. According to a comment of his made a quarter of a century later, Edward Coke did so for a Cornish borough in 1593,[129] but notwithstanding the electoral contest for the Norfolk knighthoods, or maybe on account of it, he obtained the senior place for the shire. A century earlier, in 1489, Sir Thomas Fitzwilliam had been returned both for his native county of Lincolnshire and for London, which was not a borough but an urban county. The practice in London of electing its recorder regularly had started in the 1460s. Thus, it looks as if Fitzwilliam had deliberately sought election as knight of a shire, not merely as a representative of an urban county, even though London habitually called its two senior members (of whom the recorder was the second) knights of the shire.

This review of the election to parliament of the Speakers-designate enables us to draw certain conclusions. Of the 33 Speakers during the period their constituencies can be listed:

Shires where Speakers were resident	Shires where Speakers were non-resident	Urban counties	Cathedral cities	Shire towns	Boroughs
7–17[130]	1–3[131]	4[132]	?1[133]	4[134]	5 or 6[135]

During the Tudor period there was a falling off in realizing the expectation of the Speaker being a knight of the shire, but this was hardly precipitous. It remained an aspiration for Speakers-designate to attempt, and over two-thirds almost certainly accomplished it.

Why the expectation ceased to be automatically realized is, nevertheless, of great interest. There are shreds of evidence in notes kept by members and indirect pointers in official sources that the crown's nominee as Speaker-designate was not accepted without demur, if only with no more than sullen silence. The mobilisation of the contingent from the royal household, the means whereby the crown almost invariably got its way, ensured

[129] Formerly Berkshire RO, Downshire MSS, Trumbull Add. M50, f. 56, cited in *The House of Commons 1558–1603*, ed. Hasler, i, 623. NB. At the BL, 'Misc L' has been broken up and distributed in 12 different files (without a record of the precise files being kept).

[130] ?Thomas Lovell (Middlesex or Norfolk), ?John Mordaunt (Bedfordshire), Thomas Fitzwilliam (Lincolnshire), ?Richard Empson (Northamptonshire), ?Robert Drury (Suffolk), ?(Sir) Thomas Englefield (Berkshire), ?Edmund Dudley (Sussex), ?Sir Robert Sheffield (Lincolnshire), ?Thomas Neville (Kent), ?Sir Thomas More (Middlesex), Thomas Audley (Essex), ?Richard Rich (Essex), James Dyer (Cambridgeshire), John Pollard (Oxfordshire), William Cordell (Suffolk), Sir Thomas Gargrave (Yorkshire) and Edward Coke (Norfolk).

[131] ?Humphrey Wingfield (unknown), ?Nicholas Hare (unknown) and Sir John Baker (Huntingdonshire).

[132] Robert Broke (London), Thomas Williams (Exeter), John Popham (Bristol) and John Croke (London).

[133] ?Thomas Moyle (Rochester).

[134] Sir John Baker (Lancaster), John Puckering (Bedford), Thomas Snagge (Bedford) and Christopher Yelverton (Northampton).

[135] John Pollard (Chippenham), Clement Heigham (West Looe), Richard Onslow (Steyning), Christopher Wray (Ludgershall), Robert Bell (King's Lynn) and John Puckering (Gatton). When Onslow came in for the second session of the parliament of 1563, it seems not to have been thought necessary for him to transfer to a more distinguished seat as Humphrey Wingfield had almost certainly done earlier.

the acceptance of its nominee. Even so, the members saw fit to express their disapproval. What happened in 1515, 1533 and 1536 may never be known beyond something held up the process of the Speaker's election. It may, or may not, be coincidental that in 1539 Nicholas Hare was the first Speaker not to sit for the county where he was resident, and from then on what had been custom became less frequent. This change coincides with a welter of circumstantial evidence that from late in Henry VIII's reign the return of the Speaker-designate to parliament did not go as hoped. The incidence of this evidence, when set against that for other elections where other candidates with reasonable expectations failed, suggests that from 1539, at least, steps were taken outside the capital to frustrate the crown's wishes once these became known.[136] In other words, the electorate took the opportunity to indicate its disapproval of the crown's choice. In the event these expressions achieved little more than an irritating hiccup in the process of electing a Speaker. Throughout the period the crown invariably got in the end, by hook or by crook, the man whom it wanted as Speaker.[137]

4

Thomas Lovell, Thomas Neville and Thomas Moyle seem at first sight to have lacked parliamentary experience before being chosen Speaker but this curious fact almost certainly reflects heavy losses among the names of members for so many of the earlier parliaments in the period under review (Fig. 4). In the case of Lovell he cannot have served in the parliament immediately preceding his speakership, that of 1484 where the Ricardian regime attainted him. The first Speaker who undoubtedly served in the post without any previous experience of the house of commons was, in 1584, the serjeant-at-law, John Puckering. Edward Coke, chosen in 1593, was barely better qualified as he had only sat once, in the previous assembly, that of 1589.

Age does not appear to have been a consideration in the choice of Speaker (Fig. 5). Of the men chosen in the period, eight were in their thirties (with John Mordaunt and Thomas Neville maybe barely out of their twenties).[138] The majority (18) were in their forties.[139] Sir John Baker, Clement Heigham, Humphrey Wingfield and Thomas Snagge were in their fifties, and Sir Robert Sheffield, Sir Thomas Gargrave and Christopher Yelverton in their sixties. Of these, Gargrave was the oldest, being 65 or 66 on being chosen. No pattern concerning their age can be detected during the period, beyond a

---

[136] No evidence has so far been traced as to when precisely the name of the Speaker-designate became widely known before the assembly of parliament. But it must have been virtually impossible to suppress this information once the Speaker-designate had been informed of his choice by the crown.

[137] The first documented instance of the crown's preferred choices not being returned to the house of commons occurred in Oct. 1640. This was when Thomas Gairdner failed to obtain one of the seats for London. Charles I then consulted a list of lawyers who had been elected, and settled upon William Lenthall who was, in due course, approved by the members. *ODNB*, xxi, 445–6; xxxiii, 386.

[138] Thomas Lovell, John Mordaunt, Thomas Neville, Richard Rich, Nicholas Hare, Robert Broke, William Cordell and Richard Onslow.

[139] Richard Empson, Robert Drury, Thomas Englefield, Edmund Dudley, Sir Thomas More, Thomas Audley, Thomas Moyle, James Dyer, John Pollard, Thomas Williams, Christopher Wray, Robert Bell, John Popham, John Puckering, Edward Coke and John Croke.

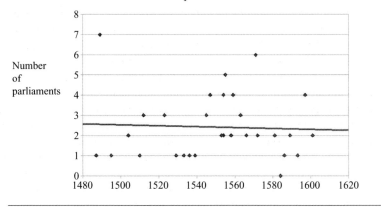

Each point is a Speaker. The vertical axis shows in how many parliaments he had sat before being chosen Speaker. The horizontal axis is the year when he became Speaker. Allowing for gaps in the extant evidence, it seems that over the period there was a gradual decline in the frequency with which, after their terms of office, Speakers continued to be members.

Figure 4: *Previous Parliamentary Experience*

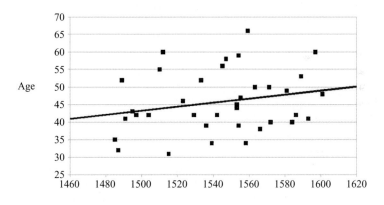

Each point is a Speaker. The vertical axis shows age in years on being chosen Speaker. The horizontal axis is the year that he became Speaker. There is much individual variation, with a slight tendency (shown by the continuous line) for Speakers becoming older on electioin as the period progressed.

Figure 5: *Age*

slight rise in their overall average age. This creates the presumption that the overriding concern for the crown was evidently not their physical maturity but the extent of their stamina and managerial skills.

If neither previous parliamentary experience nor a certain maturity were consider-ations of paramount importance in the crown's selection of a Speaker-designate, does the evidence, albeit fragmentary, enable us to infer if any such considerations existed beyond a general pragmatism? The choice of Speakers Englefield, Baker, Pollard and Puckering for a second term suggests that their handling of highly-charged issues had not gone unnoticed by the regime: with Englefield, the crown's pressing need for money; with Baker, the dissolution of the last surviving religious foundations; with Pollard, the re-establishment of the catholic church in England; and with Puckering, the difficulties arising from the presence in the kingdom of the exiled Mary Queen of Scots.

The choice of Sir Thomas Gargrave in 1559 is particularly interesting. One of the main problems facing Elizabeth I on her accession was how to end the reunion with Rome and to obtain a new Church settlement without exacerbating an already highly-fraught religious situation. In his mid-sixties Gargrave presided over an assembly younger and less experienced than its immediate predecessors. He was a trusted government official. Nevertheless, in the parliament of 1555 he had opposed the bill for the restoration of payment of annates to the catholic church and then absented himself from the house of commons for the debates on the bill to penalise exiles. He knew how opposition worked, and by inference he knew what steps to take to stop it from blocking the regime's intentions.

Successive regimes seem to have recognized the advantages of a Speaker who had revealed an independent caste of mind and behaviour. Such a man's mastery in persuasion, it was evidently hoped, could be harnessed to the advantage of the crown. This was an extension of the principle so well illustrated with Sir Thomas Gargrave: the Speaker knew, or should know, how to handle his kindred spirits. In 1504 Thomas More, barely at the outset of his career, persuaded his fellow-members to reject Henry VII's demand for money.[140] In 1571 Robert Bell so successfully spear-headed the attack upon purveyance that he was summoned before the privy council to be rebuked. Bell also had in his attack the backing of John Popham, who was to replace him as Speaker in the parliament of 1572. In 1572 (15 years before his speakership) Christopher Yelverton protested against the insufficient amount of time allowed for the consideration of a bill against Mary, Queen of Scots. Thomas Snagges's even-handed approach in 1571 to the bill encouraging church attendance and his suggestion of all dissenters from divine service to be treated equally, whatever their religious persuasions, may even have endeared him to Elizabeth I. Her government may also have spotted, long before it was generally recognized, Edward Coke's fascination with procedure and with identifying and rectifying inconsistencies. As Speaker, Coke tightened procedure and discipline.

5

The pattern of what happened under the Tudors to each Speaker after his term in office did not alter significantly from his predecessors' experience under the late Plantagenets (Fig. 6). We have already noticed that four of the Tudor Speakers were chosen for a second term.[141] These men clearly gave satisfaction to the crown in how they executed

---

[140] *The Lyfe of Sir Thomas Moore*, ed. Hitchcock, 7.

[141] Thomas Englefield, Sir John Baker, John Pollard and John Puckering.

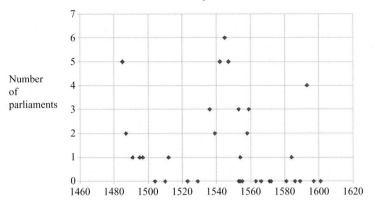

Each point is a Speaker. The vertical axis shows in how many parliaments
he sat after ceasing to be Speaker. The horizontal axis is the year when
he became Speaker.

Figure 6: *Later Parliamentary Experience*

their work in directing the house of commons. The exact extent to which former
Speakers were re-elected as members is hard to gauge, and is disguised by gaps in the
known membership, particularly in the late 15th and early 16th centuries. Whether Sir
Thomas Fitzwilliam, Richard Empson, Sir Thomas Englefield (after his second stint in
the position) and Thomas Neville re-appeared in the Commons is not known. Nevertheless, we can say that Sir Robert Drury, Sir Robert Sheffield and Humphrey Wingfield
were re-elected at least once more; Sir John Mordaunt, Sir Nicholas Hare, Clement
Heigham and Sir William Cordell twice; Sir Richard Rich and Sir Thomas Gargrave
three times; Edward Coke four; and Sir Thomas Lovell, Sir Thomas Moyle and Sir John
Baker five. Of the others, Thomas Williams and Robert Bell died while holding the
speakership, and Sir John Pollard and Richard Onslow died in the interval before the
next parliament. Both Edmund Dudley (*d*. 1510) and Sir Thomas More (*d*. 1535) were
executed for treason. Seven more became judges[142] and three either lord keeper or lord
chancellor,[143] all positions which precluded them from sitting in the lower House. Sir
Edward Coke also rose to be a justice in the common pleas, and then in the king's
bench. However, on his being discharged from the king's bench in 1616, he sat again in
the Commons throughout the 1620s. These legal figures may, beyond their personal
summonses to the upper House and the drafting of legislation, no longer have been
involved in the making of new statutes. Nevertheless they remained active in the
interpretation of the law.

[142] Sir James Dyer, Sir Robert Broke, Christopher Wray, Sir John Popham, John Puckering, Christopher
Yelverton and John Croke.

[143] Sir Thomas Audley, Sir Thomas More and John Puckering.

6

Chancellor Russell, in his draft speech intended for the opening of the parliament summoned by Edward V for 25 June 1483,[144] observed: 'yn the lower howse . . . alle is directed by the speker'.[145] Equally succinctly, John Hooker noted in 1571: 'His office is to direct and guide the House in good order, and to see the ordinances, usages and customs of the same be firmly kept and observed.'[146] Russell also explained how the Speaker must act *'quasi per tribunum'*.[147] When necessary he became the mouthpiece of the house of commons in expressing its opinions and feelings to the monarch. On such occasions he was accompanied by a representative number of members who were supposed to remain silent throughout the interview.[148]

As the person presiding over business in the Commons on behalf of the monarch, the Speaker was entitled to a reward of £100 a session.[149] Records of payment have not been traced for the majority of the Tudor Speakers. This should not be construed as evidence that such payments were not usually made nor that they were rare. Details of these payments were entered on the issue rolls of the exchequer, but none of these rolls are extant for the Tudor period. Some warrants authorising payment have been found. However, the sequence of warrants approving payment of any sort delivered to the receipt of the exchequer is severely depleted.[150]

The generosity of the payment made the Speaker the second highest paid official in the crown's service, coming only after the chancellor.[151] In addition to the Speaker's basic remuneration, the crown allowed a further equal amount for extraordinary personal expenses incurred in the performance of the work. In 1523 Cardinal Wolsey recommended the king to give Speaker More (notwithstanding his own irritation with More) a further £100 in reward. On 24 August 1523 Wolsey wrote: 'it hath been accustomed that the Speakers of the Parliamentes, in consideration of their diligence and pains taken, have had, though the Parliament hath been right soon finished, above the £100 ordinary,

---

[144] This never met on account of the usurpation of Richard III. See *History of Parliament: Register of the Ministers and of the Members of Both Houses 1439–1509*, ed. J.C. Wedgwood (1938), 465; C. Ross, *Richard III* (1981), 87, 93.

[145] *Grants, etc. from the Crown during the Reign of Edward the Fifth*, ed. J.G. Nichols (Camden Society, original ser., lx, 1854), p. xlv; A.R. Myers, 'Parliament, 1422–1509', in *The English Parliament in the Middle Ages: A Tribute to J.S. Roskell*, ed. R.G. Davis and J.H. Denton (Manchester, 1981), 482.

[146] Snow, *Parliament*, 165.

[147] *Grants, etc. from the Crown*, ed. Nichols, p. xlv.

[148] *CJ*, i, 11.

[149] *William Lambarde's Notes*, ed. Ward, 70.

[150] Evidence of payment has been traced for John Mordaunt (TNA, E404/79/45), Sir Thomas Fitzwilliam (TNA, E404/80/260), Richard Empson (TNA, E404/81 (unnumbered)), Robert Drury (BL, Harleian MS 1777, f. 75), (Sir) Thomas Englefield (TNA, E404/82 (unnumbered); E404/87/120), Sir Robert Sheffield (TNA, E404/82 (unnumbered); *LP Hen. VIII*, ii(2), 1459), Sir Thomas Neville (*LP Hen. VIII*, ii(2), 1468), Sir Thomas More (*LP Hen. VIII*, iii(2), 3267, 3270; TNA, E404/97, 15 Oct. 1523); Sir Thomas Audley (Roskell, *Speakers*, 115), Sir Humphrey Wingfield (*LP Hen. VIII*, vi, 228).

[151] The lord chancellor's emolument as chief officer of state was some £1,120: *The Report of the Royal Commission of 1552*, ed. W.C. Richardson (Morganstown, 1974), 66. His reward was intended to cover a year whereas the Speaker's reward was for a period rarely extending beyond three months, and usually no more than two.

a reward of £100 for the better maintenance of their household and other charges sustained in the same'.[152]

Two days later More thanked Wolsey for the £100 to be drawn at the receipt of the exchequer, and for the extra £100 payable 'owt of his [the King's] cofres by thandes of the Tresorer of the Chamber'. He asked Wolsey to instruct the treasurer 'that he may deliver it to such as I shall send him for hit'.[153] The privy seal warrant for payment out of the receipt of the exchequer was not issued until the following October when it was signed by More himself.[154] In the absence of issue rolls from the receipt of the exchequer for the Tudor period, it is impossible to say how punctually successive Speakers received their due. However, in 1595, nearly a decade after ceasing to be Speaker, John Puckering complained that he still had not received the £400 owing for his fees, and that while Speaker he had lost £2,000 in earnings from his legal practice. He exaggerated somewhat. He overlooked that, without transmitting any cash to him, the crown had used the money to cancel a debt of his.

The task of presiding over the Commons was not an easy one. The crown's handsome remuneration was a recognition of the difficulties facing the incumbent Speaker. Thomas Englefield dealt with sustained anger at the size of Henry VII's monetary expectations; Edmund Dudley with indignation at requests for fiscal aids that were retrospective; Thomas Neville with the outcry arising from Richard Hunne's death; Sir Thomas More with the reaction to Cardinal Wolsey's high-handedness exemplified in his demands for money supply; Nicholas Hare with concern over the Six Articles; Thomas Moyle with hysteria following George Ferrers's arrest; Sir John Baker with unease at the economic consequences of the dissolution of the last surviving religious foundations; John Pollard with disquiet at the tangled complexities of the reconciliation with the catholic church; Sir Thomas Gargrave with expectations as to the Elizabethan Church settlement; Thomas Williams with mounting pressure for Elizabeth I to marry and to secure the succession; John Puckering with disquiet as to the ambitions of Mary, Queen of Scots; and John Croke with the onslaught on monopolies. These men learnt to their cost that it was not a reward without justification. Richard Onslow's early death in 1571, when he was no more than 43 or 44 years old, was believed to have been hastened by the stress that his speakership had brought with it.[155] Not everyone succeeded in their allotted task. In 1497 Thomas Englefield presided over the least legislatively productive parliament of the period,[156] but this does not appear to have been held against him in 1510 when he was chosen Speaker for a second time. It was quickly discovered in 1571 that Christopher Wray lacked any fundamental management skills.[157]

---

[152] *State Papers, King Henry the Eighth* (11 vols, 1830–52), i, 124; *LP Hen. VIII*, i, 3267. Although this further sum was intended to cover increased personal and domestic expenditure while Speaker, this did not stop John Puckering in 1595 from complaining about the lack of any accommodation for the Speaker.

[153] *State Papers*, i, 127; *LP Hen. VIII*, ii, 3278.

[154] TNA, E404/94, 15 Oct. 1523.

[155] 'The place [that is the speakership], which Mr Onlsowe fled ever with the losse of his Lyfe', BL, Harleian MS 253, f. 33v.

[156] *PROME*, xvi, 281.

[157] J.E. Neale, *Elizabeth I and Her Parliaments 1559–1581* (1953), 187; Elton, *The Parliament of England 1559–1581*, pp. 227, 323.

Being the nominee of the crown and being remunerated by it limited how a Speaker could act. The precise extent of these ties is difficult to gauge. Two instances must suffice to indicate its amplitude. In 1585 Lord Burghley drafted Speaker Puckering's closing oration.[158] In 1601, when Speaker Croke accepted a bill curbing monopolies, Burghley's son, Sir Robert Cecil, in front of the whole House, said: 'and yow, Mr Speaker, should performe the chardge her Majestie gave unto yow in the begininge of this parleamente, not to receyve bills of this nature'.[159] From at least 1597, the royal coat of arms at the back of the Speaker's chair was a constant reminder not only of his being the person selected by the crown for the task and paid by it to direct and guide the members but also his being the personification in the house of commons of the authority of the crown, without which the House lacked any *raison d'être*.[160]

7

To conclude, throughout the Tudor period the Speaker continued to be the crown's nominee, his task to manage the house of commons on its behalf, his wages paid by it. At the opening of parliament, the knights, citizens and burgesses almost invariably accepted the crown's candidate, without more than a token protest. What substantial efforts, if any, there were to prevent that man from becoming Speaker took place outside the House, and beforehand.

[158] *Proceedings*, ii, 22–5.
[159] *Proceedings*, iii, 386.
[160] TNA, E351/322.

Chancellors, Presidents and Speakers: Presiding Officers in the Scottish Parliament before the Restoration[*]

ALAN R. MacDONALD

As a unicameral assembly for most of its history, the Scottish parliament was presided over by the chief officer of state, the chancellor. Before 1603, he presided in the presence of the monarch, who was an active participant in parliaments, in contrast to the custom in England. After the union of the crowns, the chancellor presided in the presence of the monarch's representative, the king's commissioner. As with the Speaker and the lord chancellor in the English parliament, it was customary for him to operate as an agent of the crown. He also presided over the drafting committee, the lords of the articles. During parliamentary sessions, there were also semi-formal deliberative meetings of the individual estates (prelates, nobles, burgesses and, from 1592, 'barons', that is, lairds sitting as commissioners of the shires), each presided over by one of their own number. The Covenanting revolution of 1638 led to radical procedural reform. This included replacing the chancellor with an elected 'president' (Latin *preses*), chosen by the membership at the beginning of each session. With separate meetings of the estates becoming a formal part of parliament's procedures, there was an elected president for each estate, sometimes referred to as 'Speakers' for they would speak for their estates in plenary sessions of parliament.

Keywords: Scotland; chancellor; president; Speaker; James VI; James I; Charles I; covenanters; estates

There are numerous difficulties in writing about the Scottish analogue of the Westminster Speaker. First of all, there is no historiographical tradition upon which to draw: between 1924 and 1996 not one book was published on Scottish parliamentary history.[1] Thus Scottish parliamentary historians are just beginning to explore the workings of the institution. There are also more fundamental difficulties, for Scotland's parliament had only one House. The house of lords is a more suitable comparator than the Commons since, for most of its history, the chancellor presided in the Scottish parliament. David Smith's description of the role of the lord chancellor in the Lords indicates significant commonalities between the two chancellors of the pre-union British kingdoms, in the parliamentary setting at least.[2] However, this ostensible similarity breaks down on closer examination. Although the Scottish chancellor nominally headed the judiciary and was often a trained lawyer, by the end of the 16th century, he rarely sat in the court of session

[*] I am grateful to Alastair Mann of the University of Stirling for his comments and suggestions on an earlier draft.

[1] R.S. Rait, *The Parliaments of Scotland* (Glasgow, 1924); J.R. Young, *The Scottish Parliament 1639–1661: A Political and Constitutional Analysis* (Edinburgh, 1996).

[2] D.L. Smith, *The Stuart Parliaments 1603–1689* (1999), 69.

which was presided over by the lord president.[3] In parliament, there are also problems. The House over which the Scottish chancellor presided did include prelates and peers, as in England. Yet it also included commissioners from the royal burghs, and from 1592, commissioners from the shires, so the Scottish chancellor presided over the whole institution.

Another important difference is the tradition of the king in parliament. Although a well-worn concept in the English context, it is something of a constitutional fiction: by the later middle ages, English monarchs were rarely in parliament. Officers of state did the king's business there, reporting progress, or lack of it, back to the king who remained outwith the process. In Scotland before 1603, and occasionally thereafter, the monarch really was in parliament, as an active participant on the first and last days of plenary session and usually in the deliberations of the lords of the articles. In 1563, Queen Mary sat daily with the articles and her son usually did the same, resuming the habit on his return visit in 1617 when, 'The kingis majestie and the . . . lordis of articles, with the . . . officeris of estate, satt daylie.'[4] In 1633, for the last time, the monarch participated in this process: 'the Lords of the Articles sat daylie, and the King came up daylie and sat with them'.[5] Although James I of England and Charles I spent more time in parliament than had their English predecessors, that was because James was accustomed to a parliamentary system in which the monarch was usually there.

The normal presence of the king provides one key to understanding the difference between the chancellor's role in the Scottish parliament and that of his English counterpart. In England, the lord chancellor spoke and acted for the absent monarch.[6] In Scotland before 1603, the chancellor presided in the presence of the king, so his role was largely procedural, with the king usually making the opening speech.[7] To be sure, the chancellor must have carried out his duties as president with the interests of the crown in mind, but there was no need for him to press the point because the king was sitting on the throne behind him or at the table in committee. If there was dissent, the king could ensure that the crown's view was made clear. However, just because the king was present, it did not mean that his view would always prevail. The presence of the monarch has to be seen in the context of Scottish political culture. However symbolically important the monarchy was, the person of the king was not a tremendously elevated figure. Indeed the informality and relative lack of deference in his interactions with members of the political elite might have shocked outsiders.[8] His active involvement

[3] Julian Goodare, *The Government of Scotland 1560–1625* (Oxford, 2003), 150–1.

[4] *Calendar of the State Papers Relating to Scotland and Mary Queen of Scots, 1547–1603*, ed. J. Bain *et al.* (13 vols, 1898–1969) [hereafter cited as *CSP Scot*], ii, 11; David Calderwood, *History of the Kirk of Scotland*, ed. T. Thomson and D. Laing (8 vols, Edinburgh, 1843–9), v, 492; *The Records of the Parliaments of Scotland to 1707*, ed. K.M. Brown *et al.* (St Andrews, 2007) [hereafter cited as *RPS*], 1617/5/12 [All *RPS* citations accessed Nov. 2007–Apr. 2008].

[5] John Row, *History of the Kirk of Scotland from the Year 1558 to August 1637*, ed. D. Laing (Edinburgh, 1842), 364.

[6] Smith, *The Stuart Parliaments*, 69.

[7] *CSP Scot*, xiii, pt 1, 136 (report of the king's speech to parliament in 1597); in England, in the 16th century, the lord chancellor opened proceedings with a speech: M.A.R. Graves, *The Tudor Parliaments: Crown, Lords and Commons 1485–1603* (Harlow, 1985), 20.

[8] David Stevenson, 'The English Devil of Keeping State: Elite Manners and the Downfall of Charles I in Scotland', in *People and Power in Scotland*, ed. N. MacDougall (Edinburgh, 1992), 126–44.

should not, therefore, be seen as conducive to royal domination of parliament. In 1592, James famously confronted the provost of Edinburgh in the lords of the articles over his resistance to a proposal to restrict ministers' freedom of speech in their sermons. It was the provost's view which prevailed, not the king's proposed act.[9]

1. *The Presiding Officer Before 1639*

Few have given much attention to the role of the presiding officer in the Scottish parliament. The lack of parliamentary historiography is the main cause of this. Even those who have looked closely at parliament have given little attention to its form and procedures, concentrating instead on parliamentary politics. In two extended general discussions of parliament, Gordon Donaldson made no mention of the role at all.[10] Bruce Galloway's study of the attempted union of the early 17th century merely stated that: 'The Chancellor acted as a kind of prime minister and Speaker combined, controlling the session in the royal interest.'[11] While this is not so far from the truth, the anachronistic analogy illustrates the erstwhile tendency of historians to make inappropriate, and implicitly negative comparisons with England. However, any reading of early modern English parliamentary historiography reveals that the presiding officers of the two houses of parliament were also active agents of the crown.[12] It would, therefore, be wrong to regard the actions of the chancellor on behalf of the crown in the Scottish parliament as indicative of the peculiarly subservient and impotent nature of the institution.

For details on the parliamentary process, Scottish parliamentary historians still have to resort to Robert Rait's work of 1924. Over 80 years old, it remains unsurpassed as a comprehensive study of the institution. Rait's discussion of presiding officers focused on the period after 1603 and on the roles of the chancellor and the king's commissioner.[13] His description of what happened before 1603 is, however, confused: he suggested that the king 'presided [but] did not actually conduct the business or count the votes', so 'the duty of exercising presidential control . . . naturally belonged to the Chancellor as the highest judicial officer'.[14] After 1603, this led to what Rait portrayed as confusion between the office of chancellor and king's commissioner. This transition would repay further investigation because it can shed some light on the respective roles of monarch and chancellor during the 16th century.

In a speech to the English parliament in 1607, James I described himself as 'the eldest parliament man in Scotland'. He claimed that he had complete control of the Scottish parliament through the chancellor: 'there they must not speake without the Chauncellors leave, and if any man doe . . . utter any seditious or uncomely speeches, he is straight interrupted and silenced by the Chauncellors authoritie [and] if any man in Parliament

---

[9] Calderwood, *History*, v, 161–2.

[10] Gordon Donaldson, *Scotland: James V–James VII* (Edinburgh, 1965), 276–87; Gordon Donaldson, *Scotland: The Shaping of the Nation* (Newton Abbot, 1974), ch. 4.

[11] Bruce Galloway, *The Union of England and Scotland 1603–1608* (Edinburgh, 1986), 3.

[12] Graves, *The Tudor Parliaments*, 20–1; Smith, *The Stuart Parliaments*, 69–70.

[13] Rait, *Parliaments of Scotland*, 508–13.

[14] Rait, *Parliaments of Scotland*, 508.

speake of any other matter than is . . . first allowed by mee, The Chancellor tells him there is no such Bill allowed by the King'.[15]

In 1607, James was trying to persuade a sceptical English parliament that the Scots were easy to govern and would present no problems in the more perfect union which he was trying to foist upon his reluctant realms.[16] James could tell them whatever he liked and they would have had little basis upon which to gainsay him. Whatever his distortions of how the Scottish parliament operated (he did not even mention the lords of the articles), his speech of 1607 reveals that the chancellor presided. Although no detailed account of the chancellor's role survives, some aspects of his customary functions before the Covenanting revolution of 1638 can be pieced together. An act of parliament of 1641 described the chancellor's traditonal role as 'preceiding, calling of rolles, stateing of questiones [and] asking of voyces',[17] a range of duties one might expect in a presiding officer. A few other bits and pieces can be found in records from the reign of James VI. An act of 1584 stated that the chancellor was 'to use and exerce the office of chancellarie . . . alsweill in parliamentis, previe counsell as sessioun'.[18] His role in the privy council was explicitly described in 1592 as to 'propone the mater and collect the voitis', so it would be reasonable to suppose that he did the same in parliament.[19] The English ambassador's account of the parliament of 1593 described the lord president of the college of justice, the chancellor's judicial deputy, acting as his deputy in parliament. Four years later, with the chancellorship vacant, the lord president again presided and put questions to the individual estates.[20] In 1604, in the first parliament after 1603, he was responsible for requesting a notarial record that the king's letter had been read to the estates.[21]

Rait's view was that parliament's procedures were so informal that the chancellor or the king's commissioner might preside.[22] Perhaps there was some uncertainty among those involved with parliament as to who ought to preside. In 1640, neither the chancellor nor the king's commissioner was present but the latter's absence was cited by parliament as compelling it to choose its own presiding officer.[23] That has been taken as indicating that the king's commissioner was expected to preside but it does not necessarily mean that at all.[24] The 'Act anente the electione of the precidente of parliamente' of November 1641 stated that it was 'necessary and expedient . . . that in every parliament . . . there be a president . . . chosen by his majesty or his commissioner'.[25] In 1640,

---

[15] *King James VI and I: Selected Writings*, ed. M. Rhodes, J. Richards and J. Marshall (Aldershot, 2003), 320–1.

[16] Jenny Wormald, 'The Reign of James VI, 1567–1625', in *Scotland: The Making and Unmaking of the Nation c. 1100–1707. Volume ii: Early Modern Scotland c. 1500–1707*, ed. Bob Harris and A.R. MacDonald (Dundee, 2007), 30.

[17] *RPS*, 1641/8/101.

[18] *RPS*, 1584/5/22; 1587/7/115.

[19] *RPS*, 1592/4/63.

[20] *CSP Scot*, xi, 701–2; xiii, pt 1, 136.

[21] *RPS*, 1604/4/6.

[22] Rait, *Parliaments of Scotland*, 509.

[23] *RPS*, 1640/6/4; M1641/1/1.

[24] E.g., John Scally, 'Constitutional Revolution, Party and Faction in the Scottish Parliaments of Charles I', in *The Scots and Parliament*, ed. Clyve Jones (Edinburgh, 1996), 60.

[25] *RPS*, 1641/8/215.

because the king was not there and nor was his commissioner, parliament was left with no option but to appoint its own president.

Considering the king's active role before 1603, it is not surprising that, after that date, the king's representative in parliament should have carried out most aspects of the king's former role, including touching acts with the sceptre to denote royal assent.[26] In the parliaments between 1603 and 1639 at which the monarch was absent, the commissioner made a speech on the king's behalf, conveyed his wishes to the lords of the articles and worked through others to promote the smooth passage of the crown's programme.[27] Further details of the commissioner's role can be found in King James's letter appointing the earl of Montrose to that position in 1604. It might even reveal something of the king's role in parliament before 1603, for it outlined the duties of a position with no precedent in the parliamentary setting, although the king had sent commissioners to represent him at general assemblies of the church for a number of years.[28] Montrose was to summon the estates, ensure that instructions were issued for its formal opening, fine absentees, continue the session (i.e., prorogue it), and ensure that the lords of the articles were elected.[29] So, although he was expected to participate in proceedings, he was given very little to do in the actual conduct of the session, that being left to the presiding officer.

The king's commissioner is recorded as having introduced legislation but, in spite of what Rait implied, that did not make him the presiding officer.[30] Even in 1621, when the king's secretary reported the diligence of the marquess of Hamilton as commissioner in securing the crown's programme, he did not indicate that Chancellor Dunfermline had relinquished the role of president.[31] It is therefore misleading to think in terms of confusion between the roles of chancellor and king's commissioner. In suggesting that, after 1603, either of the two might have presided, Rait was failing to appreciate that there had been a distinction between what the chancellor and the king did before 1603, a distinction which continued after 1603 between the chancellor and the king's commissioner.[32] The king or his commissioner, might intervene occasionally to press the royal view but they were not in charge of the transaction of business. James's own description of the chancellor's role in his 1607 speech makes that clear enough.[33] He made no claim for his own presidency – he was a participant but he did not routinely direct the proceedings.

In the absence of the king, the clearly-understood distinction between the roles of king's commissioner and chancellor is manifest. In the first post-union parliament, at

---

[26] *King James VI and I*, ed. Rhodes, Richards and Marshall, 321; Sir Thomas Hamilton, 'Memoriall anent the Progress and Conclusion of the Parliament Haldin at Edinburgh in October 1612', in *Maitland Club Miscellany III*, pt 1, ed. J. Dennistoun and A. MacDonald (Edinburgh, 1843), 118.

[27] Hamilton, 'Memoriall', 114; G.H. MacIntosh, *The Scottish Parliament Under Charles II 1660–1685* (Edinburgh, 2007), 18, for an example of the commissioner's speech.

[28] A.R. MacDonald, *The Jacobean Kirk 1567–1625: Sovereignty, Polity and Liturgy* (Ashgate, 1998), chs 1–4.

[29] *RPS*, 1604/4/6.

[30] Rait, *Parliaments of Scotland*, 509–10.

[31] *State Papers and Miscellaneous Correspondence of Thomas, Earl of Melros*, ed. J. Maidment (2 vols, Edinburgh, 1837), ii, no. 246; Calderwood, *History*, vii, 497.

[32] Rait, *Parliaments of Scotland*, 509–10.

[33] *King James VI and I*, ed. Rhodes, Richards and Marshall, 320–1.

Perth in 1604, the earl of Montrose was the king's commissioner. Although he was also the chancellor, he did not preside, expressly because he was the king's commissioner. Instead, Alexander Seton, Lord Fyvie, lord president of the college of justice, presided as vice-chancellor, just as he had done in 1597 when the chancellorship was vacant. He was described in the record as 'chancellor of this parliament' indicating that 'chancellor' carried the meaning of 'president', *inter alia*.[34] Soon after this, Seton received an earldom and was promoted to chancellor, Montrose having demitted office. In the parliament of 1606, the two men reprised their roles of 1604. They would have done so again in 1607 had it not been for Montrose's failing health necessitating his replacement as commissioner by Ludovic Stewart, duke of Lennox.[35] In 1612, however, Chancellor Dunfermline was appointed commissioner, repeating the situation that had arisen in 1604. The official record is silent as to who presided but a brief narrative of the parliament reveals that Dunfermline was given the option of having George Gledstanes, archbishop of St Andrews, preside as vice-chancellor, if he 'thoght not the Chancelarie and Commissionarie compatible'.[36] Since Dunfermline would rather have given up the role of commissioner than that of chancellor, he chose to do both. So, the two *could* be combined but contemporaries were well aware that the roles were distinct. Given the crown's desire to see some sensitive ecclesiastical legislation through parliament, including enhancements to episcopal powers, Dunfermline was wise to avoid the presidency of Archbishop Gledstanes.[37] James VI in person was present in 1617, so there was no royal commissioner and in 1621, although the commissioner took an active role in ensuring the success of the crown's programme, Chancellor Dunfermline presided.[38] In 1633, Charles I was present, but the chancellor, George Hay, earl of Kinnoull presided, the record explicitly noting that he also did so in the articles.[39]

Confusion as to the respective roles of commissioner and chancellor perhaps arises because, in essence, the president of parliament was an officer of the crown and, in presiding, he would promote the crown's interests along with the king's commissioner.[40] He normally presided at meetings of the privy council and conventions of the estates, to which no separate royal commissioner was sent until after the Restoration.[41] It should come as no surprise to anyone familiar with the role of the lord chancellor in the house of lords or even of the Speaker in the house of commons, that the chancellor in Scottish parliaments was not neutral.

[34] *RPS*, 1604/4/6; 1604/4/13.

[35] *RPS*, 1605/6/1; 1607/3/8.

[36] *RPS*, 1612/10/4; Hamilton, 'Memoriall', 113.

[37] MacDonald, *Jacobean Kirk*, 149; Maurice Lee, 'King James's Popish Chancellor', in *The Renaissance and Reformation in Scotland*, ed. I.B. Cowan and D. Shaw (Edinburgh, 1982), 170–82, discusses Dunfermline's character and, at 179, his low opinion of Gledstanes.

[38] *RPS*, 1617/5/4; 1617/5/7; 1617/5/10; 1617/5/14; Calderwood, *History*, vii, 497.

[39] *RPS*, 1633/6/10.

[40] *Melros Papers*, ed. Maidment, i, 17; ii, 415–6.

[41] For the chancellor presiding at conventions of the estates see *Melros Papers*, ed. Maidment, i, 165; National Archives of Scotland [hereafter cited as NAS], GD221/518: minutes of the Convention of Estates, 28 July–7 Aug. 1630.

2. *The Covenanting Revolution and Elected Presidents*

Constitutional reforms introduced in the wake of the 1638 Covenanting revolution dispensed with the automatic right of the chancellor to preside in parliament. This was of particular significance because parliamentary sessions in the 1640s were considerably lengthier affairs than had ever been known before. Much more of the deliberative process was, therefore, conducted in plenary sessions of parliament. In 1639 Charles I appointed as his commissioner to parliament, John Stewart, earl of Traquair, lord treasurer. The chancellorship was vacant and the marquess of Hamilton, keeper of the great seal in the vacancy, was in England.[42] The last of the three great offices of state, that of king's secretary, although not vacant, was held by the elderly William Alexander, earl of Stirling, who also remained in England, dying in London in February 1640.[43] Even the lord president of the college of justice, Robert Spottiswoode, who might have presided as vice-chancellor, was absent.[44] It therefore has to be assumed, in the absence of any evidence to the contrary, that the role of presiding officer was combined, as in 1612, with that of the king's commissioner.[45] In the 1639 session there was only one brief plenary meeting: on 31 August 1639, amid storms of protest about the freedom of parliament to elect its own committees, the lords of the articles were chosen. An unprecedentedly long session then ensued as the articles, unavoidably dominated by covenanters, pressed their demands on the king's commissioner who would not yield. Eventually, and without the full parliament having reconvened, the session was prorogued until 2 June 1640, with no legislation having been passed.[46] By that time, however, Charles I had good cause to desire a further prorogation: the English 'Short Parliament' had been disastrous, serving only to encourage the covenanters, against whom Charles had decided to use militarily force instead. Rather than sending a commissioner to prorogue parliament, he asked Sir Thomas Hope of Craighall, the lord advocate and a covenanter sympathiser. On 2 June, however, Craighall contrived to produce an invalid prorogation which the estates used as a pretext to continue on the basis that the only prorogation in force was that of the previous November.[47]

The very first act of the session was entitled 'Acte anent the choosing of Robert Balfour, lord Burleigh to be president of this court and sessione of parliament in respect of the absence of the kingis commissioner'.[48] This was one of many covenanting innovations that would be followed by the English parliament: in 1641, the house of lords asserted its right to choose its own presiding officer.[49] Burleigh was re-elected as

---

[42] John Scally, 'Hamilton, James, First Duke of Hamilton (1606–1649)', *ODNB*, Oxford University Press, 2005 [*http://www.oxforddnb.com/view/article/12087* (accessed 21 Apr. 2008)].

[43] David Reid, 'Alexander, William, First Earl of Stirling (1577–1640)', *ODNB*, Oxford University Press, 2006 [*http://www.oxforddnb.com/view/article/335* (accessed 21 Apr. 2008)].

[44] David Stevenson, 'Spottiswood , Sir Robert, Lord Dunipace (1596–1646)', *ODNB*, Oxford University Press, 2004 [*http://www.oxforddnb.com/view/article/26169* (accessed 21 Apr. 2008)].

[45] *RPS*, 1639/8/31/1.

[46] David Stevenson, *The Scottish Revolution 1637–1644: The Triumph of the Covenanters* (Newton Abbot, 1973), 170–6.

[47] Stevenson, *The Scottish Revolution*, 192–3.

[48] *RPS*, 1640/6/4.

[49] Smith, *The Stuart Parliaments*, 69.

president in the subsequent sessions, in January, April, May and July 1641.[50] When Charles I attended parliament in 1641, even though the vacant chancellorship had been filled by the appointment of John Campbell, earl of Loudoun, he agreed that a new president might be chosen, Burleigh having requested parliament's leave to demit.[51] Although this was explicitly not to be prejudicial to the chancellor's right to preside in parliament, the chancellor was passed over in the next three elections of a president.[52] Not until 1648 was Loudoun chosen. Even then, he did not exercise the presidency *ex officio*, as is borne out in a French diplomatic source which recorded that 'the chancellor . . . *through his office of president* [of parliament] has the advantage of being able to ask the opinion of any one he pleases'.[53] In 1651, although Chancellor Loudoun attended, Lord Balfour of Burleigh was once again elected president, confirming that there had been no reversion to the pre-revolutionary custom of the chancellor as president *ex officio*.[54] At every election of a new president between 1644 and 1651, parliament took great care to cite the acts authorising the election of a president, for these had been personally ratified by Charles I in 1641.[55]

The president exercised a role akin to that of the chancellor in the period before 1639, although almost entirely unencumbered by royal interference. The lengthier sessions of the 1640s meant that the president had a more onerous job than his predecessors, as the orders for the house, passed in July 1641, demonstrate. He was to oversee the reading of the rolls which would be done at the beginning of each plenary sitting. None might speak without his leave. Whoever was given such leave should then be allowed to speak without interruption, and all replies were to be addressed to the president. No member was permitted to absent himself from parliament without the president's leave.[56] He also had authority over who might be permitted to remain in the house during a parliamentary session.[57] He was responsible for calling votes and, in the event of a tie, he might exercise a casting vote. Although that power is not recorded in any regulations from the 1640s, in 1661, the earl of Crawford-Lindsay obtained an act in his favour, exonerating him from any responsibility for parliament's decision to end negotiations with Charles I and leave him to his English subjects in January 1647. Crawford-Lindsay's petition to parliament noted that 'by his being president he wes not to give any vote, except the votes of the house had been equall'.[58] Since there was no tie, he did not vote and was therefore not party to parliament's decision. With the massive expansion of parliament's business in the 1640s, committees also burgeoned. The president was entitled to sit on any committee as an *ex officio* supernumerary member and to preside whenever

[50] *RPS*, 1641/1/2; 1641/4/3; 1641/5/3; 1641/7/3.

[51] *RPS*, 1641/ 7/103; 1641/8/6.

[52] *RPS*, 1641/8/101.

[53] J.G. Fotheringham, *The Diplomatic Correspondence of Jean de Montereul and the Brothers de Bellievre French Ambassadors in England and Scotland, 1645–48* (2 vols, Edinburgh, 1898), ii, 417–8, 419–20, 441, 444 (emphasis added).

[54] *RPS*, 1648/3/6; M1650/5/1, 19.

[55] *RPS*, 1644/6/3; 1644/6/5.

[56] *RPS*, 1641/7/24; 1641/7/27.

[57] *RPS*, 1641/8/38.

[58] *RPS*, 1661/1/71.

he was present.[59] He also took on some of the former responsibilities of the king's commissioner, the most significant of these being the formal constitution, or fencing, of parliament.[60]

With government being carried on without the king, the president acquired a role which no chancellor would have previously presumed to occupy: he came to represent parliament itself. The first instance of this cannot have been a more dramatic demonstration of parliament's assumption of sovereignty. In June 1640, two days after his election, Lord Balfour of Burleigh subscribed a summons, directing Patrick Ruthven, Lord Ettrick, to deliver Edinburgh Castle into the hands of parliament, under the pain of treason.[61] Parliament had transformed at a stroke how treason was understood. The summons was issued in the name of the president and the estates and signed by the president, and Lord Ettrick was to deliver the castle to Burleigh 'in name of the estates'. One week later, having refused to render the castle, parliament declared that Ettrick had committed 'treasone against this kingdome'.[62]

This role was formalised on 9 June 1640, in an act declaring that the subscription of any act 'in face of parliament' by the president would be sufficient authorisation to the clerks of parliament to register it, print it and provide official copies under their signatures.[63] This was another consequence of the fact that, to be able to operate without royal authorisation, parliament had no option but to declare itself competent to act on its own behalf. Thereafter, every decision made by parliament was signed off by the president 'I.P.D.P.' (*in praesentia dominorum parliamenti*). Every act, warrant, adjournment, summons, referral of an issue to a committee, letter, commission, set of instructions to commissioners, contract to supply the army, appointment of new officers in the army, and pass granting permission to leave the kingdom was authorised with the president's signature. Similarly, letters and supplications to parliament were directed to the president. Only Charles I wrote to the estates rather than to the president in their name.[64] When Charles was present from August until November 1641, something unique occurred. Papers previously signed only by the president were also superscribed by the king. Charles had been forced to acknowledge that he shared authority with the estates. In superscribing parliament's ratification of the treaty of London, which included a promise 'never to come in the contrarie of it', he was signing an agreement with his own parliament.[65] It was a far cry from 1633 when he intimidated the estates by noting down the names of those who voted against him.

The presidential subscription of papers in the name of the estates was one of the covenanting innovations retained after 1660.[66] Even though the restoration of the

---

[59] *RPS*, 1645/1/11.

[60] *RPS*, 1644/6/3. Fencing means constituting it as a court of law.

[61] *RPS*, 1640/6/58.

[62] *RPS*, 1640/6/63; A.R. MacDonald, 'Statehood, Nationhood and Treason', in *Statehood Before and Beyond Ethnicity: Minor States in Northern and Eastern Europe, 1600–2000*, ed. L. Müller and L. Eriksonas (Brussels, 2005), 98–101.

[63] *RPS*, 1640/6/58.

[64] See, e.g., *RPS*, A1640/6/1; M16401/1; 1641/1/3. See *RPS*, *passim* and MS parliamentary papers in NAS, PA6 and PA7 for numerous examples.

[65] *RPS*, 1641/8/21. For the treaty of London, see Stevenson, *The Scottish Revolution*, ch. 7.

[66] *RPS*, M1661/1/54; 1669/10/51.

monarchy involved the reassertion of the chancellor's right to preside (it was the first act of the 1661 session), parliament remained much more of an institution in its own right.[67] It communicated directly with the king through its president, the chancellor. It is perhaps a subtle point but, before 1639, no chancellor or any other officer of state would have signed a letter in the name of parliament: no parliament would have written a letter. Instead, one or more officers of state would report to the king on proceedings, but in their capacity as officers of state, not on behalf of parliament.[68] After 1660, parliament itself could communicate with the king, indicating a significant shift in its constitutional position as an organ of government in its own right.

Just as in the period before the Covenanting revolution, circumstances arose during the 1640s in which the president could not preside. In January 1645, John Maitland, earl of Lauderdale, was ill. Parliament took this setback in its stride, electing John Lindsay, earl of Crawford-Lindsay 'to be vice president of parliament in absence and dureing the seiknes of Johne, erle of Lauderdaill'. Lauderdale died later that month and Crawford-Lindsay was elected as president in his place.[69] Later in 1645, Crawford-Lindsay himself was unable to attend and John Kennedy, earl of Cassilis was elected vice-president. The vice-presidency might also be exercised in the president's presence: when parliament passed an act in favour of Crawford-Lindsay acknowledging that the state owed him a large sum of money, propriety required that the act should be subscribed by the vice-president rather than its beneficiary.[70]

3. *Speakers in the Scottish Parliament*

So far, this article has addressed only the role of the presiding officer of the whole parliament. Yet the common understanding of the Scottish parliament as unicameral is less than half the story for much of its history. Indeed it is a crucial flaw in the way in which parliament in general and the role of the chancellor in particular have previously been discussed. However important the two days of plenary session were before 1639, most of parliament's business was not conducted in that setting and while the chancellor also presided over the lords of the articles, their deliberations are also only part of the story.[71] While the articles conducted their business, the rest of the membership did not spend all their time in Edinburgh's up-market boutiques and taverns. As well as transacting all manner of private business, they met in their separate estates 'for advising, reasoning, and preparing themselves the more deliberatlie to vote in publict', in other words, to discuss proposed legislation and agree common positions.[72] It was also a two-way process, with meetings of individual estates feeding their deliberations into the lords of the articles. The articles did not meet until ten o'clock in the morning, a

---

[67] *RPS*, 1661/1/7.

[68] Hamilton, 'Memoriall'; *Melros Papers*, ed. Maidment, i, 67–8; ii, 411–16, 421–7.

[69] *RPS*, 1645/1/13; 1645/1/32; 1645/1/34.

[70] *RPS*, 1645/11/77; 1645/11/225. A vice-president was also elected in June 1650 when Loudoun was indisposed: *RPS*, M1650/5/30.

[71] Goodare, *The Government of Scotland*, 151; A.R. MacDonald, 'Deliberative Processes in Parliament c.1567–1639: Multicameralism and the Lords of the Articles', *Scottish Historical Review*, lxxxi (2002), 23–51.

[72] Calderwood, *History*, vii, 492.

relatively late hour in a society where the working day in summer started at 5 o'clock, so there was ample time for the individual estates to deliberate.[73]

The Scottish parliament never had anything like the Speaker of the house of commons but the term 'Speaker' is not absent from Scottish parliamentary history. Its first mention dates from the reign of James I (1406–37). In 1428, the estates agreed to an act which sought to create a system of shire representation. It has been suggested, quite reasonably, that this was inspired by his experience of the English system during his captivity there between 1406 and 1424, although the detail of what James expected or intended is hard to pin down because it was never implemented.[74] However, one of its stipulations was that the shire commissioners would elect 'a wise and . . . expert man callit the commoune spekar of the parliament' who would speak on behalf of 'the commounes'. This person's principal role would not be as a presiding officer, but would be, literally, a speaker or prolocutor on behalf of those who had elected him. However, as this was akin to the original role envisaged for the Speaker of the Commons in England, there was probably an expectation that this person would preside over the meetings of those on whose behalf he would subsequently speak.

Although James I's scheme was not realized, there is later evidence that something akin to it did operate, in that individuals spoke in parliament on behalf of a whole estate. In January 1467, a spokesman appointed by the clergy and another by the burgesses spoke on debasement of the coinage.[75] In 1543, the archbishop of Glasgow protested on behalf of 'all the prelatis' against the legalisation of vernacular Scripture.[76] In 1574, the convention of burghs agreed that a commissioner might vote in parliament 'according to his conscience' unless it had been 'concludit before be the haill that ane sall *speik* and vote for all'.[77] Thus there was a mechanism whereby a single estate (and all its votes) might be represented by a 'Speaker'. It seems likely that that Speaker would have been the person who presided in the meeting of his estate at which such a resolution was agreed upon.

Whatever was the case before the Covenanting revolution, there is unambiguous evidence from the 1640s. Separate meetings of estates, probably a normal part of the deliberative process since the 15th century, obtained a more formal footing, with hours assigned for the meetings of the 'several bodies' (the individual estates), as well as committees and the full house. Their deliberations were articulated to plenary sessions through 'Speakers', at least for the burgesses and shire commissioners: the records of debates name a range of nobles but only single Speakers for the other two estates. In the case of the burghs, their Speaker was invariably Edinburgh's principal commissioner, normally its provost. In the early 1640s, the Speaker for the barons was Sir Thomas Hope

[73] *RPS*, 1605/6/28; *Registrum Episcopatus Brechinensis cui Accedunt Cartae Quamplurimae Originales*, ed. P. Chalmers (2 vols, Aberdeen, 1856), ii, 317–8.

[74] R.J. Tanner, *The Late Medieval Scottish Parliament: Politics and the Three Estates, 1424–1488* (East Linton, 2001), 30–4.

[75] *RPS*, A1467/10/13. For other instances of this, see Tanner, *The Late Medieval Scottish Parliament*, 110, 158.

[76] MacDonald, 'Deliberative Processes', 28.

[77] *Records of the Convention of the Royal Burghs of Scotland*, ed. J.D. Marwick and T. Hunter (7 vols, Edinburgh, 1866–1918) [hereafter cited as *RCRBS*], i, 25 (emphasis added).

of Craighall; in the later 1640s, Sir Archibald Johnston of Wariston, took on the role.[78] These men spoke for their estate in parliament having already presided over the separate meetings of those estates: whenever the convention of burghs met at Edinburgh, it was convened by Edinburgh's senior commissioner and Edinburgh's commissioners always took precedence among the burgesses in parliament. Status was also important for the selection of the Speaker of the shire commissioners. Although Sir Thomas Hope sat for the tiny county of Clackmannanshire, he was also king's advocate.[79] Johnston of Wariston's parliamentary career began as commissioner for Midlothian, in which Edinburgh sits and which therefore took precedence among the shires in parliament. Yet his being chosen as the Speaker for the barons probably had more to do with his role in the covenanting movement (he co-authored the National Covenant) and his status as a lord of session from 1641, king's advocate from 1646 and clerk register from 1649.[80] It is, therefore, not surprising that, in 1641, the leading covenanting noble, Archibald Campbell, earl of Argyll was elected president of the estate of nobles.[81] Similarly, in 1648, the natural choice was James, duke of Hamilton, Scotland's senior noble and leader of the moderate covenanters in the deal with the king known as the Engagement. A brief parliamentary diary written by Hamilton in the spring of 1648 has recently been identified.[82] It records three meetings of the estate of nobles, at all of which the duke of Hamilton was 'elected to preseid' by his peers.[83]

It is impossible to know exactly what went on in these separate meetings of the estates as very few of their papers survive and reportage is frustratingly laconic. It is clear, none the less, that a significant part of the deliberative process was conducted in that setting.[84] There were, therefore, up to five different presiding officers in any parliamentary session before 1633 (when the king forbade the separate meetings of the estates 'contrare to the forme practised in all other Parliaments before').[85] The chancellor presided in the two brief plenary sessions and in meetings of the lords of the articles; the Speakers of each of the three estates before 1592 and the four estates from that year until 1633 presided over meetings of the individual estates. During the 1640s, with the clerical estate having been abolished, parliament reverted once again to three estates each with its own president or Speaker. After 1660, although the lengthy, deliberative plenary sessions were retained, there was no revival of the meetings of individual estates, with the apparent exception of the burghs.[86] In 1685, in an obsequious address to James VII, they reminded

---

[78] *The Historical Works of Sir James Balfour*, ed. J. Haig (4 vols, Edinburgh, 1824), ii, 87, 105; iii, 177, 277, 253, 422–3.

[79] *The Parliaments of Scotland, Burgh and Shire Commissioners*, ed. M. Young (2 vols, Edinburgh, 1992), i, 360.

[80] *Parliaments of Scotland*, ed. Young, i, 381–2.

[81] *RPS*, A1641/7/42.

[82] J. Scally, 'The Rise and Fall of the Covenanter Parliaments, 1639–51', in *The History of the Scottish Parliament. Volume ii: Parliament and Politics in Scotland: 1567–1707*, ed. K.M. Brown and A.J. Mann (Edinburgh, 2005), 146 n. 28; National Library of Scotland [hereafter cited as NLS], MS 8482.

[83] NLS, MS 8482, ff. 20, 65, 71.

[84] Goodare, *The Government of Scotland*, 151, makes this point while discussing the chancellor's role.

[85] Row, *History*, 364.

[86] E.g., *RCRBS*, iii, 532–44 (1661). The convention met repeatedly between January and July while parliament was in session. This pattern was repeated in 1663, 1681 and 1706; J.D. Mackie and G.S. Pryde, *The Estate of the Burgesses of the Scots Parliament* (St Andrews, 1923), 43–8.

him that their loyalty to his predecessors had uniquely secured to them the 'great priviledge . . . to meett apairt and by themselves as a third state of parliament'.[87]

4. *Conclusion*

The Scottish parliament was not like the house of lords or the house of commons – it was like the Scottish parliament. As Michael Graves has argued, generalizations about representative assemblies across Europe tend to break down because of the different local conditions within which they developed and operated.[88] Therefore there is little utility in thinking in terms of the Scottish equivalent of the Speaker of the house of commons. Yet this does not mean that comparative history cannot provide useful insights. Difference is as interesting and telling as similarity. It is only by looking more closely at the Scottish parliamentary process in its own contexts, not through the distorting lens of the Westminster system, that it will be possible to achieve a clearer understanding of its place in the polity of early modern Scotland and in relation to the rest of Europe.

[87] *RCRBS*, iv, 50–1.
[88] M.A.R. Graves, *The Parliaments of Early Modern Europe* (2001), 1, 197.

Speakers in the 17th-Century Irish Parliament*

COLEMAN A. DENNEHY

In Ireland in the 17th century before the Battle of the Boyne, there were only five parliaments held. For these parliaments there was a total of 16 different individuals who acted as Speaker or made an attempt to become Speaker in the Commons or the Lords. This article will attempt to consider the possible criteria that may have been important in assessing the suitability of the candidates and also to see how many of those 16 are found to be suitable according to these conditions. We can be assured that the vast majority of those appointed and selected were politically reliable and that other issues such as legal training and legal experience are also common among most. However, ethnicity, religion (including attitudes to others' religion), family and marriage contacts, and administrative experience show that the Speakers did not always share a common background. To a certain extent, it may be deduced that these differences may be reflective of the changing political scene in Ireland over the course of this short 17th century. The performance and attributes of those who failed to become Speaker can also be useful in a study that attempts to understand the qualifications deemed desirable in a Speaker in 17th-century Ireland.

Keywords: Ireland; Irish parliament; lord chancellor; Speaker; Wentworth; Ormond; Davies; Mervin; jacobite; Restoration; Dublin

There were just five parliaments in Ireland between the accession of the Stuart dynasty and the Glorious Revolution. One was in the reign of James I (1613–5), two were in Charles I's reign (1634–5, 1640–8), and there was one each in the reigns of his two sons (1661–6, 1689). The jacobite parliament of 1689 was subsequently declared illegal and void by the Williamite administration and its journals burned by the common hangman some six years after. Sixteen men became Speakers or aspired to become Speakers of one or other house of parliament. Sir John Davies, the poet and lawyer, was the Speaker of the house of commons for the 1613–5 parliament. He was followed in this role by Nathaniel Catelin in 1634–5 and later by Sir Maurice Eustace in 1640–8. Following the interregnum, Sir Audley Mervin was elected Speaker for the Restoration parliament (1661–6) and finally, Sir Richard Nagle served as Speaker in the jacobite house of commons. In usual circumstances, the lord chancellor was the Speaker of the Irish house of lords. This was the case when Archbishop Thomas Jones sat on the woolsack in 1613–5, Sir Adam Loftus (later Lord Loftus of Ely) in 1634–5 and Sir Richard Bolton in the 1640s. During Bolton's impeachment it was agreed that Sir William Ryves, a judge, would serve. Archbishop John Bramhall, although not lord chancellor, filled the role in 1661 and 1662. Sir Maurice Eustace, the lord chancellor and no longer needed

* I would like to thank Dr Hazel Maynard for reading an advance draft of this article and making very useful recommendations for its improvement.

as one of three lords justices (a committee of governors) of the kingdom took up the role until his death in 1665, which was followed by the appointment of Archbishop Michael Boyle to both the seal and the woolsack. Lord Chancellor Fitton was Speaker in the single-session parliament of 1689.

The role of the Speaker was similar to that in the parliament of England. He, with assistance from the clerk, organised the day-to-day undertaking of business, chaired meetings, and was, on formal occasions, the mouthpiece of the House. The Speaker in the Lords, usually being the lord chancellor, had additional responsibilities in his role both as the head of the legal arm of the kingdom in the House, and also as the chairman of the highest court in the kingdom. Naturally in a position of potentially huge importance, the government of the day had an interest in seeing the role performed by a loyal servant. As a general rule, the lord chancellor and other Speakers in the Lords were such loyal servants and, in general, their performances were helpful.[1] There was no selection process when the lord chancellor was available, but when not, it was influence from Whitehall that decided the matter. The king had a strong role in recommending Sir William Ryves in 1640, but in 1661 the lords justices were permitted to select the Speaker[2] and Archbishop Bramhall was selected, although the choice would seem to be very much in keeping with the prevailing opinion in Whitehall and reflective of the wishes of Ormond and Clarendon.[3] The situation in the Commons was a little different. Formally, the Speaker could be chosen from any of the members, but the government almost always exerted influence. As Wentworth pointed out to the Commons in 1634: 'it was not worth their contention, considering the power of allowance was undeniably in the King, and that if he rejected, they were still to chuse another, and another, till his Majesty approved thereof; and that it would be taken as an ill presage of some way-wardness or forwardness of Mind reigning in them, if they should go about to deny such for their speaker as should be recommended by his Majesty's Privy Council'.[4] There is no example of a chosen Speaker being rejected. As in England, in reality, Dublin Castle usually chose the preferred candidate and he was usually the one elected. In 1634, 1640 and 1689 there was no competition.[5] In 1613, the catholics had put forward their own candidate, Sir John Everard, who, having been deemed defeated, prompted a (probably pre-arranged) walkout.[6] In 1661, there was another competition, which saw two royal officers go against each other. Sir William Domville, despite having royal support, was favoured by the minority and Orrery and Mountrath encouraged the king to assent to

---

[1] The only possible exception to this rule is the serious breakdown in the relationship between Wentworth and his lord chancellor, Lord Loftus of Ely, although this was to happen several years after the dissolution of parliament and did not have any negative implications in parliament: Hugh Kearney, *Strafford in Ireland, 1633–41: A Study in Absolutism* (Cambridge, 1989), 72.

[2] *CSP Ireland, 1633–1647*, p. 288.

[3] Bodl., Carte MS 31, f. 159; Bodl., Clarendon MS 74, ff. 383–6; National Archives of Ireland, MS M.2449, f. 234.

[4] *The Earl of Strafforde's Letters and Dispatches with an Essay towards his Life by Sir George Radcliffe*, ed. William Knowler (2 vols, 1739), i, 276–92.

[5] David L. Smith, *The Stuart Parliaments, 1603–1689* (1999), 79.

[6] 'A Document on the Parliament of 1613 from St Isidore's College, Rome', ed. Brian Jackson, in *Analecta Hibernica*, xxxiii (1986), 47–58; John McCavitt, *Sir Arthur Chichester: Lord Deputy of Ireland, 1605–16* (Belfast, 1998); Tadhg Ó hAnnracháin, 'Imagining Political Representation in Seventeenth-Century Ireland', in *Community in Early Modern Ireland*, ed. Robert Armstrong and Tadhg Ó hAnnracháin (Dublin, 2006).

the wishes of the Commons.[7] This is an important event in the history of parliamentary privilege, as it is the only time in the 17th century, and perhaps the first time in the history of the Irish parliament, that the election of the Speaker of the Commons, Sir Audley Mervin, went against royal wishes. The king surely regretted this minor democratic experiment as Mervin was regarded by many historians as being obstructive to the government programme.[8]

In addition to Domville and Everard, one other was left disappointed. James Barry, Lord Barry of Santry, the lord chief justice of the king's bench, considered himself apt for the speakership of the Restoration house of lords, but failed to gain it.[9] Lord Chancellor Eustace had suggested him for the woolsack at the council table in advance of the 1661 meeting of parliament, but was overruled by Lords Justices Mountrath and Orrery in favour of Archbishop Bramhall. Orrery said that it would be 'for the betterment of the established church after the miseries the 1640s and 1650s had brought' and also cited his experience, Bramhall being 'a person well known in the rules & proceedings of the Howse[,] have two passte sat'. But Barry of Santry had a decent claim, being the next senior legal figure after the lord chancellor, and the appointment of Sir William Ryves, a judge, as Speaker in 1640 had also established a precedent of sorts. Feeling slighted, he entered a protest to the privy council, and for such an affront, the council had him 'severely chastis'd and confined to the Castle' for two days until he relinquished his claim.[10]

The position of Speaker was invariably political. The Speaker was expected to influence the House as much as was possible, within the rules of his office, in favour of the government. But while political subservience was important, so, too, was the legal training and experience that most Speakers of the Lords and Commons had. Their connections with, and dependence upon, patrons in government were important in securing positions, as could be family connections, religious outlook, racial or ethnic background and, of course, their political background. A study of the men who were appointed and elected to the position may also tell us much about what was expected of them and what was deemed important qualities in the Speaker.

Many of those who held the position had some education at one of the inns of court in London. Of the Speakers and those who wished to be Speaker in the Lords, only the ecclesiastics, Jones, Bramhall and Boyle, had not been educated at the London inns. In the Commons, almost all studied in the inns in London, except Sir Audley Mervin, who became a member of the King's Inns at Dublin at the mature age of 55 years, although some previous legal knowledge was obvious from his speeches in

---

[7] Fergus M. O'Donoghue, 'Parliament in Ireland under Charles II', University College, Dublin MA, 1970, p. 46; *CSP Ireland, 1660–1*, p. 256.

[8] The criticism of Mervin seems a little unfair, for although it must be acknowledged that his printed speeches of spring 1663 caused discomfort for Ormond and the government and possibly danger to the kingdom, he did preside over the provision of a very generous financial settlement. The early biographers of Ormond seem to have pushed a strong anti-Mervin line that has been followed by most subsequent historians: see Coleman A. Dennehy, 'The Restoration Irish Parliament, 1661–6', in *Restoration Ireland: Always Settling and Never Settled*, ed. Coleman A. Dennehy (Aldershot, 2008), 56–7, 65–6.

[9] Barry was raised to the peerage as Baron Barry of Santry in 1661.

[10] Bodl., Carte MS 31, f. 159; Bodl., Clarendon MS 74, ff. 383–6; National Archives of Ireland, MS M.2449, f. 234.

parliament in the 1640s.[11] Despite having the reputation of one of the most brilliant common lawyers in Ireland of his day, Sir John Davies was twice suspended from the Middle Temple for violent misbehaviour, although he did spend part of one of those suspensions in the company of the Dutch jurist, Paul Merula in Leiden.[12]

In terms of legal experience, the subjects of this study present more of a mixture. For the Lords, the three archbishops naturally had little conventional legal experience, yet they did all sit on the privy council, Jones and Bramhall had experience of the prerogative courts in Dublin, and all heard suits on ecclesiastical causes.[13] Of the remaining Speakers of the Lords, most had a previous career conducive to appointment to such an important position. Sir Adam Loftus, later Lord Ely, was the nephew of the Elizabethan lord chancellor, and had a wealth of experience in the judiciary. He was appointed a master in chancery in 1598, sat on the privy council from 1609 and was appointed as lord chancellor in 1619. He was three times lord justice and sat on the court of castle chamber (Ireland's star chamber) for over 30 years, although he was humiliated and deprived by Wentworth at the end of the 1630s.[14] Sir Richard Bolton served as recorder of Dublin, solicitor general, chief baron of the exchequer and the treasurer of the King's Inns at Dublin in advance of his promotion to lord chancellor. He also published one of the first collections of Irish statutes.[15] Although never a lord chancellor, Sir William Ryves's legal career made him at least as well qualified as many other Speakers. He held several positions of importance in the Middle Temple and acted as a justice on the Carmarthen circuit in advance of his taking up the role of attorney general on the advancement of Sir John Davies to the position of chief justice of the king's bench in London. He was created second justice of the king's bench in 1636.[16] Lord Chancellor Eustace took over as Speaker from Archbishop Bramhall in summer 1662 when the return of Ormond as lord lieutenant freed him from the lord justiceship. He conducted a very successful private practice as a barrister in the late 1620s and early 1630s. His appointment as prime serjeant in 1634 was followed by his elevation to master of the rolls in 1645. He practised again as counsel in the later 1650s and was made lord chancellor in 1660.[17] Barry of Santry, a candidate who was never made Speaker, was, nevertheless, very well qualified. He pipped Eustace to the post of prime serjeant-at-law in 1629 and became second baron of the exchequer in 1634. He was in private practice

[11] Anthony R. Hart, 'Audley Mervyn: Lawyer or Politician?', in *Explorations in Law and History*, ed. W.N. Osborough (Dublin, 1995), 86–7, 98.

[12] Hans S. Pawlisch, *Sir John Davies and the Conquest of Ireland: A Study in Legal Imperialism* (Cambridge, 1985), 16–7.

[13] Helen Coburn Walshe, 'Jones, Thomas (c.1550–1619)', *ODNB*, Oxford University Press [*http://www.oxforddnb.com/view/article/15086* (accessed 13 Oct. 2008)]; John McCafferty, 'Bramhall, John (bap. 1594, d. 1663)', *ODNB*, Oxford University Press [*http://www.oxforddnb.com/view/article/3237* (accessed 3 Oct. 2008)]; Toby Barnard, 'Boyle, Michael (1609/10–1702)', *ODNB*, Oxford University Press [*http://www.oxforddnb.com/view/article/3131* (accessed 4 Oct. 2008)].

[14] John G. Crawford, *A Star Chamber Court in Ireland: The Court of Castle Chamber, 1571–1641* (Dublin, 2005), 101–2.

[15] F.E. Ball, *The Judges in Ireland* (2 vols, New York, 1927), i, 331.

[16] Ball, *The Judges in Ireland*, i, 336–7.

[17] Brid McGrath, 'A Biographical Dictionary of the Membership of the Irish House of Commons, 1640–1641', University of Dublin PhD, 1997, pp. 150–2.

during the interregnum and by 1655 was acting as a justice of the assize in Ulster, and with the Restoration was advanced to be chief justice of the king's bench.[18] The strangest of all appointments to the woolsack was that of Alexander Fitton, created Lord Gawsworth in May 1689. He was called to the bar in 1662 but spent the majority of the Restoration incarcerated due to an unsuccessful suit for the possession of Gawsworth, culminating in a hearing in the English house of lords, and a subsequent publication by Fitton which was deemed a scandalous libel by the Lords.[19] His appointment as lord chancellor would appear to have been due to little more than his conversion to Roman catholicism and perhaps some sort of attachment to the king.[20] It certainly cannot have been due to his legal experience as he had very little outside of his own case. His imprisonment precluded any practice and he never held office before attaining office in Ireland as lord chancellor.

None of the Commons' Speakers had as successful a legal career as Sir John Davies. He served as solicitor general of Ireland from 1603 and was upgraded to the more senior position of attorney general in 1606 and made king's serjeant in England in 1612. Later, after leaving Ireland, he was appointed as chief justice of the king's bench in England in 1626, but died after a hearty meal the evening before taking up office, in accordance with the prophecy of his mentally-unbalanced wife.[21] Davies worked with gusto towards the total transformation of the Ireland he found on his appointment in 1603 into a state where English common law was supreme and the last vestiges of the Gaelic Irish brehon law were removed. He extended the circuit system to all four provinces, removed many of the medieval privileges of the towns, and shifted the religious balance in the house of commons in favour of the protestants.[22] Sir John Everard, Davies's competitor for the Speaker's chair in 1613, had all of the attributes necessary for the chair but one, his religion. After his education at the Inner Temple he was called to the bar in 1590. He held judicial positions in Tipperary in the later 1590s and was appointed second justice of the queen's bench in summer 1602. He held this position until he was pressurised out of it by Chichester and Davies in early 1607, despite the former holding him in a high professional regard.[23] Nathaniel Catelin followed in the position of Speaker. He was not necessarily a lawyer of lesser ability, but certainly did not have the reputation someone such as Davies had. He was a second serjeant from 1627 until his death in 1637. In tandem with this central government position, he was also recorder of Dublin, which led

---

[18] A.R. Hart, *A History of the King's Serjeants at Law in Ireland: Honour Rather than Advantage* (Dublin, 2000), 163. Aidan Clarke, *Prelude to Restoration: The End of the Commonwealth, 1659–1660* (Cambridge, 1999), 199–200.

[19] *LJ*, xi, 554.

[20] Victor Stater, 'Fitton, Alexander, Jacobite Baron Fitton (d. 1699)', *ODNB*, Oxford University Press [*http://www.oxforddnb.com/view/article/9520* (accessed 30 Oct. 2008)]; Ball, *The Judges in Ireland*, i, 363–7; Thomas Davis, *The Patriot Parliament* (3rd edn, Dublin, 1893), 14.

[21] The wife was Eleanor Touchet, sister to the 2nd earl of Castlehaven, which in itself may go some way to explaining her deficiencies. She specialised in combining scriptural anagrams with prophecy: see Pawlisch, *Sir John Davies*, 27–33.

[22] Humphry William Woolrych, *Lives of Eminent Serjeants at Law of the English Bar* (2 vols, 1869), i, 186–219; Ball, *The Judges in Ireland*, i, 231–4.

[23] McCavitt, *Sir Arthur Chichester*, 98; Richard H.A.J. Everard, 'The Family of Everard: Part I', *The Irish Genealogist*, vii (1988), 334–7.

to a split in his loyalties in 1628 that nearly cost him his position.[24] The legal career of Sir Maurice Eustace, the Speaker in the Commons in 1640–8 (and later lord chancellor) has been described above. He was followed in that office by Sir Audley Mervin, who served in the Restoration parliament. Mervin's legal career is less convincing. Despite having some legal knowledge in advance of his acceptance into the King's Inns, he seems to have had no substantial legal practice in advance of his appointment as prime serjeant-at-law in 1660, which was surely a political one.[25] Sir John Temple, a temporary Speaker of the Commons during Mervin's absence in London, had a speedy rise to the chair. He entered one of the inns of court, probably Gray's Inn, in May 1650 and was by 1654 pleading in chancery in Dublin. He was appointed solicitor general of Ireland in 1660.[26] Sir William Domville was Mervin's fellow contestant for the Speaker's chair in 1661. His career had been one which had been built up in England where he had practised as a successful attorney since his call to the bar in 1640. By 1657, he had been called as a bencher in Lincoln's Inn and in 1660 was appointed as attorney general.[27] Finally, Sir Richard Nagle was the Speaker of the Commons in the jacobite parliament in the summer of 1689. Unlike Fitton, he had a substantial background in law. He began his legal education at Gray's Inn, London, before being called to the bar in Dublin. His legal career seems to have been successful. Later commentators described him as 'a cunning Irish lawyer . . . he was a man of great parts, educated among the Jesuits and therefore very inveterate'.[28] Nagle was close to Tyrconnell and replaced Domville as attorney general two days after Tyrconnell formally secured the Irish administration from Clarendon. He remained influential at James II's court in exile.[29] The legal knowledge and record of the various Speakers of both the house of commons and the house of lords highlights the sophisticated legal knowledge that was, in most cases, deemed necessary to fulfil such an important function as a Speaker of a house of parliament.

The extent of the experience of the lord chancellors and Speakers in the administrative affairs of royal government previous to an appointment or election was rather mixed. Thomas Jones, the first lord chancellor, had a considerable role in central government previous to his appointment. His rise was due to the fact that he was a protégé of Adam Loftus, archbishop of Dublin and lord chancellor (1581–1605), whom Jones succeeded in both secular and ecclesiastical employment, and whom one commentator considered 'in very truth a shadow of him'.[30] His appointment to the see of Meath in 1584, being superior to all the other bishoprics, entitled him to a seat on the privy council. He seems to have been an active member of the council, and acted on

[24] Hart, *A History of the King's Serjeants*, 54–5; 'The King's Serjeant at Law in Ireland: A Short History', in *Explorations in Law and History*, ed. W.N. Osborough (Dublin, 1995), 53–4.

[25] Hart, 'Audley Mervyn', 99.

[26] Ball has him attending Lincoln's Inn and Handley has him entering Gray's on the same date: Francis Elrington Ball, 'Some Notes on the Irish Judiciary in the Reign of Charles II, 1660–85', in *Journal of the Cork Historical and Archaeological Society*, ix (1903), 91–2; Stuart Handley, 'Temple, Sir John (1632–1705)', *ODNB*, Oxford University Press [*http://www.oxforddnb.com/view/article/27115* (accessed 17 Oct. 2008)].

[27] Ball, 'Some Notes on the Irish Judiciary', 88.

[28] Quoted in James McGuire, 'A Lawyer in Politics: The Career of Sir Richard Nagle, c.1636–1699', in *European Encounters: Essays in Memory of Albert Lovett*, ed. Judith Devlin and Howard B. Clarke (Dublin, 2003), 119.

[29] McGuire, 'A Lawyer in Politics', 124, 127–8.

[30] Ball, *The Judges in Ireland*, i, 236.

several brief occasions as a lord justice in 1614 and 1616.[31] Sir Adam Loftus, the nephew of the lord chancellor of the same name, who succeeded Jones in 1619, can also be considered experienced in government and his career took a similar path to that of his predecessor. He was appointed judge martial in 1597 and took an active part in the suppression of Tyrone's rebellion. He was made a privy councillor in 1609 and a judge in the admiralty court in 1612 and acted as a lord justice on three separate occasions in 1622, 1629–33 and 1636.[32] Bolton, Speaker of the house of lords in the 1640s, attained civic office in Dublin, being appointed recorder in 1605. His posts as attorney general and later baron of the exchequer meant his involvement in the administration at privy council level, but his close association with Sir Thomas Wentworth and his policies meant his heavy involvement in the administration of the state.[33] All three lord chancellors were accused of maladministration, Bolton being unsuccessfully impeached, although these accusations were hardly uncommon in the early 17th century. Despite his prominence within Wentworth's administration, John Bramhall never attained a seat on the council during the 1630s. He did, however, gain some administrative experience in central government working towards a re-energised Church of Ireland and became very unpopular in the process with major landowners who had prospered on the back of advantageous leases of church lands. This included drafting legislation for the 1634–5 parliament. Bramhall also worked hard against the Scottish influence in politics and religion in the north of Ireland.[34] At the Restoration, Bramhall was elevated to the archiepiscopal see of Armagh.[35] The unsuccessful candidate for the woolsack, Barry of Santry in 1661, was held in high favour by Strafford, but does not seem to have sat at the council board, being a second baron of the exchequer. At the Restoration he was heavily immersed in the work of the convention, being its chairman.[36] Eustace seems not to have had such a large amount of experience in administration until after the interregnum, although like all royal attorneys, he would have had regular contact. He was Speaker in the 1640–8 house of commons and was made lord chancellor at the Restoration in 1660 and acted as a lord justice for two years. Boyle's administrative career began during the wars of the 1640s. Unlike much of his extended family, he was staunchly royalist and acted as a diplomat between the various competing interests at the

---

[31] Ball, *The Judges in Ireland*, i, 315–7.

[32] Crawford, *A Star Chamber Court in Ireland*, 101–2.

[33] Crawford, *A Star Chamber Court in Ireland*, 102–3.

[34] McCafferty, 'Bramhall, John (bap. 1594, d. 1663)'; John McCafferty, *The Reconstruction of the Church of Ireland: Bishop Bramhall and the Laudian Reforms, 1633–41* (Cambridge, 2007).

[35] James McGuire, 'Policy and Patronage: The Appointment of Bishops, 1660–1', in *As by Law Established: The Church of Ireland Since the Reformation*, ed. Alan Ford, James McGuire and Kenneth Milne (Dublin, 1995), 116.

[36] Robert M. Armstrong, 'Eustace, Sir Maurice (1590x95–1665)', *ODNB*, Oxford University Press [http://www.oxforddnb.com/view/article/67049 (accessed 22 Oct. 2008)]. The Irish convention of 1660 remains quite distinct from the assemblies in England of the same name in 1660 and 1689. Although elected from the traditional parliamentary constituencies, only half of the normal number of MPs were returned and there was no house of lords. It is generally not considered a parliament by Irish historians. For an account, see Clarke, *Prelude to Restoration*. In many respects it was similar to the catholic confederate assembly which usually sat at Kilkenny during the 1640s war, which was used as a political forum for the catholic side in the civil wars and like the protestant convention, was a unicameral assembly, elected by the usual parliamentary constituencies and parliamentary franchise (except protestants were obviously not involved). For the best account, see Micheál Ó Siochrú, *Confederate Ireland, 1642–9: A Constitutional and Political Analysis* (Dublin, 1999).

end of the period. At the Restoration his loyalty and possibly his family name worked in his favour and his elevation to the see of Cork, Cloyne and Ross was followed soon after by a seat on the privy council. His negotiations on behalf of the Irish church in London in 1661–2 raised his stock with Ormond, this favour being responsible for his elevation to Dublin and later to Armagh, and was made lord chancellor on the death of Eustace in 1665.[37] Fitton's experience of central administration in Ireland was non-existent previous to his return to the kingdom in 1687 on his appointment as lord chancellor. He obviously had some involvement in government affairs after this point, although the main business of the jacobite council, overturning the Restoration land settlement and catholicising the army, judiciary and local government, seems to have been dominated by Tyrconnell and his coterie of Irish judges and other legal figures.[38]

Of the Commons' Speakers, Davies, as has been mentioned above, was very influential in the Irish administration, probably second only to the lord deputy, Sir Arthur Chichester. Catelin and Eustace must have had some influence and experience being serjeants-at-law and, in theory at least, superior to the attorney general and solicitor general. It was less than a year before the sitting of the Restoration parliament that Domville, Mervin and Temple were welcomed into the royal administration. The transfer of landed property in the jacobite period created a mammoth administrative workload for Nagle. He was appointed two years in advance of parliament as attorney general and worked hard with Tyrconnell in attempting to substantially adapt the Restoration land settlement in favour of the Old English community.[39] Everard, the defeated candidate in 1613, was the only one with relatively little experience of central administration. Whilst the experience of a prospective Speaker must have been important in that they undertook a large amount of administrative work in their capacity as Speaker, without a doubt, the primary consideration was the reliability of the Speaker to push forward the legislative programme of Dublin Castle and look after royal interests in general. Nagle, Eustace, Catelin and Davies were utterly obedient to directions from the administration. It cannot be a coincidence that the only major breakdown between Dublin Castle and the house of commons in spring 1663, took place during the only parliament where a Speaker (Mervin) was freely elected by the Commons without any firm indication of a preferred candidate by the administration. The position of Mervin as prime serjeant-at-law, which made him a part of the administration, was given to him because of his prominence during the early months of the Restoration rather than zealous royalist convictions.[40]

[37] Barnard, 'Boyle, Michael (1609/10–1702)'.

[38] Eoin Kinsella, ' "Dividing the Bear's Skin Before She is Taken": Irish Catholics and the Land in the Late Stuart Monarchy, 1683–91', in *Restoration Ireland*, ed. Dennehy, 161–78.

[39] J.G. Simms, *Jacobite Ireland, 1685–91* (2nd edn, Dublin, 2000).

[40] His appointment should be seen in the same fashion as those of Monck, Mountagu, Cooper, Howard, Annesley, Morrice, Holles and Northumberland to the English privy council on Charles II's return in May 1660; many were included to promote stability in the immediate future and perhaps because they were more dangerous if left out of the council. A further example of this inclusive approach in Ireland is the appointment of both Mountrath and Orrery as one of three lords justices. Orrery (formerly Lord Broghill) had served in the highest office in Cromwellian Scotland and Mountrath (formerly Sir Charles Coote, jnr) was also heavily involved in Cromwellian politics and had declared for parliament early in the wars. R. Hutton, *The Restoration: A Political and Religious History of England and Wales, 1658–1667* (Oxford, 1986), 127; Patrick Little, *Lord Broghill and the Cromwellian Union with Ireland and Scotland* (Woodbridge, 2004), 91–123.

How relevant was religion to the position of Speaker? When the monarch was a protestant, the Speakers were protestant, and when the monarch was a catholic, as in the reign of James II, so, too, were the Speakers. However this is a simplistic approach, and if we delve a little deeper, there may be more to learn. We may begin with the catholics. Both Everard and Nagle were born catholic and remained so throughout their lives, even though at times there was no obvious worldly or practical advantage to be had. From Everard's perspective, things became progressively worse. He lost his position in the judiciary due to his continued refusal to take the oath of supremacy in the early years of Lord Deputy Chichester's administration, while several protestant Irish-born men thrived in the judiciary in Ireland, particularly Thomas Dongan (a former recusant, appointed second justice of the king's bench in 1644), James Donnellan (third justice of the common pleas in 1637, later chief justice of the common pleas in 1660), Lord Barry of Santry, and even Richard Kennedy (second baron of the exchequer in 1660). Although the judiciary was primarily in the hands of English born judges, under Ormond and Wentworth those with Old English or even Gaelic Irish names could do well. There can be no doubt that in a parliament so sharply divided by religion, Everard lost the election for Speaker on account of his religion. Had he conformed he may have been worthy of the chair, but it is unlikely he could have usurped Davies as the candidate of the castle. Certainly Chichester was complimentary of his legal skills even at the time of his being harried out of office.[41] However, had he remained as a judge he would, more than likely, have been an assistant in the lords. Nagle's role as Speaker was certainly dependent on his being catholic but he also had the attributes of other speakers in terms of training and experience. Had he conformed during the Restoration period he may well have attained the office that his religion precluded him from. The situation regarding Fitton is substantially different. He languished in the king's bench prison for much of the Restoration and was granted liberty after the death of Charles II in 1685 and the subsequent decline in the fortunes of his counter-claimant for the Gawsworth estate in Cheshire, the earl of Macclesfield. It has been suggested that his conversion to catholicism on his release was a *politique* one, the success of which was emphasized by his appointment as lord chancellor. It is impossible that he would have been appointed had he not converted.

For the Speakers of protestant faith, all were of the established religion. Indeed Jones, Bramhall and Boyle were archbishops of the primatial see of Armagh when they performed the office of Speaker in the Lords. Mervin was suspect as a presbyterian, although his excuse that he risked losing Londonderry and its garrison, of which he was commander in the 1640s, by failing to take the covenant seems to stand up to scrutiny.[42] For the rest of the Speakers in the Restoration period, it may be easier to judge their religious outlook by their opinions and actions against those outside of the Church of Ireland. According to John McCafferty, Bramhall in the 1630s concentrated on making the Church of Ireland strong rather than 'direct confrontation with the Catholics'.[43] If

---

[41] *CSP Ireland, 1603–6*, pp. 279–80, 299, 332, 401, 430; *CSP Ireland, 1606–8*, pp. 44, 90, 120. Everard was compensated for his loss of earnings by Chichester on condition that he never took a case against the king.

[42] Indeed the *Commons Journals* show that Mervin was at the forefront of the campaign by parliament against the covenant. Robert Armstrong, *Protestant War: The 'British' of Ireland and the Wars of the Three Kingdoms* (Manchester, 2005), 114–5. *CJ Ireland*, i, 324–6.

[43] McCafferty, 'Bramhall, John (bap. 1594, d. 1663)'.

anything, Bramhall reserved most of his venom for the Scots-presbyterians of the north. Eustace and Boyle, whilst not necessarily sympathetic to catholicism, were no enemies of catholics in parliament.[44]

Of the pre-civil war Speakers of the Commons, the earlier ones tended to make the most stringent moves against catholics in Ireland. Davies consistently pushed a vigorous policy against recusants, part of his 'civilizing mission', which resulted in the resignation of Everard as a justice of the king's bench in 1607.[45] Loftus, as soon as he took over as lord justice with the earl of Cork in 1629, moved quickly to close down 16 catholic mass houses and other institutions in Dublin causing a riot.[46] Those appointed by Wentworth tended to follow his lead in the conclusion that although he may have had no love for catholicism in Ireland, moving against its church structure was useless without a well-established Church of Ireland in place. Veronica Wedgwood argued that Nathaniel Catelin was appointed as Speaker in the Commons in 1634 because it would placate catholic opinion until the money bills had been consented to.[47] Irish historians have not recognized his apparent sympathies for catholicism as a reason for his appointment although he did defend the city of Dublin (in his position as recorder) against the attempt by the lords justices to bring more troops into the city in contravention of the city's privileges during the catholic riots mentioned above.[48] Bolton and Ryves's views towards catholics are more difficult to gauge. Bolton seems not to have held a particular animus towards catholics in Ireland, despite his debt to anti-catholic patrons such as Chichester, Sir Oliver St John and Cork. In general, he tended to tie himself to the prevailing power in Ireland, which meant he was closely linked with Wentworth (which was a cause of his attempted impeachment) and then Ormond. He was heavily involved in the negotiations with the confederate catholics both in 1643 and 1646.[49]

Some of the Speakers owed much to family connection, particularly Loftus, Boyle and Sir John Temple. However, given the meteoric rise in power of figures such as Cork and Wentworth with little family background, it was possible to rise to the woolsack or chair from relative obscurity.[50] None of the Speakers in the Lords held a peerage whilst on the woolsack, except Viscount Loftus, who had been ennobled just a few years earlier.[51] The lay lord chancellors generally tended to be commoners in the early modern period, the only previous noble one being Lord Trimleston in 1538.[52] There are some examples of family links being used to forge a career. It is surely no coincidence that Viscount Loftus was a nephew of a previous lord chancellor, Sir John Temple was the son of the

[44] Dennehy, 'The Restoration Irish Parliament, 1661–6', 54–6.

[45] Pawlisch, *Sir John Davies*, 103–21.

[46] Raymond Gillespie, *Seventeenth-Century Ireland: Making Ireland Modern* (Dublin, 2006), 92–3.

[47] C.V. Wedgwood, *Thomas Wentworth, First Earl of Strafford, 1593–1641: A Revaluation* (2nd edn, 2000), 150.

[48] Hart, *A History of the King's Serjeants*, 54–5.

[49] Ó Siochrú, *Confederate Ireland*, 77–9, 230–1.

[50] Nicholas Canny, *The Upstart Earl: A Study of the Social and Mental World of Richard Boyle, First Earl of Cork, 1566–1643* (Cambridge, 1982), 41–6.

[51] Lord Barry of Santry was not appointed, despite his strenuous efforts, and Eustace, although awarded a peerage at the Restoration, never accepted it. This trend of non-aristocrats chairing meetings of the house of lords is something that is replicated in England in the period: Smith, *The Stuart Parliaments*, Appendix iii, 241–2. A possible exception is Fitton, who was ennobled after James II had fled from England (although still *de facto* king of Ireland) and so his title is not always recognized.

[52] S.G. Ellis, *Ireland in the Age of the Tudors* (1998), 370–1.

master of the rolls, or that Michael Boyle was the son of an archbishop and a cousin of the primary scion of the Boyle family. These factors are seen as a primary reason why Boyle was appointed as bishop of Cork in 1660, although it has been pointed out that his attainment of the seal and woolsack was the result of a strong relationship with Ormond in the years between.[53] Ryves was related to the wife of Sir John Davies but, because of the Davies's marital difficulties, this was not necessarily an advantage.[54] It would seem then, that it was not familial relationships but political connections and loyalties and perhaps even ability, which influenced appointments of Speakers.

Nor was the marriage policy of the various Speakers of much use to them in their elevation to positions of importance within the chambers. Few of the 16 subjects of this article gained political influence by marriage. Only Lord Barry of Santry and Sir Audley Mervin attached themselves to women of distinctly political families, when they respectively married the daughters of Sir William Parsons, a lord justice, and Martha Clotworthy, the daughter of Sir John Clotworthy, Viscount Massereene. Boyle could be also included in this number as he married Mary O'Brien, the sister of Murrough O'Brien, earl of Inchiquin. Most others, whilst having married well locally, seemed to attain no real benefit in their careers by acquired family contacts, and even the star of the Clotworthy and Parsons family shone less bright in the Restoration after their allegiances in the 1640s and, if anything, may have worked as a disadvantage.

Some trends can be discerned in relation to birthplace and ethnicity. In the earlier part of the century, particularly the first two parliaments (1613–5, 1634–5), the offices were dominated by the New English interest, the term used to describe English immigrants in Ireland between the Reformation and 1649. This is no surprise. What is more interesting is the resurgence in the standing of the Old English community in the Restoration and the jacobite periods. The Speaker in James II's parliament was likely to be Old English, as Tyrconnell's *quo warranto* campaign against the boroughs ensured that the majority of returns to the jacobite parliament was not just overwhelmingly catholic, but was overwhelmingly Old English too.[55] But Eustace and Barry of Santry could also trace their families back to the centuries of the Anglo-Norman invasions, as could Nagle and Everard. Eustace, as a lord justice, had suggested Barry of Santry for the woolsack in 1661.[56] Ormond appointed Eustace to the position of lord chancellor; the lord lieutenant being a protestant, like Eustace, of Old English origin and with an extended family containing more catholics than protestants. If Inchiquin's ethnicity was enough to preclude support for him from the English parliament in the 1640s, then the Old English tag was not yet enough to destroy the reputation of Barry of Santry or Eustace.[57] Indeed Barry of Santry had taken employment in judicial affairs during the interregnum and was

---

[53] McGuire, 'Policy and Patronage', 115; Barnard, 'Boyle, Michael (1609/10–1702)'.

[54] Ball, *The Judges in Ireland*, i, 336.

[55] J.G. Simms, *The Jacobite Parliament of 1689* (Dundalk, 1969), 4–6.

[56] Bodl., Carte MS 31, f. 159; Bodl., Clarendon MS 74, ff. 383–6; National Archives of Ireland, MS M.2449, f. 234.

[57] Little, *Lord Broghill and the Cromwellian Union*, 49, 54. Interestingly enough, despite the enmity of the civil war period, Orrery saw fit to give his proxy to Inchiquin in the 1660s, by which time Inchiquin had converted to catholicism: Coleman A. Dennehy, 'Parliament in Ireland, 1661–6', University College Dublin MLitt, 2002, p. 237.

chairman of the all-protestant convention and so could hardly have been deemed too close to the catholic party by Orrery and Mountrath.[58]

If the omission of the Gaelic Irish from important positions within parliament and the administration at large is understandable in the context of 17th-century Ireland, then so, too, is that of the Scots. The lack of any Scottish figure in this article is easily explained by two particular facts. The first of these is that the Scottish legal system was, and is, considerably different from that of the English one (upon which the Irish system was, and is, heavily based). In keeping with the premise that legal education and experience is quite important in the *curriculum vitae* of a prospective Speaker, it would be difficult to find Scottish figures in Ireland with such experience. The second, and probably the more important, issue is that Dublin Castle never had a decisive Scottish influence in the 17th century and would not have been likely to want to see a figure of a Scottish background in a position of any importance, particularly during the administrations of Wentworth and Ormond. The Gaelic Irish were absent in the same fashion, although there are examples of some men with Gaelic Irish surnames, if that be a suitable method to denote ethnicity, to be found in the judiciary such as Kennedy, Donnellan and Dongan.

The involvement of Speakers and aspirant Speakers in the mid-century wars may also be of use in a comparative study of these chairmen in identifying their political allegiances when the political environment became sufficiently pressurised. Jones, Davies, Everard and Catelin were all dead by the beginning of the civil wars in Ireland. Loftus, by autumn 1641 no longer lord chancellor, retired to North Yorkshire soon after the outbreak and played no significant part in the wars.[59] Of the Speakers of the Commons in the Restoration period, only Mervin has a war record worth speaking of. Temple was only nine years old when the fighting began and spent the interregnum pursuing his legal education and career. Domville did the same and spent little or no time in Ireland in the 1640s or 1650s, which may have been one of the reasons why he failed to convince a majority of the Commons of his suitability in 1661. Nagle, after the parliament of summer 1689, became secretary for war and later followed James II into exile at St Germain en Laye, as did Fitton.

No Speaker in the house of lords can really be described as a traitor to the monarchy, although Barry of Santry was found assisting the English parliament in raising money for the war effort in Ireland in 1648–9 and undertook some legal office during the interregnum.[60] Bolton and Eustace stayed at their judicial and parliamentary posts throughout the wars, Eustace, in particular, supporting the royalist cause in the Irish parliament and being imprisoned in Chester until 1655, when he returned to private legal practice in Dublin, apparently under the protection of Henry Cromwell.[61] Boyle and Bramhall worked actively against parliament in the 1640s. Bramhall spent most of the two decades on the Continent and Boyle remained in Munster isolated from Cromwellian government.

One would imagine that previous experience of parliament would be deemed useful in acting as chairman. This was certainly not the case, however, in the Irish house of

---

[58] Clarke, *Prelude to Restoration*, 200.

[59] W.N. Osborough, 'Loftus, Adam, First Viscount of Ely, 1568–1643', *ODNB*, Oxford University Press [*http://www.oxforddnb.com/view/article/16935* (accessed 22 Oct. 2008)].

[60] Clarke, *Prelude to Restoration*, 200.

[61] Armstrong, 'Eustace, Sir Maurice (1590x95–1665)'.

commons in the 17th century. Everard, Catelin, Domville and Nagle had no experience at all of the chamber to which they were supposed to bring order, although the lack of regular meetings made experience difficult to establish on occasion. Temple sat in 1661 for less than three months in advance of his election. Eustace sat for the borough of Athy in Kildare and Mervin as knight of the shire for Tyrone in the parliament previous to their appointment. Davies was the only Speaker of the Commons with experience in the English House (which operated in a similar fashion). He sat for the borough of Corfe Castle in Dorset in 1601 and heavily criticized the government over monopolies.[62] Speakers in the house of lords tended to have more parliamentary experience. Three of them (Bolton, Ryves and Barry of Santry) had been members of the Commons and had also later held judicial office, and were, therefore, legal attendees on the House, in advance of their appointment as Speaker. Barry of Santry, as has been mentioned above, was the chairman of the convention at the beginning of the Restoration. Loftus and Eustace had both been members of the Commons, in Eustace's case, twice. Jones had been created bishop of Meath just in time to attend Perrot's parliament as far back as 1585. It can be considered fortunate that Speakers could get any experience at all when one takes into account the fact that in Ireland in this period, as many as 28 years could pass between parliaments. Boyle had only a few months' experience of parliament. Fitton did not spend any time as a member of parliament, but must have had some awareness of its procedural rules in England, having spent plenty of time at the bar of the house of lords pleading for estates in his case against the earl of Macclesfield and later for his enlargement.

In all, the Speakers from the earliest journal records in 1613 to the point where parliament became a more permanent institution in the 1690s have several common-alities. Legal training and legal and administrative experience were normally required. However, the ethnic and religious affiliations of the various Speakers of both the house of commons and the house of lords mirrored the outlook and vision of the prevailing administrations then resident in Dublin Castle, for despite the fact that parliament undertook many judicial, legislative and administrative functions, in the religiously and ethnically divided and highly-politicised Ireland of the 17th century, political reliability was absolutely essential.

---

[62] J.E. Neale, *Elizabeth I and her Parliaments, 1584–1601* (1957), 381–3.

The Reputation and Authority of the Speaker and the Speakership of the House of Commons, 1640–60

STEPHEN K. ROBERTS

The speakership during the civil war and interregnum has received scant attention by historians. This article considers the occupants of the Speaker's chair as a group, making some observations about their age and background, including within its scope the short-lived and irregular speakerships of men such as Sir Sampson Eure and Henry Pelham. The popularity of the Speaker within the Commons is found to have depended much on his perceived competence and goodwill, while his reputation in the country at large depended greatly on the unpredictable cut and thrust of political opinion. The speakership of William Lenthall in the Long Parliament is examined in some detail and judged to be exceptional in a number of respects, not least in his grappling with the explosion in the number and power of executive committees. Lenthall's dealings with the press suggest that he was well aware of the uses of print as well as its potential for damage to his reputation. The contemporary allegations of venality aimed at Speakers are examined with respect to individual occupants of the office and are also set in the context of fee-taking by Commons' officials. While this period seems not to have been a particularly important one in terms of lasting procedural innovation in the chamber, it was significant in heralding the possibility of a separation between the person and office of Speaker. The article provides as an Appendix an authoritative list of Speakers in this period.

Keywords: Speaker; speakership; house of commons; Long Parliament; protectorate; committees; printing; corruption; venality; fees

The 20 years of the civil wars and interregnum might be expected to provide evidence of change and development in the office of Speaker. Momentous changes in the functions, scope and authority of the parliaments which they chaired, not to mention the often turbulent and usually experimental relationship between parliaments and the executive, might be presumed to have affected the functions and standing of the speakership. In fact, a great deal remains opaque about precisely how the Speaker's work related to that of managers of the government's business, and where the balance lay between the Speaker's authority in the chair and his power behind the scenes of daily life in the Commons. Indeed, treatment of the speakership is largely absent from the modern literature on parliaments of the 1640s and 1650s.[1] In certain respects, Speakers

---

[1] There is scant treatment in, e.g., P. Little and D.L. Smith, *Parliaments and Politics during the Cromwellian Protectorate* (Cambridge, 2007). There is a short useful summary of the speakership in the context of procedure in D.L. Smith, *The Stuart Parliaments* (1999), 68–71. All the Speakers mentioned in this article will, in due course, have their biographies in *The History of Parliament: The House of Commons 1640–1660*, ed. S.K. Roberts (forthcoming). For this article I have drawn on draft articles by David Scott on Sir Thomas Widdrington and

in this period conformed to certain patterns which had been long established, in how they were selected and from what backgrounds they came. In the conventions governing procedures in the House, too, this period is suggestive of a cautious rather than radical approach to the job of the Speaker, if the surviving summaries of procedural change can be relied upon. In other, more outward respects, however, these were challenging and exceptional times for the speakership. In no respect was this more the case than in the public reputation of the Speaker. Eleven men occupied the office in an English parliament between April 1640 and the final dissolution of the Long Parliament in March 1660, but because of Speaker Lenthall's various occupations of the chair there might more properly be said to have been 14 speakerships, including periods where the Speaker was acting during another's illness. There were no standing deputy Speakers. Lenthall's multiple occupancy gives a clue to a critical feature of this period: his own exceptional qualities as Speaker during the Long Parliament, in his own reputation and political prominence on the one hand, and in the character and scope of the House over which he presided, on the other. It may have been the extraordinary character of Lenthall's speakership that accounts for the cautious, not to say lack-lustre performances and reputations of those who followed him in the chair. This article can do no more than outline suggestions for further research, by identifying some of the more striking aspects of the office and its occupants.

All Speakers except two in this period were common lawyers who had been called to the bar: in the words of Edward Hyde: 'men of that profession had been always thought the most proper for that service'.[2] No single inn of court dominated their backgrounds, although none of them had attended the Inner Temple or the minor inns. The exceptional figures among them were Francis Rous, who had attended the Middle Temple but was never called to the bar there, having broken off his studies to engage in godly scholarship; and Henry Pelham, a lawyer but not a barrister-at-law whose brief speakership was in more immediate ways exceptional. The parliament over which Rous presided was itself *sui generis*. Each member of the nominated assembly of July–December 1653 had been summoned to Westminster by warrant of the lord general of the army, rather than by the usual process of writ, election and return. Indeed, this assembly only adopted the title of parliament by its own deliberate act when the members had assembled. Rous was called chairman until this decision in favour of continuity with precedent was adopted, and even then his occupancy of the chair was confirmed from month to month, limiting his tenure of the office.[3] The principal quality of Rous's that recommended him to his colleagues was his devout godliness, an attribute that was little less than a *raison d'être* and certainly a defining feature of this particular assembly. Only a little less significant an aspect of Rous's background was his deep and impressive learning, acquired not only in the two universities of Oxford and Leiden but also during the course of a lifetime of private study. To clinch his suitability, this half-brother of the parliamentary icon, John Pym, had himself sat in four parliaments before 1653.

---

[1] *(continued)* Henry Pelham and my own pieces on Sir John Glanville, Sir Sampson Eure and Thomas Bampfylde. I have also drawn on my own article on William Lenthall in the *Oxford Dictionary of National Biography.* I am most grateful to Paul Seaward for help with listings of Speakers.

[2] Edward Hyde, earl of Clarendon, *History of the Rebellion and Civil Wars in England*, ed. W.D. Macray (6 vols, Oxford, 1888), i, 221.

[3] A. Woolrych, *Commonwealth to Protectorate* (Oxford, 1982), 151.

As well as egregious in his piety, Rous was exceptional among the Speakers in a rather less enviable way. At the time of his coming to the chair he was around 72 years of age, making him its oldest occupant. Not that his compeers in the office were a notably youthful lot: typically a Speaker in this period would be in his fifties when coming to the post. William Lenthall was relatively young at 49 years when he first ascended to the chair in November 1640, but in marked contrast, at his last incarnation as Speaker on the eve of the final dissolution of the Long Parliament in January 1660 he was 69 years old. There was a growing tendency to favour the elderly in selecting Speakers in this period, which may have reflected the inclination towards gerontocracy in the pattern of membership of the House as a whole. The exceptional parliament in this respect was the single parliament of Richard Cromwell, which met in January 1659. The initial choice on this occasion favoured Chaloner Chute, a Middle Temple man aged 64 years who personified the general trend. But when Chute fell into what was to prove a fatal illness, the House seems deliberately to have gone for a younger man, Sir Lislebone Long, at 46 years the youngest up to that period. When illness quickly overtook Long, too, members dug their heels in to insist on an even younger choice. Thomas Bampfylde was a mere 36 years old during his brief tenure.

Bampfylde was led to the chair by his supporters, a tradition which was well established by this period and was comparable with ceremonial initiation procedures in other prestigious arenas of politico-legal public life, such as admissions to the order of serjeant-at-law.[4] Sir Lislebone Long was led, despite objections from some members that that ritual was 'not parliamentary'.[5] Bampfylde made a show of unwillingness, which also seems to have been traditional by this time. Bampfylde had been mentioned in connection with the chair during the 1656 parliament, and during that assembly had been a vocal critical commentator on the chairing of Speaker Widdrington.[6] This previous history suggests that Bampfylde had set his cap at the position of Speaker and the show of reluctance was indeed mere form. The physical show of unwillingness was a close relative of the expressions of unworthiness which were made by the Speaker on reaching the chair, some of which found their way into print, as in the case of Speaker Lenthall.[7] This should, of course, be distinguished from the very genuine reluctance which soon overtook Speaker Lenthall in his tenure during the Long Parliament. By November 1641 he was complaining of the long hours in the chair, certain that 'he could not hold out to sit daily seven or eight hours'.[8] A few months later he was keen to escape from the job, and persisted in a querulous tone for many years afterwards, to which his colleagues proved largely deaf.

Whether unworthy or reluctant or not, every Speaker had to be acceptable to a majority of his colleagues and had to enjoy their confidence if his tenure was to be at all successful. In the cases of the Speakers of the two parliaments of 1640, it was equally important that they were acceptable to the king. The practice was that the king nominated the Speaker before parliament met. Having been apprised of the king's

---

[4] As described in J.H. Baker, *The Order of Serjeants-at-Law* (Selden Society, suppl. ser., v, 1984).

[5] *Diary of Thomas Burton*, ed. J.T. Rutt (4 vols, 1828), iv, 92.

[6] *Diary of Thomas Burton*, ed. Rutt, i, 9, 12, 118, 290–1, 295; ii, 9–10, 149, 192.

[7] *Master Speaker his Speech* (1659), 3.

[8] *The Journal of Sir Simonds D'Ewes*, ed. W.H. Coates (New Haven, 1942), 172–3.

wishes, the members would be expected to select that individual and present him to the king as their own choice. The procedure accorded with the culture of selection of members themselves in the constituencies. Sir John Glanville, Speaker of the parliament of April that year, had enjoyed the support of the queen during his legal career, was a long-established recorder of both Bristol and Plymouth and a veteran of six previous parliaments. Despite what was a felicitous choice from the crown's viewpoint, the parliament ran into the sands within three weeks. Glanville did not run according to the expected form. He criticized the ship money judgment that had pronounced in 1637 in the king's favour, and in committee denounced the tax in an artless outburst that contributed to the king's decision to summon the Commons to the Lords for a dressing down. Glanville pleaded illness, was kicked upstairs to a senior legal post, that of king's serjeant, and did not find a seat in the parliamentary elections of the autumn.

The selection of William Lenthall to preside over the parliament that met in November seemed inauspicious from the outset. The king's declared intended candidate for Speaker, Sir Thomas Gardiner, the recorder of London, failed to secure a seat. Lenthall was thought the best that was available from a fairly thin crop of lawyers returned to sit. Hyde, who proved a relentless critic of Lenthall, considered his best attribute 'no ill reputation for his affection to the government of church and state'.[9] In fact, the reforming members themselves may have entertained higher hopes of Lenthall than Hyde's dismissive remarks suggest. He had been noticed in the April assembly and had done well in chairing important committees, which would have done his reputation among the members no harm at all.[10] Further back than that, Lenthall had acted as principal defending counsel in the prosecution the government brought against the feoffees for impropriations in 1633.[11] This puritan trust had bought up church livings in order to fill them with godly protestant ministers and lecturers, and in the absence of parliaments in the 1630s, was one focus, among a small number, for puritan resistance to Caroline policies. A record of association with those who resisted the personal rule would have given Lenthall at least some standing and credibility as a friend of remedial parliamentary action in the eyes of the leaders of reform in the Commons.

Hyde's dismissal of Lenthall as merely the best of a bad bunch needs, therefore, to be appraised critically. Lenthall's speakership may mark a significant tilt in the balance of nominating authority between king and parliament. In later assemblies, when the king was succeeded by republican sovereign powers, there were examples of Speakers whose elections to the chair owed little or nothing to manipulation by the executive. The two best examples are probably Francis Rous (1653), whose seniority and godliness set him apart among his contemporaries in the chamber; and Thomas Bampfylde (1659), a vocal critic of Cromwellian governments. On the other hand, Sir Thomas Widdrington (1656) was vastly experienced as a parliamentarian but by the time of his speakership had also served in high office as a commissioner of the great seal and as serjeant-at-law: hardly a back benchers' choice. The tenure of Sir Sampson Eure, brought to the chair at the

---

[9] Clarendon, *History of the Rebellion*, i, 221.

[10] *The Short Parliament (1640) Diary of Sir Thomas Aston*, ed. J.D. Maltby (Camden, 4th ser., xxxv, 1988), 19, 23, 36, 77, 95, 107, 129.

[11] E.W. Kirby, 'The Lay Feoffees: A Study in Militant Puritanism', *Journal of Modern History*, xiv (1942), 17–18.

royalist Oxford parliament in January 1644, showed how, when unimpeded by partisan political considerations, the king would continue to select along traditional lines. Eure was a prominent lawyer who had in 1641, in fact been an effective chair of an important committee at the Westminster parliament, responsible for steering through a bill to grant £400,000 in taxation to the king. He had also, by being made a king's serjeant in June 1640, long been suborned to the king's cause. His selection at Oxford seems to have been carefully planned, even if commentators mentioned others as contenders for the office. A balancing case in opposition-free selection is that of Henry Pelham who presided over the Long Parliament at Westminster after Lenthall and the independents had fled to the army for safety during unrest in London in the summer of 1647. Pelham's tenure turned out to last for a mere seven days. He was sponsored by the presbyterians who remained at Westminster, but his politics are hard to read from his behaviour in the Commons. Clearly he was sympathetic to the presbyterians or he would not have been selected, but his most obvious qualifications were long parliamentary service (six parliaments before the Long Parliament) and prominence as a lawyer. The implication is that his distance from openly partisan conduct in committees was a recommendation, even in the prevailing fraught and dangerous political climate.

The popularity of Speakers among their parliamentary colleagues was a tender plant, easily blasted by unpleasing words or gestures from the chair. Sir Thomas Widdrington was brought to the chair in September 1656 on the nomination of John Lisle, a government officeholder, but by April 1657, Thomas Burton, in his parliamentary diary, was beginning to record his errors in the chair on matters of procedure. 'We were growing a little angry . . . the Speaker was more to blame'; 'The Speaker stood up and reported, and said, I am a yea, a no I should say. This caused an alternate laughter all the House over, and some said he was gone'; 'The Speaker was at a loss to explain his meaning.'[12] Thomas Bampfylde seems to have waited on Widdrington's mistakes, like a fielder in the slips anticipating the catch from a hapless batsman. When Bampfylde was himself in the chair in 1659, he was brought to the chair in an unusual display of unanimity by presbyterians and Commonwealthsmen. He was soon attracting critical comment, however, some noting how he took 'a little too much on him, grandly', others wishing for the return of the sick man he had replaced.[13]

In his standing among his fellow parliamentarians, as in so many other respects, William Lenthall is a case apart, because of starkly contrasting assessments of his character. Hyde dwelt on his 'very narrow timorous nature', a quality Lenthall incidentally is said to have shared with Widdrington, 'naturally a cautious and timorous man' according to another critic.[14] It is hard to square this picture of Lenthall with the figure who defied Charles I so memorably on 4 January 1642. Even in his more quotidian performances in the chair, Lenthall could be authoritative, for example, in March 1641 telling the House not to skip from one topic to another.[15] He was certainly assertive, whether in expressing opinions contrary to the 'duty of his place', or denouncing members for their alleged shortcomings in helping the parliamentarian cause during the

[12] *Diary of Thomas Burton*, ed. Rutt, ii, 10, 70, 73.

[13] *Diary of Thomas Burton*, ed. Rutt, iv, 243, 254.

[14] Clarendon, *History of the Rebellion*, i, 221; Philip Warwick, *Memoires of the Reign of Charles I* (1702), 381.

[15] *The Journal of Sir Simonds D'Ewes*, ed. W. Notestein (New Haven, 1923), 461.

civil war.[16] Like Burton on Widdrington, the diarist Sir Simonds D'Ewes liked to record Lenthall's frailties, but unlike Burton introduced a more personal note of dislike into his recording. D'Ewes habitually sat near the Speaker's chair and took grim satisfaction in noting what he considered examples of Lenthall's lapses into unbecoming conduct, such as his 'fleering' (jeering or scornful laughter) at someone called to the bar of the House.[17] Both Lenthall and Widdrington were inclined to ask the opinion of the House when they ran into difficulties. Lenthall asked whether he should attend the trial of Thomas Wentworth, earl of Strafford in May 1641 and later that year sought clarification from the chamber on a procedural point.[18] Widdrington waited on the direction of the House when it came to pronouncing sentence on the quaker, James Naylor, his anxiety captured in Burton's unforgiving reportage: 'What shall I say to him? Shall I ask him any questions? or, if he speak, what shall I answer? Shall I barely pronounce the sentence, and make no preamble to it? I can do nothing but by your directions. I pray you inform me.'[19]

The reputations of Speakers inside the Commons doubtless rose and fell according to how popular were their judgments and how obliging their responses to requests by their colleagues. Their reputations outside the House were much more volatile. They were also, where possible, carefully managed. In this respect, the reputation of Speaker Lenthall probably deserves a full-length study of its own. Following his dignity and steadfastness during the confrontation of January 1642, he found himself presiding over a parliament which by the following year was developing a range of executive powers which no previous parliament had ever arrogated to itself. The volume of business that passed through his hands was enormous, the precise scale of it probably incalculable. In earlier parliaments the Speaker had been the conduit for the many petitions which came before the Commons for consideration. After 1642, added to this were the letters and reports from generals, colonels of regiments, naval commanders, county committees, mayors of corporations and from a host of other reporters and informants, a proportion, but by no means all, of whose messages are preserved in the Nalson MSS, the Tanner MSS and other collections.[20] The growing importance and power of parliament in the civil war years naturally led to the enhancement of the reputation and authority of the Speaker. Distant Plymouth sent Lenthall (*qua* Speaker, not mentioning his name in the civic record) a roll of Spanish tobacco in 1644.[21] The town was enduring a long siege, and the gift was intended to help cement the bond between corporation and the parliament it supported, serving, too, as a useful reminder of the trading interests of western ports. A search of municipal accounts of other towns would doubtless turn up comparable gifts, which had in more normal times tended to be showered on more local dignitaries.

Lenthall's official reputation rose even higher after the execution of the king. As the officer presiding over the commonwealth in which sovereignty was vested in a unicameral parliament, with the house of lords abolished, he was positioned at the apex of social

[16] BL, Harleian MS 163, f. 245; Harleian MS 165, ff. 190, 190v.

[17] BL, Harleian MS 163, ff. 177v, 178v.

[18] *D'Ewes Journal*, ed. Notestein, 453; *D'Ewes Journal*, ed. Coates, 224.

[19] *Diary of Thomas Burton*, ed. Rutt, i, 161.

[20] Bodl., Tanner MSS; see also the Nalson MSS in the same repository, and the strays in the Main Papers of the Parliamentary Archives.

[21] Plymouth and West Devon RO, 1/132, f. 258.

and political precedence. In June 1649, Lenthall filled the place of the king in the City of London ceremonial at its banquet. A frigate, *The Speaker*, was launched in 1650 and when Lord General Oliver Cromwell entered the capital in triumph after the battle of Worcester in September 1651, he was invited to join Lenthall in his state coach.[22] Van Weesop's portrait of Lenthall and his family, which currently hangs in Speaker's House at the palace of Westminster, may be impossible to date precisely, but is evidently a product of Lenthall's glory days. Invoking domesticity and the harmony of private life, the portrait is, in fact, an artefact of the Speaker's supreme standing in the body politic, and must, at the time of its unveiling, have been reminiscent to many of Van Dyck's 'great piece', representing Charles I as father of his people.[23] The singular honour surrounding the office of Speaker in a parliamentary republic was never lost sight of by its supporters. In political polemic surrounding the demise of the Cromwellian protectorate and the revival of the commonwealth, the Speaker was apotheosised as 'the greatest man in England' by republicans.[24] Public symbols of the office were also inevitably the focus of popular discontent, as when a display in London of the Speaker's arms was broken down in July 1652.[25]

Lenthall would doubtless have been delighted if his personal reputation had always matched the grandeur of official representations of him and his office. On the contrary, however, his unseemly ambitiousness and interest in the spoils of office began to be noted by observers quite early in his speakership. D'Ewes recorded Lenthall's crude lobbying for the office of master of the rolls in December 1642, which coloured the diarist's observation of the confused nominations in the House for that post a few months later. D'Ewes thought the process was rigged to favour Lenthall.[26] By April 1643, D'Ewes was convinced that the Speaker was showing favour to the most radical figures in the House, anathematised by the diarist as the 'fiery spirits', because they had promised Lenthall the office and an award of £6,000.[27] Hyde shared D'Ewes's view of Lenthall's acquisitiveness, but during the early years of the civil war these were private opinions that were circulating among MPs rather than damaging personal attacks on Lenthall. It was more demeaning when suggestions of Lenthall's partiality began to circulate beyond Westminster, as they did as early as the summer of 1641.[28] Worse still was an accusation of treachery to the cause of parliament. An example is the serious public allegation in July 1645, made outside the Commons by lobbyists, including the radical army officer, John Lilburne, that Lenthall had organised the sending of £60,000 to Oxford as clandestine help for the king's cause. Lenthall defended himself from the Speaker's chair against these charges, and Lilburne was made to appear before the committee for examinations and subsequently imprisoned.[29] The canard that Lenthall was a closet

[22] S. Kelsey, *Inventing a Republic* (Stanford, CA, 1997), 127–8.

[23] R. Cust, *Charles I: A Political Life* (Harlow, 2005), 158.

[24] *Diary of Thomas Burton,* ed. Rutt, iv, 319, 346–8.

[25] *The Diary of John Harington, MP 1646–53*, ed. M.F. Stieg (Somerset Record Society, lxxiv, 1977), 77.

[26] BL, Harleian MS 163, ff. 244, 289.

[27] BL, Harleian MS 163, f. 356v.

[28] J. Adamson, *The Noble Revolt* (2007), 331.

[29] BL, Harleian MS 166, f. 245; *The Copy of a Letter to a Friend* (1645), (BL, E296.5); S.R. Gardiner, *History of the Great Civil War* (4 vols, 1901), ii, 332–3.

royalist as well as being a supporter of the 'fiery spirits' and later of the independents proved durable, however, and even in the early days of the commonwealth persisted among his detractors.[30]

Lenthall's exceptional qualities derived partly from the extraordinary character and duration of the Long Parliament. In 1648 Lenthall was reckoned to be earning £2,000 a year from the speakership, 'besides rewards for courtesies (not to say bribes)'.[31] Most Speakers of the period were in office for too short a period to acquire the patina of cupidity. Even so, the rewards of the post in normal times were significant. Each private bill attracted a fee to Speaker and clerk, so that one historian has described the Speaker as 'the most zealous promoter of private legislation'.[32] In an attempt at fending off his critics, Speaker Lenthall in 1660 retrospectively computed his earnings from private bills at £5 a bill to amount to £2,220 for the entire course of the Long Parliament.[33] Widdrington attracted notice in February 1658 as combining the speakership with the lucrative post of treasury commissioner. The Speaker's salary was £1,820, and Widdrington was alleged to have made an extra £1,500 in the 14 months the second protectorate parliament had been sitting, from processing private acts and granting naturalisations alone.[34] These earnings were within the rules by which parliaments were conducted at the time, but reports of Speakers' self-interested dealings appeared in the products of a fertile, febrile and virtually unregulated press.

Parliament had been quick to avail itself of the power of the printing press from the collapse of censorship by the Stuart government in the early 1640s. One analyst has calculated that judged only by surviving products of the press, 13% of the output of London presses between 1641 and 1648 was sponsored by the houses of parliament, with a high point of some 23% in 1645.[35] William Lenthall was the first Speaker in English history to have to deal with an unfettered press. The unflattering reports of his conduct would not have acquired the staying power they did, had they not been crystallised in reportage. Not that a manifestation in printer's ink was a precondition for heavy-handed intervention by the Commons' authorities. John Lilburne's rumour-mongering about Lenthall in 1645 was by word of mouth, and it was only after his interrogation by the committee of examinations that Lilburne resorted to the press to vindicate himself. Most importantly, print was a tool that could be used by both sides: there was no sense in which either parliament or the Speaker himself were handicapped by any self-imposed restraint in dealing with distasteful scribblers. Lenthall personally used the press in a number of ways. When he and the independents were forced by the rising tide of mob violence in London to take themselves to the New Model army for protection in the summer of 1647, he put out a declaration, printed in Oxford, a city by then safely under parliamentarian control, to justify his departure. Lenthall had feared for his life during the intimidation by the crowd, having been pushed, jostled and nearly prevented from

---

[30] *Ten Articles Already Proved Upon Oath* (1649), (BL, 669.f.14.52).

[31] C. Walker, *The History of Independency* (1648), (BL, E463.19), 166.

[32] J.H. Willcox, 'Some Aspects of the Early History of Committees of the Whole House', *Parliamentary Affairs*, vii (1953), 415.

[33] *A True Narrative of the Particular Profits and Gaines made by Me William Lenthall* (1660), 5.

[34] *A Narrative of the Late Parliament* (1658), 10.

[35] *Printing for Parliament, 1641–1700*, ed. S. Lambert (List and Index Society, special ser., xx, 1984), p. ix.

getting into his coach, and his declaration is a dignified and cogent plea for the resumption of order and the 'free and parliamentary way of proceeding'.[36]

This was a direct appeal to the public, written in the language reminiscent of Lenthall's better-known defiance of Charles in 1642. He was alive to other uses of the media. Walter Frost, secretary to the Derby House committee, was described in 1648 as Lenthall's 'newshound' for acting on his behalf to ferret out breaking stories.[37] Frost was an intelligence agent and counter-revolutionary propagandist.[38] Drafts of publications remain in Lenthall's surviving papers, and at least one newspaper editor, Marchamont Nedham, thought Lenthall capable of having correspondence manufactured for propaganda purposes.[39] Lenthall was never out of the public eye during the 20 years of the civil wars and interregnum, and the reports of him that appeared in print were rarely flattering. Stories of his avariciousness and his covert royalism refused to go away, and in 1653 after the ejection of the Rump Parliament by Cromwell he was compared unfavourably with Balaam's ass (the talking donkey of the Old Testament) in a squib distributed about London.[40] These themes returned with a vengeance during the later 1650s, before, during and after the revivals of the Long Parliament, when Lenthall was again in the Speaker's chair. In 1657 he was even said in print to have been in the pay of the pope.[41] In June 1660, as in August 1647, he decided to hit back. Two pamphlets vindicating Lenthall appeared, one in the first person, the other in the name of 'J.N.' apparently in response to a request from 'G.G.'. The same printer's ornaments adorn both publications, and it is likely that both were simply variants of a text prepared by Lenthall himself.[42] Both texts dwell on Lenthall's outlay on official entertaining; the arrears of the money promised him by the king in the early days of the Long Parliament; the shortfall from profits of office consequent upon the collapse of business in the law courts; and the exaggerations in the reported potential for fee-taking in the Commons.

Lenthall's use of the press suggests that he was mindful of the possibilities as well as the destructive power of print, but there were more traditional remedies open to a Speaker who considered himself publicly traduced. The liberties of parliamentary privilege were well established and zealously defended. One of these liberties was the right of parliament to act against those who wilfully misrepresented its actions. Vague in origin and elastic in scope, this aspect of privilege provided a rationale for the executive actions of the Long Parliament, including its raising armies against the king and its reach into local communities with tax-raising powers. Against this momentous backdrop, assaults on the integrity of the Commons by individuals were small change, and challenges to the integrity of the Speaker smaller still. Ironically, given the volume of comment in print on parliament's doings, it remained a breach of privilege to report them without licence. In times of greater press regulation, it was once again realistic for a Speaker to refer to

---

[36] *A Declaration of Master William Lenthall Esquire* (Oxford, 1647).

[37] J. Peacey, *Politicians and Pamphleteers* (Aldershot, 2004), 244.

[38] G.E. Aylmer, *The State's Servants* (1973), 254–5.

[39] Peacey, *Politicians and Pamphleteers*, 239.

[40] *Ten Articles Already Proved Upon Oath* (1649), (BL, 669.f.14.52); *Lenthall's Lamentation* (1653); Numbers xxii: 21–35.

[41] *Truths Triumph over Treacherous Dealing* (1657).

[42] *An Account of the Gaines of the Late Speaker William Lenthall* (1660); *A True Narrative of the Particular Profits and Gaines made by Me William Lenthall*.

hostile report as a privilege matter. Speaker Widdrington did so in June 1657, complaining from the chair that he was being blamed by the London vintners' company for some aspect of excise legislation currently before the House that affected their interests: 'There is a great reproach upon me. I bear all the blame in the business of the Vintners.' On that occasion, a few members spoke in supportive terms of the Speaker's position and called for punishment of offending interests outside the House, but Widdrington himself reined in his colleagues to prevent any parliamentary retaliation.[43] More personally, Lenthall complained in December 1640 of an injury to his servant: the offender, albeit a justice of the peace, was sent for as a delinquent.[44]

In contrast to the burgeoning executive power of the Long Parliament, the quasi-headship of state of the Speaker under the commonwealth and the controversy surrounding the reputation of the Speaker outside parliament, this period saw no obvious increase in the power of the Speaker in procedural matters in the Commons itself. He remained the servant of the House. Lenthall sometimes made substantive contributions to debate, as in November 1642 when he offered his view on possible peace negotiations with the king.[45] He was by convention denied a voice in debate, however, and could be jumped upon by members for breaching that rule.[46] The language used in recording the Speaker's interventions and pronouncements tended to be couched in elaborate courtesies, concealing any more direct, behind-the-chair dealings that may have driven his decisions. Even so, it is the case that Lenthall had to request leave to speak in February 1641 in order to present an order on episcopacy that he considered the sense of a rather overheated House.[47] Bampfylde prefaced one of his interventions in March 1659 by making it clear that he was well aware of that rule.[48] If the surviving records of debates convey the tenor of them at all accurately, there was no culture of deference to the chair. Rather, there was a sense of difficulties being shared frankly. In 1641–2 alone, Lenthall articulated to the House his problems framing questions; allowed himself to be corrected by the insufferable D'Ewes when he slipped up over the protocols between the Houses and the king; and at other times listened as members rose to correct those correcting him.[49] He was blamed for allowing members to speak more often than they should have and was told not to plead a case when two members had a spectacular falling out. The criticisms of him by members were sometimes couched in the second person, the convention of third person discussion of other members apparently not applying in his case.[50]

Most of these exchanges took place within the heat of debate. A number of procedural decisions reached the *Commons Journal* as a matter of record, however. In December 1640

[43] *Diary of Thomas Burton*, ed. Rutt, ii, 237; *CJ*, vii, 453, 454, 514, 568.

[44] *D'Ewes Journal*, ed. Notestein, 193; *Proceedings in the Opening Session of the Long Parliament: House of Commons. Vol. ii: 21 December 1640 – 20 March 1641*, ed. M. Jansson (Woodbridge, 2000), 54.

[45] BL, Add. MS 18,777, f. 65v.

[46] BL, Harleian MS 163, f. 245.

[47] *Proceedings . . . of the Long Parliament*, ed. Jansson, ii, 400–1.

[48] *Diary of Thomas Burton*, ed. Rutt, iv, 204–5.

[49] *D'Ewes Journal*, ed. Notestein, 437; *D'Ewes Journal*, ed. Coates, 224; *Private Journals of the Long Parliament 3 January to 5 March 1642*, ed. W.H. Coates, A.S. Young and V.F. Snow (New Haven, 1982), 444, 473–4.

[50] *D'Ewes Journal*, ed. Notestein, 236, 462; *Private Journals . . . 3 January to 5 March 1642*, ed. Coates, Young and Snow, 338.

it was recorded that in divisions, those voting for preserving the orders of the House should stay in, while those voting for change should go out, and the following month in January 1641, it was taken as a rule that the Speaker should not chair a sitting with fewer than 40 members in attendance.[51] Of course, as the presiding officer, the Speaker had to enforce the rules and the changes of rules, and so *ipso facto* most rule changes affected the Speaker. It is doubtful whether procedural innovation – or apparent innovation, since many such rules were surely codifications of existing practice – can be attributed to Speakers themselves. One area with potential for further scrutiny for evidence of change is the frequency and duration of periods in which the Commons sat as a committee of the whole House. On such occasions, the Speaker stood down in favour of an alternative chairman. This was a procedure with origins in the parliaments of Elizabeth I, generally in the interests of flexibility in debate.[52] Some of these sessions could be lengthy. When Lenthall was Speaker of the first protectorate parliament, the early months of that assembly were taken up with review and revision of the constitution. Between 19 September 1654 and 4 January 1655, Bennet Hoskins, the member for Hereford, presided at sessions of the committee of the whole House on 40 occasions. As Hoskins sat in spite of hostile petitioning by constituents who reported his crypto-royalist past, his continual re-appointment to chair the highly significant discussions of the constitution must have been a deliberate expression of the will of the House and a tacit show of defiance towards the government of Lord Protector Cromwell. The committee of the whole had been a useful mechanism in the parliaments of the 1620s, utilised as a means of freeing debates from the restrictions which limited contributions from individual members.[53] In 1654–5 it was not simply convening to debate, but was breaking into sub-committees to examine individual subject areas of the bill on government. The sub-committees took votes to make their decisions and reported them back to Hoskins, who, in turn, read them to the House.[54] While these procedures were by no means an attack on the authority of the Speaker, they did create potential for an alternative focus for parliamentary activity, and in this particular example a way for country interests to register their voice.

As the reach of the Long Parliament extended further over the country during and after the civil war, executive committees of parliament were established by order of both Houses, some like the committee for the navy and customs, a committee of men from both Commons and Lords, others like the committee for plundered ministers, from the lower House only. The most important and durable of these bodies had their own regular meetings, venues and clerks; kept their own records and issued orders and letters in effect on their own authority. How this growth of executive power related to the office of Speaker is hard to determine. Certainly there was no regular mechanism by which the powerful executive committees had to make reports of their actions to the Speaker; nor, given the sheer volume of business transacted, could there realistically have been. Nevertheless, the Speaker was in most cases brought within the scope of what amounted

---

[51] J. Hatsell, *Precedents of Proceedings in the House of Commons* (2nd edn, 2 vols, 1785), ii, 123, 134.

[52] Willcox, 'Some Aspects of the Early History of Committees of the Whole House', 415.

[53] C. Russell, *Parliaments and English Politics 1621–1629* (Oxford, 1979), 38–9.

[54] S.K. Roberts, 'Bennet Hoskins', draft article for the History of Parliament: House of Commons 1640–60. Copyright remains with the History of Parliament Trust.

to an administrative devolution of authority. The business of raising taxation from parliament's friends and enemies illustrates the principle. As early as April 1643, the Speaker was to receive the accounts of the weekly assessment.[55] The oaths of subordinate officers such as sequestrators and excisemen were taken before him or certified to him, and when in 1645, compounding for delinquency was an option for royalists, they had to apply to the Speaker for passes to visit Goldsmiths' Hall in order to file their cases.[56] As Lenthall himself freely admitted in 1660, his interest in these cases was cemented with the award to him by the Commons of £5 for each delinquent admitted to composition.[57] The net effect of these developments was to swell the workload before the Speaker's clerks, and to bind him by financial incentive to the machinery of penal taxation.

Most of the powerful executive committees of the Long Parliament became the preserve of the independents.[58] Contemporary private diary entries on Lenthall's willingness to be suborned by the 'fiery spirits' in 1642–3 have already been noted. Private observation of Lenthall's partiality quickly spilled over into public comment.[59] By March 1644 he was being associated with the politics of the independents, an identification which persisted through the turbulence of 1647 to the trial of the king and beyond. The immediacy of Marchamont Nedham's reports in *Mercurius Pragmaticus* of Lenthall as a tool of the independents is compelling, but in the factionalised politics of that parliament it is hard to envisage how a modern-style, strictly impartial speakership could have functioned. Hyde's insistence on Lenthall's personal weakness was his explanation of Lenthall's surrender to faction, but the Speaker was not protected from other members by a large staff or by an extensive or hallowed code of conduct. In the normal course of events the Speaker was often apprised of sensitive information before it reached the floor of the House. Reports without number from the field armies were addressed to him, for example, as were diplomatic communications, and he had ample time to study these before he read them to the House. In January 1644, D'Ewes confided to his Latin diary how the Speaker and a group of unnamed other MPs were privy to messages about peace proposals denied the rest of the House.[60] The Speaker was at the centre of all ceremonies. Much of this was routine, such as his daily taking the chair which signalled prayers and the start of the day's proceedings. But he was also invariably at the centre of special important occasions, such as the visit of the Dutch ambassadors in July 1644, when they were seated next to him in places of honour.[61] His privileged position made him a natural target for determined politicians intent on pursuing their own agenda, and occasionally Lenthall inadvertently let slip that he had been lobbied hard by particular individuals privately. An example is when in March 1643 he accidentally revealed that he

---

[55] *Acts and Ordinances of the Interregnum, 1642–1660*, ed. C.H. Firth and R.S. Rait (3 vols, 1911), i, 124.

[56] *Acts and Ordinances*, ed. Firth and Rait, i, 203, 438; *Calendar of the Committee for Compounding with Delinquents, 1643–1660*, ed. M.A.E. Green (5 vols in 1, 1889–92), p. vii.

[57] *A True Narrative of the Particular Profits*, 4–5.

[58] J. Peacey, 'Politics, Accounts and Propaganda in the Long Parliament', in *Parliament at Work*, ed. C.R. Kyle and J. Peacey (Woodbridge, 2002), 59.

[59] J. Peacey, 'Perceptions of Parliament: Factions and "The Public" ', in *The English Civil War*, ed. J. Adamson (Basingstoke, 2009), 94.

[60] BL, Harleian MS 483, f. 12.

[61] BL, Harleian MS 483, f. 94; *CJ*, iii, 559–60.

had been closeted with the French general, Bernard de la Valette, duc d'Épernon, honoured by Charles I with the order of the garter.[62]

No Speaker was entirely immune to political influences. Lenthall's reputation as a placeman of the independents emerged and remained prevalent during a period when control of the executive was vigorously contested. Other Speakers in this period were brought to the chair in parliaments in which executive authority was clearly determined, but they were mostly the products of either the king's choice, as in the case of Glanville of the Short Parliament, or were close to the protectoral government at the time of their appointments. At the time of his election in 1656, for example, Widdrington was a treasury and trade commissioner and a commissioner of the great seal, and was thus evidently a government client. It cannot credibly be argued that the politics of the parliaments of the 1650s were without faction, but neither were they chaotically factionalised. A recent study has analysed parliamentary faction in terms of 'interests', which were at least stable and, to a large extent, predictable.[63] It is noticeable that in the more stable political climate presided over by the protectoral government, Lenthall's speakership of 1654–5 attracted less critical comment than did his chairing of the Long Parliament. Of all the speakerships of 1640–60, Thomas Bampfylde's brief occupancy of the chair was, arguably, coloured most overtly from the outset by factional politics, as he had a known history of opposition in parliament to protectoral policies and had no significant record of government service: in this last respect rather like Lenthall in November 1640, in fact.

Lenthall was captured by the independents because he was largely defenceless to prevent it, and endured hostile comment from the enemies of the independents as a consequence. But is there any relationship between this vilification of the Speaker as partial and venal and the huge increase, alluded to earlier, in the volume of political business passing through the Speaker's office? The Tanner and Nalson MSS show how detailed and nuanced were the reports reaching him from every parliamentarian county committee and interest group in the country. To what extent was Speaker Lenthall a witting participant in all the transactions in his name behind his chair? It is obvious that many informants of the House wrote to the Speaker impersonally *qua* Speaker, not presuming any personal relationship with the man himself. It is equally clear from the *Commons Journals* in the 1640s that letters back to the provinces from the House were prepared for the Speaker to sign by members with expert knowledge, and that he could not in any meaningful way have been cognisant of all instruments that passed under his own hand, any more than he can have personally supervised the parliamentary printing undertaken in his name. The speakership had always been a symbol of Commons' authority, but in conditions of civil war Lenthall's person, more than his office, came to personify faction, self-interest and the other evils attributed by parliament's enemies to the institution itself. In such circumstances, it is more interesting to encounter examples of letters of intelligence to Lenthall from those who clearly knew him well, and who had things to convey to him that presumed a closer relationship than the merely formal. In

---

[62] BL, Harleian MS 163, ff. 336, 336v.

[63] Little and Smith, *Parliaments and Politics*, ch. 5, which takes issue with, among others, P. Gaunt, 'Oliver Cromwell and his Protectorate Parliaments: Co-operation, Conflict and Control', in *'Into Another Mould': Aspects of the Interregnum*, ed. I. Roots (2nd edn, Exeter, 1998), 70–100, and D. Hirst, 'Concord and Discord in Richard Cromwell's House of Commons', *English Historical Review*, ciii (1988), 339–58.

November 1645, for example, John Ashe, member for Westbury, provided Lenthall with an account of progress in the recruiter elections in the west country. Making it clear that he was on business instigated by the Speaker himself, Ashe advised him to begin discussions with other regional leaders, offered snide comment on the conduct of one colleague, conveyed good wishes from another and vouchsafed that a third's outlook was improved since his wife had joined him in the field.[64] Such examples indicate that there were limits to the impersonal in the Speaker's chamber, no clear distinctions between what was Lenthall's official file, his clerks' in-tray and his personal folder.

It is doubtful whether the period 1640–60 saw an increase in the power and authority of the Speaker. Measured by procedural change in the Commons' chamber, this was a period of limited reform which did not benefit the Speaker in terms of his standing *vis-à-vis* the members. Speakers still depended on the goodwill of the House for their success in 1660, as they had done in 1640. Nor was there a significant or lasting change in the type and quality of Speakers and the selection procedure surrounding their chairing. The speakership of Lenthall was exceptional, but it has been suggested here that this owed more to the extraordinary scope and self-image of the Long Parliament and the Rump Parliament rather than to any inherent qualities he may have possessed: nowhere more so than in the case of Lenthall's reputation, flayed in a hostile and partisan London newspaper market. Lenthall was also unique in his willingness to embrace the expanding new medium not only for parliament's benefit but also for his own. As the pretensions of parliament dwindled in the mid to late 1650s under the aegis of the protectoral government, so the speakership retreated to become less visible and less controversial and also less busy, compared with the heyday of the 1640s and early 1650s. It is paradox enough that Lenthall was a case apart in attracting on the one hand fame as a defier of the king, and on the other opprobrium as a man with deep pockets and no principles. A further twist in the reputation of this exceptional figure is that while he came to personify the heights and depths of the Long Parliament's reputation, during his tenure we can dimly discern a potential distinction between the person and the office of the Speaker.

Appendix

List of Speakers and Dates 1640–60

If only because of the prominence of the Speaker in the order of precedence, it is curious that no list appears in the Royal Historical Society's *Handbook of British Chronology*, not even in the most recent edition.[65] At least four previous listings have been made for this period. A.I. Dasent's list in *The Speakers of the House of Commons* (1911), 384–6, provides start dates of the speakerships and gives no biographical dates for the Speakers. P. Laundy, *The Office of Speaker* (1964), 455–7, is the fullest, providing full dates, biographical dates and brief notes. A more recent list of all Speakers to the present, with biographies of all

---

[64] Bodl., MS Nalson v, f. 29.

[65] *Handbook of British Chronology*, ed. E.B. Pryde, D.E. Greenway, S. Porter and I. Roy (Royal Historical Society Guides and Handbooks No. 2, 3rd edn, Cambridge, 1996).

except former ones still living, is to be found in the *Oxford Dictionary of National Biography* online. Another is in D.L. Smith, *The Stuart Parliaments 1603–89* (1999), 43. In matters of dating, the *Oxford Dictionary of National Biography* provides years only, whereas Smith provides months in addition. All these lists omit the speakership of Eure at Oxford. Smith also omits Pelham and Whitelocke; *Oxford Dictionary of National Biography* also omits Say. The biographical dates provided below are based on the most recent work on the biographies of these Speakers at the History of Parliament Trust. Opening dates of speakerships below are when the Speaker was elected, which was not always on the first day that the parliament sat; closing dates are based on days the House sat. The issue of legitimacy in this period goes far to explain the omissions and contradictions. Here the authority for the Speaker's tenure and dates is the *Commons Journal*, except in the cases of Eure and Say. The rival parliament Eure chaired at Oxford seems not to have been prorogued or dissolved, so its terminal date is taken to be that of the surrender of Oxford to parliament. In the case of Say, his appointment was regularised before Lenthall retired sick. Lenthall proposed to take ten days' leave, but a newspaper report provides the date of his return, 21 January 1660.[66]

1. John Glanville (c.1586–1661)	13 Apr.–5 May 1640
2. William Lenthall (1591–1662)	3 Nov. 1640–27 July 1647
3. Sir Sampson Eure (c.1592–by 1659)	22 Jan. 1644–?24 June 1646 (Oxford parliament)
4. Henry Pelham (1597–after 1660)	30 July–5 Aug. 1647
5. William Lenthall (1591–1662)	6 Aug. 1647–20 Apr. 1653
6. Francis Rous (1580/1–1659)	5–6 July 1653 (chairman); 7 July–12 Dec. 1653
7. William Lenthall (1591–1662)	4 Sept. 1654–22 Jan. 1655
8. Sir Thomas Widdrington (c.1600–64)	17 Sept. 1656–4 Feb. 1658
9. Bulstrode Whitelocke (1605–75)	27 Jan.–17 Feb. 1657 (acting)
10. Chaloner Chute (c.1595–1659)	27 Jan.–*d.* 14 Apr. 1659 (sat for last time on 9 Mar. 1659)
11. Sir Lislebone Long (1613–59)	9–14 Mar. 1659 (acting)
12. Thomas Bampfylde (c.1623–93)	16 Mar.–15 Apr. (acting); 15–22 Apr. 1659
13. William Lenthall (1591–1662)	7 May 1659–13 Oct. 1659; 26 Dec. 1659–16 Mar. 1660
14. William Say (c.1604–65)	13–21 Jan. 1660 (acting)

[66] *CJ*, vii, 811; *The Publick Intelligencer*, 212 (16–23 Jan. 1660), 1036.

The Speaker in the Age of Party, 1672–1715

PAUL SEAWARD

The discussion by King Charles II and his senior advisors in 1672 of the choice of a new Speaker for the forthcoming parliamentary session reveals both the way in which the appointment was prepared and the government's considerations in the appointment. Prominent among them was the Speaker's personal influence, and his personal views on the great issue to be debated, the Declaration of Indulgence. The choice of Sir Job Charlton, and the behaviour of his successor, Sir Edward Seymour, in the chair, mark a new phase in the history of the speakership, in which Speakers are less likely to be lawyers, for whom the office was a step on the road to high legal office, and more likely to be significant political leaders with their own influence and following. After the 1688 revolution, the tendency for Speakers to be party political leaders became still more marked. Nevertheless, the country ideology espoused by several of them, including Paul Foley, Robert Harley and the tory, Sir Thomas Hanmer, provides a pedigree for the model of the impartial speakership whose invention is often attributed to Arthur Onslow.

Keywords: parliament; Speaker; party; parliamentary management; Restoration; revolution of 1688; whig; tory

Sir John Eliot, writing of the re-election of Sir Thomas Crewe as Speaker in 1625, was said to have referred to the speakership as an office 'frequently filled by nullities, men selected for mere Court convenience'.[1] Unfair as it may have been to the many able and distinguished men who filled the office, the remark reflected the fact that early-17th-century Speakers were rarely leading political figures, and more often competent lawyers *en route* to the senior legal judicial offices. But between the 1670s and the early 18th century the post was occupied by a series of ambitious and powerful politicians, aiming at the major offices of state, who were appointed not because of their legal expertise or simply for their compliance with government, but because of their own political influence within the house of commons. The change was closely associated with the importance of the Commons in post-Restoration politics, with the longer and more regular parliaments and sessions of the 1660s and 1670s and particularly after the revolution, and with the development and acknowledgement of explicit parties within the House. The appointments in 1673 of Sir Job Charlton, and, in rapid succession, Edward Seymour, just as a debate about religious toleration and persecution was moving ominously into a divisive confrontation about the rights of the crown and its relationship with the Church, mark the beginning of this phase in the history of the speakership.

---

[1] Quoted by Philip Laundy, *The Office of Speaker* (1964), 194.

In November 1672 the Cavalier Parliament was in recess. Since its first meeting in May 1661 in the first flush of Restoration enthusiasm for the crown and the Church, it had become much less manageable and every session was accompanied by speculation about its dissolution. The new session, expected to begin the following February, would be exceptionally problematic. Early in 1672, the king had renewed war with the Dutch republic in an attempt to seek revenge on the Dutch: the previous naval war of 1664–7 had ended with the humiliation of a Dutch fleet sailing up the Medway barely challenged by the English navy. The war was also something of a defiance of parliament: the English navy had been laid up in 1667 because the house of commons had failed to provide adequate funding to set it out that year; this time the war was begun without seeking endorsement or funding from parliament. The first year of the war had not gone as well as had been planned, and the government could only carry it on with parliamentary funding. Moreover, at the same time as he had declared war, the king had introduced a policy of toleration for religious nonconformists – the 1672 Declaration of Indulgence. As the house of commons had decisively rejected a similar declaration in 1663, and debates in 1668 and 1670 had clearly shown that overall the House continued to be opposed to removing religious disabilities of any kind, this was another move which could not help but provoke serious opposition.

In such a situation, there could be nothing more critical to the government than a strong and effective Speaker. Sir Edward Turnor, the Speaker since the beginning of the Cavalier Parliament in 1661, had been appointed lord chief baron of the exchequer in May 1671, in the middle of a long recess, leaving a vacancy. On 24 November 1672, about three months before parliament was expected to meet, the question of a successor was discussed at length in the committee on foreign affairs – an inner and relatively informal group of the king's privy council in which the king met his most senior advisors. The meeting was minuted, as usual, by the under secretary of state, Joseph Williamson, and although his scribble is often difficult to decipher, his extensive notes, more extensive than on any other subject in the committee's minutes, provide a remarkable indication of the concerns and interests of the government in the speakership.[2]

The meeting began with a point of universal agreement: Robert Milward, who was present at the meeting, was 'unanimously agreed as without exception the best': a traditional Speaker, a safe pair of hands, without any evidence of strong political ambitions of his own. Milward was a senior lawyer, called to the bar in 1638 and currently acting as a Welsh judge; he had been chairman of the committees of ways and means and supply in 1661 and 1666, and in his parliamentary career had chaired numerous other committees. Milward was attending the meeting, probably because he was one of the three commissioners of the privy seal, and was a lynchpin of the government's management of the Commons.[3] He hastily disclaimed any ambition for the post: 'he is not able to serve by reason of his indispositions of body', Williamson wrote down. Asked to propose an alternative, Milward suggested Sir Thomas Jones

---

[2] TNA, SP104/177, f. 107: 24 Nov. 1672.

[3] For Milward's role in the Cavalier Parliament in the 1660s, see Paul Seaward, *The Cavalier Parliament and the Reconstruction of the Old Regime, 1661–67* (Cambridge, 1989), 83; *The History of Parliament: The House of Commons, 1660–1690*, ed. B.D. Henning (3 vols, 1983) [hereafter cited as *HPC, 1660–90*], iii, 69–70.

instead. Jones was a lawyer too, slightly more senior than Milward, like him a Welsh judge and a serjeant-at-law, though with much less parliamentary experience. Later on in the meeting Sir Thomas Osborne (shortly to become the earl of Danby, and the architect of the policy pursued by Charles II in the late 1670s of seeking a firm alliance with the supporters of the Church in the Commons) returned to cajoling Milward, assuring him that 'the king's work will not be long we hope', and he was joined by the lord chancellor, the earl of Shaftesbury, one of the chief architects of the declaration and to become Danby's determined opponent. Milward vehemently insisted that he was unable to take on the post: 'before God by his great infirmities he cannot serve in that place'. He was evidently unconvinced by the secretary of state, the earl of Arlington's suggestion that he might take the chair on a temporary basis. The outgoing Speaker, Sir Edward Turnor, was called in to provide advice, and told the meeting 'that according to the ancient custom the chair of the Committee of Privileges was chosen Speaker', as he had been himself. This pointed to Sir Job Charlton. Charlton was a serjeant-at-law, king's serjeant since 1668, and like Milward and Jones, a Welsh judge. He was formidably experienced in the chair and in the House: he had chaired the committee of privileges and elections since the beginning of the Cavalier Parliament, and had also chaired the committee of ways and means. The problem with Charlton was that he was regarded as one of the leaders, perhaps the leader, of those in the House who supported the Church of England, and one of the architects of the legislation against nonconformists in 1661–5. Andrew Marvell referred to him in his satirical account of the house of commons of 1667 as 'awing' 'the mitre troop'. He could be assumed to oppose the Declaration of Indulgence.[4] Turnor's own suggestion, though, was William Montagu, the queen's attorney general, who had never chaired the senior committees of the House, although he was a senior lawyer and an extremely experienced parliamentarian, and also someone who had had some experience in helping to manage the king's interest.[5] Shaftesbury intervened to cast doubts on Montagu, although his grounds for doing so are (except for concerns about his 'quickness') illegible; others thought him too 'modest'. The secretary of state, Henry Coventry (generally regarded as, like Charlton, something of a defender of the Church) returned to Charlton: he was as 'stout as anything'.

Sir John Duncombe, the chancellor of the exchequer threw in several more names. One was a senior lawyer, Edward Thurland, the duke of York's attorney general.[6] A second was the phenomenally industrious and extremely influential Sir Thomas Meres. Trained in the law and called to the bar, though there is little evidence of him practising, Meres was generally seen as a powerful 'country' and pro-Church politician.[7] The third was another bumptious hyperactive country politician – though one rather more attuned to the government's current policy of favouring dissenters – Edward Seymour. Seymour was said to be 'equall to every body', although there was one major reservation, sadly illegible: it may have been that Seymour was not a lawyer, not just not practising, like Meres, but not even trained in the law. Not since the middle ages had there been a Speaker who lacked legal training. There was an irony here, since one of the participants

---

[4] See Seaward, *Cavalier Parliament*, 83–4, 96–7; *HPC, 1660–90*, ii, 44–6.

[5] *HPC, 1660–90*, iii, 90–2; Seaward, *Cavalier Parliament*, 83.

[6] *HPC, 1660–90*, iii, 562–4.

[7] *HPC, 1660–90*, iii, 48–58.

in the discussion was the earl of Shaftesbury, the first lord chancellor for very many years not to have been a lawyer. One man Duncombe ruled out: Serjeant Maynard, an eminent lawyer, premier king's serjeant, and much in evidence in government business in the Commons.[8] The reasons Duncombe gave for his preference for Meres or Seymour are impossible to read, but seem to imply that once made Speaker they would be prevented from frustrating the government's business. The lord treasurer, Lord Clifford, thought Seymour 'magisterial', a man who 'keeps the House well in awe': 'no body better'; Meres he thought, perhaps merely, 'able'. Clifford was a very close neighbour of Seymour: their estates at Ugbrooke and Berry Pomeroy in Devon were within about ten miles of one another, and Clifford's parliamentary borough of Totnes was Berry Pomeroy's nearest town. Clifford may have been responsible for finding Seymour government office in 1665, and when lord treasurer he had already relied heavily on his heavy-handed but effective chairmanship of the committee of ways and means.[9] The duke of Buckingham, later in the meeting, also vigorously supported Seymour, who had been regarded as attached to his interest for some time. Sir Robert Long, a key and very senior exchequer official, preferred Meres: he 'doubts not of his zeal to serve the King', and he proposed that the king should talk to him. But there was a major problem with Meres, which the king himself pointed out: 'he loves his own opinion' he said. Long laconically replied: 'he'll be of yours'. But the king made it clear that he assumed that Meres would 'boggle the Declaration', which seems to have sunk his candidacy.

The meeting returned to Charlton. The key problem, as Shaftesbury said, was his 'zeal' – for the Church – and 'his own opinion against the king's measures'. According to Sir John Duncombe, Charlton was, anyway, wanting to be excused on grounds of his health. Coventry was Charlton's closest supporter and answered the objections against him: he acknowledged his 'zeal', but said that this was 'only when he is left to himself and knows not your Majesties pleasure. But otherwise dares say he will submit to the king in this great conjuncture.' Coventry had to answer doubts, too, about Charlton's tendency to 'passion', and his health: he pointed out that he ought to be able to manage these as well in the chair of the House as he had done in the chair for committees of the whole House. Arlington said that 'the great talent is honesty in this parliament. If Sir Job Charlton has that, it will recompense the want of anything else.' At the end of the meeting the king said that he would think further about the matter and 'commanded an absolute silence in all that has been said here'.

The king still was said not to have made up his mind before the next recorded meeting a week later, on 1 December; but at that meeting it seems that it was decided to offer it to Sir Job Charlton, though the expectation was that he would refuse. The merits of an alternative were further discussed; the king had heard 'good things said of Sir Thomas Meres' from Sir Robert Long and Sir Robert Howard, the two treasury officials.[10] Against expectation, however, Charlton accepted. He was nominated in the

---

[8] Maynard may have been ruled out on grounds of age: he was almost 70, although he continued to sit in the house of commons until he was past his mid-eighties. See *HPC, 1660–90*, iii, 38–44, and Seaward, *Cavalier Parliament*, 82–3.

[9] D.T. Witcombe, *Charles II and the Cavalier House of Commons, 1663–1674* (Manchester, 1966), 110. For the commissionership of prizes, see Seaward, *Cavalier Parliament*, 89–95; see also *HPC, 1660–90*, ii, 91–4; iii, 410–20.

[10] TNA, SP104/177, f. 101.

House by Henry Coventry and elected Speaker on 4 February 1672, the first day of the new session. The lord chancellor – Shaftesbury, his opponent in the committee discussion – in approving his appointment on behalf of the king said ambiguously: 'Such a House of Commons; Such a Speaker!', and went on, perhaps pointedly: 'For with reverence to the Holy Scripture, upon this Occasion, the King may say, *He that is not with Me, is against Me.*'[11]

Charlton was instantly plunged into controversy when he had to deal with a motion against the issuing of writs in the recess by the new lord chancellor, Shaftesbury. Charlton lasted for about a week-and-a-half of a vigorous onslaught against Shaftesbury, a man whom he had tried to have removed from any chance of power in 1660, and against the Declaration of Indulgence, a policy with which he was almost certainly at odds. On 10 February the Commons voted against the declaration; on 14 February – conceivably reacting to either speculation or a tip-off that the government's strategy was to get the Lords to disagree with the Commons' vote[12] – they decided not to ask the Lords to concur with it. Whether Charlton buckled under the strain of a confrontation between the king and the Commons on a scale not seen since the Restoration, whether he found it impossible to square the government's policy with his own views, or whether the government simply decided that he was not sufficiently reliable in the circumstances, is not clear. On 15 February, the Speaker 'being much indisposed' only arrived at 11 am to adjourn the House to the following Tuesday, the 18th. On that day, his letter of resignation was read to the House, together with the letter he had written to the king asking to be excused. One of those discussed the previous November, Edward Seymour, had already been making what may have been a none-too-subtle pitch to succeed to the job, acting as chair of the committee of supply on 7 February when it quickly voted £1,250,000 to support the war, and speaking on 10 February in favour of the declaration; another, Sir Thomas Meres, may also have had an eye on the prize when in the debate on 10 February he announced his conversion to liberty for tender consciences.[13] But it was Seymour who, on the 18th, was nominated as Speaker by Henry Coventry, and accepted without division. The diarist Sir Edward Dering noted that Seymour, 'being presently agreed upon, took the chair in his sword and belt, a thing hardly ever seen before in that place' – lawyers normally wearing their gowns, and swordless.[14]

The discussion in the foreign affairs committee emphasizes the arduous nature of the speakership in the 17th century – Milward's horror at the prospect of taking it on is quite palpable – and how important it was for bringing clarity and direction to the proceedings of the House. But what is most interesting about this discussion – apart from the existence of any record of it – is the extent to which it was not just the candidates' abilities which was under discussion, but their own political stances, and the extent to which factions supporting different candidates are discernible within the committee. The foreign affairs committee had been faced with an intensely difficult choice: anticipating a problematic session in which the government's current stances would come under extreme scrutiny and pressure, they needed a Speaker of great authority and influence. The men with the

---

[11] *CJ*, ix, 246.

[12] See TNA, SP104/177, ff. 143, 144v, 146.

[13] Anchitell Grey, *Debates of the House of Commons from the Year 1667 to the Year 1694* (12 vols, 1763), ii, 22–3.

[14] *The Parliamentary Diary of Sir Edward Dering*, ed. B.D. Henning (New Haven, 1940), 121.

greatest authority in the House were, however, deeply opposed to the government's present policy. Charlton and Meres were both regarded as highly qualified for the speakership, but there was extreme nervousness about their stances; Charlton, moreover, was strongly backed by the one man within the discussion, Henry Coventry, most closely identified with the Church interest, and strongly opposed by the earl of Shaftesbury, that interest's most obvious opponent. Mere's backers, apart from Sir John Duncombe, are unclear, although later he seems to have been connected with the earl of Arlington, one of Danby's rivals.[15] Seymour's main supporters in the foreign affairs committee meeting were Clifford, Sir Thomas Osborne, both of them regarded as associates of the duke of Buckingham, and Buckingham himself. Clifford resigned office as lord treasurer in June 1673 within four months of Seymour's appointment. He was replaced by Osborne, who became Viscount Latimer in July and earl of Danby in June 1674.

The storm raised against the Declaration of Indulgence in the 1673 session, resulting in its withdrawal, was, to many, confirmation that the government would be unable to pursue an effective policy of religious comprehension or toleration through the Cavalier Parliament. It resulted in the king's abandonment of any attempt to do so, his acceptance of Osborne as the leader of an alliance with the Church and its supporters in the parliament, and to the bitter departure from the government of another of the participants in that discussion, the earl of Shaftesbury, one of the prime figures behind the Declaration of Indulgence. In its aftermath came confirmation that Charles II's heir, his brother James, duke of York, had converted to the Roman catholic church, something which itself brought a new and highly dangerous edge to religious politics.

Seymour, in the chair, became a key ally of and party manager for Danby. Both men had previously been associated with the duke of Buckingham, so a connection must have been already established. Seymour was believed to have a particular influence over the members who sat for Devon and Cornwall. Danby's lists of court supporters in the late 1670s refer to specific individuals who are to be managed by the Speaker.[16] His appointment to the privy council on 9 April, and to the treasurership of the navy, were unsubtle indications of his closeness to government and assimilation into Danby's growing parliamentary management machine. When the Commons reassembled after the recess over the summer of 1673, an immediate attack on Seymour was also a token of the current perception that he was close to one of the factions within the court. On 27 October Sir Thomas Littleton moved that Seymour be replaced by a temporary Speaker: he complained that he was a privy councillor, and alleged that there was:

> hardly a precedent, at least not since the Reformation – Speakers, in Queen Mary's time, were chosen for the re-establishment of the Roman religion[17] – You might be made a Privy Counsellor afterwards, as a reward of your service, but not whilst you are Speaker – Other offices you hold inconsistent with that Chair, and have admittance to the most secret councils, and how improper is that, we having no man to

[15] Meres was described as such by Danby in 1674: *HPC, 1660–1690*, iii, 53.

[16] Andrew Browning, *Thomas Osborne, Earl of Danby and Duke of Leeds* (3 vols, Glasgow, 1951), iii, 80–4.

[17] A reference to Sir Clement Heigham, Speaker 1554–5, who was a member of the council before his election. Sir Edward Dering noted other precedents mentioned in the debate – Sir Thomas Hungerford (though Sir Walter Hungerford, 1414, seems to be meant) and Sir William Cordell (1558) – and one who was not, Sir John Baker (1545, 1547).

present our Grievances but you! You are too big for that Chair, and for us; and you, that are one of the Governors of the world, to be our servant, is incongruous – And as Carteret, Treasurer of the Navy, in that place [which you hold] took up the main business of a Session; by way of supposition, if that should happen again, were it proper for you to be in the Chair? For who [then] will be so much concerned?[18]

Littleton had both factional and personal reasons for attacking Seymour: an assocation with Arlington, a grudge against Danby, and a sense of entitlement to the office of treasurer of the navy, from which he had been evicted by the lord treasurer in 1671.[19] The motion was not pressed to a division, and Seymour survived what was, in effect, a motion of censure on the chair.

Given that his appointment had much to do with the assumption that he would support the Declaration of Indulgence, Seymour's association with Danby throughout his alliance with the Church was opportunistic and ironic. Nevertheless it lasted while Danby's management of the Cavalier house of commons ran into acute difficulties in the face of a determined campaign against that alliance, of the king's reluctance irrevocably to commit himself to the alliance with the Netherlands against France, which formed the other element of Danby's political strategy, and of the personal hostility to him of key politicians within court and outside it. The emergence of a 'country party' coalition against Danby and its prolonged fight to secure the dissolution and replacement of the Cavalier Parliament made his alliance with Seymour even more critical to his survival. During 1675, despite sniping against him personally, Seymour's tough-minded management of Danby's interests in the House was regarded as remarkably effective.[20]

As Danby's regime began to collapse, however, Seymour came under increased pressure. The most controversial moments of his speakership came in 1677. At the end of May, the king responded to an address of the Commons for an alliance with the Dutch States General by requiring the House to adjourn to July, an instruction which Seymour carried out over a barrage of protests that it was against the privilege of the House and reminders of how Sir John Finch had been forcibly prevented from adjourning on the king's instructions in 1629. In July, December and January 1678, the Speaker repeated the offence when the House was required to continue the adjournment while the king continued his negotiations with the Dutch and the French.[21] When the House did finally resume, on 28 January 1678, William Sacheverell attempted to deliver a charge against him. Why this was not pressed is unclear, although it is possible that Seymour had already found it expedient to switch his allegiances. Seymour escaped any significant censure in the debate, resumed at length on 9 February largely to divert attention from more politically immediate matters.[22]

---

[18] Grey, *Debates*, ii, 182–215.

[19] For which, see *HPC, 1660–90*, ii, 750. Littleton's son, also Sir Thomas, held the same post when Speaker, from 1699 to 1700 (*The History of Parliament: The House of Commons, 1690–1715*, ed. Eveline Cruickshanks, Stuart Handley and D.W. Hayton (5 vols, Cambridge 1982) [hereafter cited as *HPC, 1690–1715*], iv, 647), as did Sir Arthur Onslow during his speakership from 1734 to 1742.

[20] See *HPC, 1660–90*, iii, 415.

[21] Browning, *Thomas Osborne*, i, 232, 239, 255.

[22] See Browning's explanation, *Danby*, i, 262.

Danby's parliamentary management, and its central element, the alliance with Seymour, were now in tatters. When in April the government, at another awkward moment in negotiations with the Dutch, wanted to adjourn the Commons again very soon after the Easter adjournment, there was clearly a case that Seymour, so tainted by the previous adjournments, should not be in the chair when it happened, and arrangements were made for him to be absent, claiming indisposition, on 11 April, and to be replaced by a new Speaker, Sir Robert Sawyer. It was widely, and probably accurately believed, however, that Seymour and Danby had finally fallen out. Danby's opponents made as much capital of this as they could, claiming to regret Seymour's absence. His reinstatement on 6 May injected an element of farce into the situation, but also underlined Danby's inability to reassemble a workable leadership in the Commons; they may also indicate Seymour's own attempts to deal with the opposition leaders. Seymour was certainly attempting to ingratiate himself with them during the autumn, when Danby regarded him and his 'party' as among his own enemies. Seymour, he said in a bitter minute to the king, had been 'the promoter of the most desperate addresses and proceedings of the House of Commons the last sessions'.[23] Seymour's courtship of Danby's opponents paid dividends when, after the eventual dissolution of the Cavalier Parliament at the beginning of 1679 and the assembly of its replacement in March, Danby tried to promote Sir Thomas Meres, one of the men passed over six years earlier, as Speaker. With the backing of the opposition leaders Seymour secured the election by acclamation. In probably the most notorious speakership election, the king withheld his consent, and required the Commons to elect someone else. A confrontation ensued in which the court's ability to manage events collapsed entirely. The issue was only resolved after a prorogation when a third candidate, Serjeant Gregory, was accepted as a compromise.

Seymour's troubles in 1678–9 showed how, as the opposition to Danby began to coalesce, it had quickly identified the speakership as a target to be gained, or at least neutralised. After Seymour, the office returned to the lawyers – William Gregory (1679) had been made a king's serjeant in 1677; William Williams (1680, 1681) was a practising lawyer, though he never, apparently, took silk; Sir John Trevor (1685, 1690–5) was king's counsel from 1673. But except in this, the Speakers of the exclusion crisis had moved away from the pre-civil war model: no longer could they be regarded unproblematically as crown nominees. Speaker Gregory, even though accepted as a compromise, was plainly close to the opponents of Danby, regarded as an ally by Shaftesbury and recommended to the House by two of their leaders, William Russell and Lord Cavendish.[24] Williams was subservient to the opposition leaders and as 'pliant to them as a spaniel dog', according to one very hostile – and tory – memoirist.[25]

Their experience indicated the impact of the development of whig and tory parties on the speakership. Before the civil war the Speaker had had to serve two masters, the crown and the Commons collectively. Now he had parties to worry about as well. After

---

[23] Browning, *Danby*, ii, 71.

[24] *HPC, 1660–90*, ii, 436.

[25] Mark Knights, *Politics and Opinion in the Exclusion Crisis, 1678–1681* (Cambridge, 1994), 125.

the revolution the slide towards a partisan speakership became much more marked.[26] Henry Powle, the Speaker of the convention, had been a whig candidate for the speakership in 1679, when he had been one of a handful of whig leaders. Sir John Trevor was reappointed in 1690 because of his tory credentials, and was acknowledged to be a shrewd manipulator of individual members. His successor, Paul Foley, was a major political leader in his own right.

Paul Foley was elected on 14 March 1695, following Trevor's disgrace, in a contest against the court candidate, Sir Thomas Littleton (the son of Seymour's antagonist). Both figures were significant politicians. Littleton was a lawyer, who, as chairman of the committees of supply and ways and means from 1693, had been a key manager and speaker on behalf of the government. Foley, like most of his predecessors, was also a lawyer, called to the bar in 1668 and a bencher at the Inner Temple from 1687. A leading 'country' whig by 1690, he had played a central role in the commission of public accounts set up by statute in the beginning of 1691. Intensely hostile to the court, and willing to form alliances with 'country' tories, Foley and his colleagues, particularly Robert Harley, had used the commission as a platform from which to dominate the house of commons and present to the king alternative political and financial strategies to those of his ministers. His election as Speaker recognized his leadership of a coalition of country forces, increasingly of a tory complexion. He used the office, as he had used the commission, to offer to the king an alternative model of political leadership to that provided by the whig junto. His balancing act, between the roles of parliamentary chairman, a leader of the 'country' party and a potential minister, collapsed in the face of his inability to convince the more extreme country politicians, many of them tory, that there was value in any co-operation with an essentially whig government. In 1698 he ceded the post to Littleton. Littleton's inglorious tenure came to an end with the 1701 election, after which he was persuaded to stand down, and to be absent in order to avoid nomination, in favour of Foley's old colleague, Robert Harley.

Harley, like Seymour, was not a lawyer. He had become the undisputed leader of the country opposition to the junto whigs following Foley's death in 1698. Although he was increasingly closely allied, and even identified, with the tories, in February 1701 he won the speakership with the support of whigs who were prepared to view him as a symbol of country independence. As David Hayton has put it, the speakership offered Harley an opportunity to 'hold the reins of Commons management but still argue that he had not betrayed his often reiterated Country principles by joining the Court'.[27] After the second election of 1701, however, Harley's country credentials had become tarnished by his party connections. Before the ensuing speakership election in December 1701 he was being referred to in whig propaganda as 'a leader of the Tory party', and only barely defeated Littleton (the candidate preferred by the king himself) in 'one of the fullest Houses ever known'. His speakership was talked of in almost completely partisan terms. The historian Gilbert Burnet and the parliamentary diarist Sir Robert Cocks recounted

---

[26] The best account of the speakership from the revolution to the Hanoverian succession is David Hayton's, in the introductory survey to *HPC, 1690–1715*, i, 348–54; what follows owes much to it and to the biographies of the respective Speakers – Foley, Hanmer and Harley by Hayton, Bromley and Littleton by Andrew Hanham, Smith by Paula Watson and Sonia Wynne – in the remaining volumes. Details of the careers of the Speakers are taken from those biographies.

[27] *HPC, 1690–1715*, iv, 262.

between gritted teeth numerous instances of his ability to bamboozle whigs through his procedural answers to his party's political problems. The closeness of the speakership to the administration was signalled by his swearing in as a privy councillor and his acceptance of the post of secretary of state in 1704 while he was still Speaker. Both damaged his already awkward relationship with the tories, which deteriorated further with the ministry's resistance to their Occasional Conformity Bill. He abandoned the role of Speaker after the elections of 1705, no doubt because he had lost much tory support over occasional conformity (tories had already planned to supplant him in 1704), and because the gains of the whigs in the election of 1705 and the increasing whig hue of the government made a whig Speaker a more obvious choice.

His successor, John Smith, was also a party manager who had already served as a lord of the treasury in 1694–1701 and as chancellor of the exchequer in 1699–1701. His candidacy was announced to government placemen by Lord Treasurer Godolphin, and though it was supported by senior ministerial tories – Harley himself and Henry St John – it was opposed, though unsuccessfully, in a tory campaign of unusual sophistication. Smith was succeeded, in turn, by Sir Richard Onslow in 1708, far less of a ministerialist, and more than acceptable to back bench whigs because of his attacks on placemen in 1705–8. In 1710 the tories regained the chair with the election of William Bromley, member for their intellectual and spiritual home, Oxford University. A leader of the party in the Commons, he was one of the principal architects of the attack on occasional conformity and the defence of Dr Sacheverell. Seen by Lord Treasurer Harley as a valuable link to the more extreme back bench tories, by 1711, however, he was actively encouraging them to carry out a programme of disruption of government business.[28] Sir Thomas Hanmer, Speaker in 1714–15, appealed to tories because of his consistent resistance to ministerial blandishments, although he directly led a much smaller group of pro-Hanoverian tories, and his support for the Hanoverian succession won him the acquiescence of the whigs.

In 40 years the speakership had undergone a transformation from Eliot's legal 'nullities'. Harley, Smith, Onslow and Bromley, had all attended one of the inns of court, but none had been called or gone on to practise law; Hanmer (like Seymour) could not pretend to having a legal education of any kind.[29] Seymour had set out a new blueprint for the speakership: no longer ambitious lawyers, keen to vindicate the government's trust and prove themselves worthy of senior legal office, they were now more likely to be party barons and managers. Still men with experience and enough procedural knowledge to avoid embarrassing themselves and their supporters, their real importance lay in the influence they wielded over a group of personal followers (such as Seymour's leadership of the west country members, or Hanmer's pro-Hanoverian tories) or more generally, because of their political leadership, over a much larger faction or party.

Yet the transformation of the role from procedural chairman to leading party manager was not, quite, the whole story. The criticism directed at Seymour in 1673 for accepting a place on the privy council and a lucrative office – contested and ineffective as it was – indicated that a measure of independence from the court was expected, by some, at

---

[28] *HPC, 1690–1715*, iii, 353–4.

[29] Hanmer was referred to in 1705 as a 'young lawyer'; perhaps in a misunderstanding of the honorary LLD conferred on him by Cambridge that year: *HPC, 1690–1715*, iv, 188.

least, in a Speaker. The country tradition espoused by Foley and Harley preserved and may have deepened the sense that the Speaker, however much a party leader, should remain independent of the court and had some sort of responsibility to maintain parliamentary and 'patriot' values. Foley's explicit presentation of those values during his speakership was a natural response to Trevor's removal and expulsion for corruption in 1695. But it also reflected the strength of the 'country party' tradition in the house of commons in the 1690s, and a recognition in a time of confused party allegiance that a successful Speaker would need to appeal to a variety of factions within the House. Burnet attributed Foley's election in 1695 to his reputation as a 'patriot' through his 'constant finding fault with the government, and keeping up an ill humour, and a bad opinion of the Court'. Foley went out of his way to emphasize his independence of the court, saying in his speech accepting the position that 'whatever his failings might be, he would still preserve clean hands', and refusing a place on the privy council, which he claimed would be incompatible with the speakership.[30] On his re-election in 1696, he lectured the House on maintaining the standing orders and the honour and dignity of the House, 'whereof they owed very much of their liberties and properties in all times, lest by any misbehaviour of theirs they should bring the House into contempt and thereby endanger the making a way for the overthrow of their constitution'.[31] He supported initiatives for the parliamentary nomination of a council of trade, and country projects against the corruption of the Commons. That one aspect of Foley's conception of the office had put down roots was suggested by the debate on his successor, in which criticism was directed at the idea of having an officeholder in the chair of the House.[32] Harley, like Foley, paraded 'country virtues' and on his first election pronounced that he had 'come in clean, and will go out so'.[33] The speakership suited men like Sir Richard Onslow or Sir Thomas Hanmer, who, despite their immersion in party politics, regarded themselves as above the sordid search for political place: Hanmer was described by the duke of Berwick as a man who 'will never publicly take any part but that of the parliament, where he thinks to be always the top man'.[34]

The period of intense party competition which might be said to have begun in 1673 and continued until the Hanoverian succession was a period of rapid, and sometimes contradictory, political change and development. If it laid down a model of the speakership which was explicitly partisan, at the same time it not only preserved the ideal of the Speaker as independent of the court, but even strengthened it. It was not quite the non-partisan and impartial model of the speakership which is familiarly associated with Arthur Onslow's tenure from 1728 to 1761; but there was in it something of his conception of the office as an end in itself, rather than a stepping-stone to higher preferment. The conduct in the office of the power-broker Sir Edward Seymour, or the archetypical tory, William Bromley, and many of the others, may have suggested that the speakership could develop into an office with the essential responsibility for management of the Commons on behalf of a party-based government. But the fastidiousness exhibited

[30] *HPC, 1690–1715*, iii, 1068.
[31] *HPC, 1690–1715*, iii, 1068–9.
[32] *HPC, 1690–1715*, iv, 647.
[33] *HPC, 1690–1715*, iv, 262.
[34] *HPC, 1690–1715*, iv, 197.

by Hanmer and Arthur Onslow's uncle Sir Richard, and the ideas espoused by Foley, anticipating Arthur Onslow's influential country whig ideology of independence, suggested that the speakership could also become the repository for a set of *parliamentary* values which – despite the deftness or 'dexterity' exhibited by Seymour or Harley or many of the others on behalf of the governments they supported – could never be completely squared with the blacker managerial arts required in an age of party government.

The Speakership of the House of Lords, 1660–1832

RUTH PALEY

The speakership of the house of lords was a lucrative and prestigious post, held by individuals who either as lord chancellor or lord keeper carried out a range of high-profile and demanding judicial duties. There seems to be a contradiction between this and the time-consuming but largely empty ceremonial duties appropriate to this role in the conduct of business in the theoretically self-regulating house of lords. This article suggests that the apparent insignificance of the Speaker's role was a façade that disguised the chancellor's ability to influence the conduct of business in the Lords as well as to exercise leadership and electoral influence over the membership of the Commons. Nevertheless, the precise level of power that he was able to exercise was mediated by the nature of the political infrastructure within which he operated, his own personal and political skills and his relationships with the crown and its other ministers.

Keywords: party politics; parliament; electoral management; lord chancellor; lord keeper; law; lawyers; peers

1. *Lord Chancellors and Lord Keepers*

Until the very recent past the speakership of the house of lords was co-terminous with the office of lord chancellor or lord keeper. The difference between the two offices was minimal. The title 'lord keeper' was usually held by a commoner and 'lord chancellor' by a peer but the distinction was by no means cut and dried. Edward Hyde, better known by his later title as earl of Clarendon, became lord chancellor in 1658, whilst still a commoner. It was a further two years before he was created a peer. The political context of his appointment, during the interregnum, was unusual. But John Somers (who had been lord keeper since 1693) similarly became lord chancellor in April 1697 as a commoner. He was not promoted to the peerage until the following December. Conversely, Sir Francis North remained lord keeper even after he had been created Baron Guilford in 1683 whilst William Cowper, who had been appointed lord keeper in 1705 and became a peer in December 1706, was not given the title of lord chancellor until May 1707. By an Elizabethan statute the power and status of the keeper of the seals was identical whether he was deemed to be a lord keeper or a lord chancellor.[1] The essential difference between the two offices appears, therefore, to have been a matter of bureaucratic formality. During the period under review, lord chancellors were appointed by letters patent, lord keepers by

[1] 5 Eliz. I, c. 18.

taking delivery of the seals.[2] For convenience, therefore, I will use the term lord chancellor throughout this article to refer to both offices because, in reality, the critical difference did not relate to the name of the office but to the status of the holder. Whether called lord keeper or lord chancellor a commoner who held the seals was not a member of the house of lords and so could not (in theory at least) participate in its debates.

After 1660 it became customary for all those who had custody of the seals to be rewarded with a peerage. There were only three exceptions to this rule: Sir Orlando Bridgeman (1667–72), Sir Nathan Wright (1700–5) and Charles Yorke (1770). Bridgeman and Wright were both lord keepers at a time when the offer of a peerage might take many years of faithful service. After the Hanoverian succession promotion to the peerage was usually very much speedier. There were only two exceptions, one of whom, Charles Yorke, has already been mentioned. Had he lived Yorke would have been created Baron Morden but he killed himself just three days after accepting office and before his patent could be sealed. Robert Henley, who was appointed lord keeper (the last individual to hold this title) in 1756 had to wait four years for his peerage. Henley was something of a political lightweight. His appointment was a compromise one, brokered as part of the negotiations for the creation of the Pitt-Newcastle ministry, and owed more to Pitt's refusal to consider the re-appointment of Philip Yorke, earl of Hardwicke than to Henley's own abilities. George II was reluctant to offer the peerages demanded by other candidates for the post. He disliked Henley because of his earlier involvement with the political faction associated with Frederick, prince of Wales. Henley's willingness to do without a peerage was an important factor in reconciling the king to his appointment.[3]

Irrespective of the name by which it was known, the office of keeper of the seals was a plum post and one that was very well rewarded. Additional monies were payable to the chancellor in his capacity as Speaker of the Lords; indeed the post was surprisingly lucrative. In 1706, over and above his salary of £4,000 a year and the various other sums that he received as chancellor, William Cowper received £1,091 12s. 6d. from fees on private bills in his capacity as Speaker of the house of lords.[4] In 1811 John Scott, Lord Eldon, was reported to have received sums ranging from just under £3,000 to nearly £7,000 a session from fees as Speaker of the House in addition to some £10,000 a year in emoluments as lord chancellor.[5]

2. *The Chancellor and the House of Lords*

The presence of the Speaker was clearly believed to be crucial to the orderly conduct of business in the house of lords, although as will be seen, estimating the full extent of his influence poses something of a conundrum. In the very early days of the Restoration,

[2] Bohun notes, however, that there have been instances of lord keepers being appointed by letters patent in the distant past. William Bohun, *Cursus Cancellariæ; or, The Course of Proceedings in the High Court of Chancery* (1723), 21.

[3] He was created Baron Henley early in 1760 as part of the preparations for the trial of Laurence Shirley, 4th Earl Ferrers. He had to wait for the accession of George III before being declared lord chancellor and was promoted to an earldom (Northington) in 1764.

[4] Hertfordshire Archives and Local Studies [hereafter cited as Hertfordshire ALS], DE/P/F102, DE/P/F69: diary of 1st Earl Cowper.

[5] *The Times*, 12 July 1811, p. 3.

when the House consisted of a small group of presbyterian peers, they feared that the crown might stop the House from meeting and deliberating by preventing the attendance of their Speaker. It was this fear that lay behind the resolution:

> That it is the duty of the lord chancellor, or lord keeper of the great seal of England, ordinarily to attend the Lords House of parliament; and that in case the lord chancellor or lord keeper of the great seal be absent from the House of Peers, and that there be none authorized under the great seal from the king to supply that place in the House of Peers, the lords may then choose their own speaker during that vacancy.[6]

An incident in 1722, when the lord chancellor, Thomas Parker, earl of Macclesfield, was unexpectedly detained at St James and consequently failed to arrive at the House until the late afternoon or to arrange for a substitute to attend in his place, demonstrated just how essential the Speaker's presence was. The House was unable to enter into the business of the day and, despite a substantial attendance of members, was unable to prevail upon any of them to stand for election as temporary Speaker: it was reported that Charles Seymour, 6th duke of Somerset, actually 'ran out of the House' when he was nominated. If he did do so, he did not return for he is not mentioned in the attendance list. Nicholas Lechmere, Baron Lechmere, who is named in the attendance list, was equally reluctant and 'hid himself'. A motion for an immediate adjournment as an expression of the House's resentment of the insult to 'the greatest council in the kingdom, to which all other councils ought to give way' was lost, but 25 of those present insisted on entering a protest on the grounds that because 'the dignity of our House has not been of late years increasing; so we were unwilling that any Thing we conceive to be a gross neglect of it should pass without some Note in our Records, that we were sensible of such neglect, and did not approve it'.[7]

The Macclesfield incident was clearly accidental, and in practice the crown never did try to use the absence of the Speaker as a means of preventing the House from transacting business. On the contrary, it ensured that during periods of vacancy or absence his place was supplied by salaried deputies or commissioners. Occasionally, especially in the later part of the period under review here, the absence of both Speaker and deputies did lead to an election, but such elections were always foreseeable and consequently the results seem to have been planned beforehand. In 1780 the House elected the lord president, Henry Bathurst, 2nd Earl Bathurst; in the early 19th century the House customarily elected the chairman of committees. The only overtly political manipulation of the Speaker's presence in the House appears to have been the somewhat farcical proceedings on the afternoon of 22 April 1831 when Henry Brougham, Baron Brougham, twice left the woolsack (and the chamber) in order to delay the proceedings of the House. He knew that as a result of the impasse over the Reform Bill the king had been persuaded to dissolve parliament and to do so in person. Brougham dodged in and out of the chamber (taking the seal with him), forcing the election of a temporary Speaker each time, in order to prevent the passage of a wrecking motion (opposing the dissolution) before the king could arrive.[8]

[6] *LJ*, xi, 54, 58.
[7] HMC, *Lonsdale*, 123; *LJ*, xxi, 67–43.
[8] *LJ*, lxiii, 510–11.

To date only one document has been discovered that provides an insight into what it was like to act as Speaker of the house of lords. In November 1754, the chief justice of the court of king's bench, Dudley Ryder, was appointed to deputise as Speaker for Lord Hardwicke. Although an accomplished lawyer who had reached high office, Ryder's diaries reveal a conviction that his success depended on careful research in order to master both the appropriate legal procedures and the details of cases presented to him. Before taking his seat on the woolsack he conducted similar research into the minutiae of the work that he was to undertake as Speaker of the house of lords. He recorded that it was the job of the Speaker to open the day's proceedings by declaring that the House was in session as soon as the mace was laid on the table. He went on to observe that:

> The House cannot sit . . . till the Speaker comes. When he comes, he asks if it is your lordships' pleasure to go to prayers, on which the youngest Bishop then in the House reads prayers. When that is done, Speaker takes his place, and the House being then sitting, he does nothing himself, till something is begun either by the House or from without or upon foot of orders of the day.

> But if anything is moved to be done, the speaker puts the question 'Is it your Lordships' pleasure that such a thing be done?' If no debates arise upon it, he says of course ordered. If a debate arises, every Lord has the right to say what he pleases, and the Speaker's business is to see that nothing indecent or contrary to the rules of the House is said or done.[9]

Thanks to Ryder's notes we also know that it was the Speaker's task to appoint tellers at a division 'but not of the first rank or old members', that it was also his duty to go with his chancellor's purse to the bar to accept messages from the Commons and that whilst sitting on the woolsack he asserted the dignity of his office by keeping 'his hat on always except when he speaks, or pulls it off by way of civility to any Lord. When counsel come to the bar with three bows, the Speaker pulls off his hat to each bow, but sitting.'[10] Other sources establish that every motion had to be submitted to the Speaker in writing and that it was the act of the Speaker reading the motion that placed it formally before the House.[11]

When the House voted it was the Speaker who judged the result by listening to the volume of voices but his decision in such cases was not final; any peer who objected might compel a formal division instead. This is what happened in December 1711 when Lord Keeper Sir Simon Harcourt declared that the yeas had carried a motion for an amendment to the address, only for Arthur Annesley, 5th earl of Anglesey, to rise in protest and to demand that the question be put. His opponents declared that no question could be put after the Speaker had said 'let it be ordered' but Anglesey insisted that 'this saying "yeas have it", without dividing the House would not do, whilst there was any Lord would say he had said no . . .' and forced a division. Despite the much-vaunted

[9] Harrowby MSS Trust, Sandon Hall, Stafford, vol. 432: Ryder notebook, nd [c.Nov. 1754].

[10] Harrowby MSS Trust, vol. 432: Ryder notebook, 23 Sept. 1755.

[11] Anita J. Rees, 'The Practice and Procedure of the House of Lords 1714–84', University of Aberystwyth PhD, 1987, pp. 368–9.

decorum of the House, some of those on Anglesey's side 'hopped and skipped about' to obstruct the tellers, providing light relief and 'sport' for spectators.[12]

3. *The Self-Regulating House*

In contrast to the speakership of the Commons the function of the Speaker of the Lords was very much a passive one. In his capacity as Speaker the lord chancellor presided over, rather than chaired, proceedings. He could not adjourn the proceedings without seeking the approval of the House so that on a day-to-day basis his major duty was simply to put the question. Admittedly these duties could on occasion offer considerable scope for partisan intervention. In July 1663, Clarendon succeeded in defusing a privilege issue resulting from the unsuccessful attempt by George Digby, 2nd earl of Bristol, to impeach him by adjourning the House before the relevant motion could be debated; when critics accused him of ignoring opposition to the adjournment he explained that he simply had not heard anyone challenge the motion to adjourn.[13] The presiding officer certainly did, on occasion, frame the question. In November 1705 the motion put by Daniel Finch, 2nd earl of Nottingham, for an address to the queen concerning the actions of the Scots parliament in relation to the succession and union, led to a prolonged debate over the precise wording of the address. Cowper recorded with some pride in his diary that although the phraseology agreed upon was based on suggestions by Sidney Godolphin, Lord (later earl of) Godolphin, the question as put to the House was: 'the first Q[uestio]n I worded as Speaker in L[or]ds House'.[14] A century later the lords were clearly shocked to be told by the lord chancellor, John Scott, Baron Eldon, that they had been debating an issue on which the motion had been put and carried 90 minutes earlier. Not surprisingly: 'Some astonishment was expressed by some noble lords, that the putting the question had not been heard. Earl Stanhope [Charles Stanhope, 3rd Earl Stanhope] said, that the noble and learned lord had put and carried them in a parenthesis. The lord Chancellor observed, that he had merely said, "ordered," conceiving there was no objection to the motion.'[15]

The apparent passivity of the Speaker's role in the house of lords stemmed from the nature of its proceedings because the Lords, unlike the Commons, was a self-regulating body. Even something as basic as deciding which of two peers might speak first if both rose at the same time was a matter for the House to decide rather than its Speaker. When in May 1733, Allen Bathurst, Baron (later Earl) Bathurst and Thomas Pelham Holles, duke of Newcastle, both rose to speak to an issue relating to the South Sea Company: 'The Lord Chancellor [Peter King, Baron King] pointed to the Duke of Newcastle, and the Lord Bathurst not offering to sit down, Lord Carteret [John Carteret, 2nd Baron Carteret] stood up, and said, That if there was any Dispute which Lord was to speak, the Lord Chancellor was not to determine the Question, but the Opinion of the House was to be asked upon it.'

---

[12] *The Wentworth Papers, 1705–39*, ed. J.J. Cartwright (1883), 222–3.

[13] Bodl., MS Carte 33, f. 34.

[14] *Private Diary of William, First Earl Cowper*, [ed. E.C. Hawtrey] (Eton, Roxburghe Club, xlix, 1833), 13.

[15] Hansard, *Parl. Debs*, 1st ser., xi, cols 709–10.

Bathurst then reminded the House that it was customary for the House to give priority to the peer who had made the motion: 'because it is to be expected that he has something to say, or some farther Motion to make in Consequence, or in Explanation of the Motion'. Accordingly it would have been his right to have been heard even if he had not been the first to stand.[16]

In spite of – or perhaps because of – this system of self-regulation, it was considered that the standard of behaviour in the Lords was far higher than in the Commons. As William Murray, earl of Mansfield, once pointed out, the Commons 'too often descended to altercations and personal reflections' whilst the Lords behaved 'like gentlemen'.[17] The sharp cut and thrust of debate that was characteristic of the Commons was thought to have no place in the Lords, where decorum was preferred to eloquence and where it was not unusual for the peers to lapse into periods of silence.[18] The reality, of course, did not always match the ideal. Debates in the Lords, as in the Commons, did indeed descend into petty squabbling and personal attacks. It was, perhaps, particularly ironic that Mansfield was acting as Speaker on 10 December 1770 when a motion to clear the House provoked an 'indecent and . . . unprecedented uproar'. The uproar was so great that even when Mansfield stood up with his hat off to explain order the tumult 'prevented also any information from the woolsack'.[19] But the decision to censure such behaviour or to call an individual to order properly belonged to the House, not to its Speaker. In reality there certainly were occasions when the Speaker did call the House or individual speakers to order.[20] He should not, however, have done so unless he were himself a peer and stepped away from the woolsack in order to act in his capacity as a member of the House. During one such altercation in 1817, Lord Chancellor Eldon denied that it was his responsibility to enforce discipline other than 'equally with any other noble lord in the House'. Nevertheless, only minutes earlier he had made his views quite clear when he declared that 'if their lordships permitted any thing so disorderly to proceed, he would not sit ten minutes on the woolsack to hear it'. Since the allegedly 'disorderly' peer, Robert Grosvenor, 2nd Earl Grosvenor, had chosen his words with extreme care, this incident also provides an example of the partisanship of the Speaker. Eldon's comments from the woolsack acted as a signal to other government supporters to use the issue of order as a way of silencing him.[21]

It was symptomatic of the ideal of self-regulation that when in debate the lords addressed the House rather than the Speaker and that the Speaker had (in theory at least) no role in deciding the order of business. The business of the House was arranged

---

[16] E. Timberland, *The History and Proceedings of the House of Lords 1660–1742* (4 vols, 1742), iv, 139.

[17] *Cobbett's Parliamentary History*, xviii, 282.

[18] See, e.g., the account of the Lords' reception early in 1709 of the address from the Commons for the queen to remarry and the debate in November 1780 concerning a quarrel between Augustus Henry FitzRoy, 3rd duke of Grafton and George Fermor, 2nd earl of Pomfret: BL, Add. MS 61129, f. 19; J. Almon, *Parliamentary Register* (17 vols, 1775–80), iv, 18, 19.

[19] *LJ*, xxxiii, 23.

[20] During the debate over the Grafton/Pomfret quarrel in Nov. 1780, Lord Chancellor Thurlow was reported to have called Pomfret to order three or four times: Almon, *Parl. Reg.*, iv, 13.

[21] *The Times*, 22 Feb. 1817, p. 1. The issue before the House was the report of the secret committee; Grosvenor disputed the findings of the committee but was careful to confine his remarks to a suggestion that it might not have heard all the relevant evidence rather than openly to allege that its findings were politically biased.

through a series of motions made by individual peers proposing that a particular subject be discussed so that the decision to do so could be entered as an order for that item to come on for debate on a particular day. The assumption was that individual peers would take responsibility for conducting their measures through the House. Failure to do so was likely to disrupt the course of business. On 22 June 1808, William Wyndham Grenville, Baron Grenville, was expected to move a resolution to put the House into committee to discuss the bill for renewing the charter of the Bank of Ireland. Although it was almost the last item of business of the day Grenville had still not arrived when it came on, so that 'a conversation ensued between the lord chancellor, Lords Holland [Henry Fox, 3rd Baron Holland] and Stanhope [Charles Stanhope, 3rd Earl Stanhope], respecting the propriety of discharging, or passing over, the order of the day'. It was, perhaps. fortunate for them that in the event no decision was required: Grenville arrived in the nick of time and rose to make his motion.[22]

Where the measure was one proposed by the government it was expected that this would be undertaken either by the minister concerned or by some other leading government spokesman – by the end of the period, the leader of the House. Accordingly a change of administration could cause problems. In 1783 the new administration, led by William Cavendish-Bentinck, 3rd duke of Portland, failed to move for the second reading of the Irish Judicature Bill. Portland excused himself from any responsibility for doing so because the bill had been proposed by the previous administration and it was, therefore, a matter for the House to decide 'when to proceed with it, and in what manner'. Thomas Townshend, Baron (later Viscount) Sydney, who had been responsible for introducing the bill into the Commons before his elevation to the peerage and who had then moved the first reading in the Lords protested that he would have moved for the second reading had he still been in government, but that since he was not he had forborne making the requisite motion, thinking it 'extremely indecent and improper' to do so.[23]

By convention, each order of the day was taken in the sequence in which it had been entered – they were not prioritised by order of importance. On 18 December 1775, for example, the single most important item of business was the committee stage of the bill to prohibit American trade but debate over ways of dealing with the recalcitrant and imminently revolutionary American colonies had to wait until the House had dealt with several other issues, including a petition for a private act and a local enclosure bill.[24] The order of business could be changed and individual items of business could be postponed to another day, but again this was by agreement of the peers who 'were competent to postpone or anticipate, as they might think proper'.[25] In theory this was not a matter for the intervention of the Speaker although in practice there was scope for manipulation. In March 1743 Francis Hastings, later 10th earl of Huntingdon, then styled Lord Hastings, reported that: 'The Tories wanted to bring in something today and Lord Chancellor would not let them . . . I saw a great many noblemen speak to him about it,

---

[22] Hansard, *Parl. Debs*, 1st ser., xi, col. 976. No indication of the problem is to be found in the *Lords Journal*, nor is Grenville listed amongst those present: *LJ*, xlvi, 748, 752.

[23] Almon, *Parl. Reg.*, xi, 109–10.

[24] *LJ*, xxxvii, 537.

[25] Almon, *Parl. Reg.*, xiv, 122.

but he ordered the order of the day to be read and never minded.'[26] In 1757 when members of the House wanted to proceed urgently with the examination of witnesses concerning the court martial of Admiral Byng rather than the business that had been scheduled, it was Hardwicke's suggestion that the House could proceed if it first reversed its own orders.[27] Similarly on 8 February 1804, an appeal set down for a hearing that day was postponed on the motion of the lord chancellor (Eldon).[28] A decision by Lord Chancellor Thurlow in 1781 suggests that it was also possible for a member to withdraw a motion without consulting the House. Thurlow's pronouncement was greeted with ironic gratitude by Charles Lennox, 3rd duke of Richmond, who was acutely aware that the decision was a partisan one intended to favour his opponents – Richmond having himself been 'a witness to several instances of a contrary nature' in the recent past.[29]

Once an order had been read the issue had to be resolved before the House moved on to the next item of business. The lord chancellor was ideally placed to influence just how strictly the House should observe this rule and to indulge in a little creative manipulation. On 5 May 1783, after the third reading of the Loan Bill had been properly brought before the House, William Petty, 3rd earl of Shelburne,[30] made a long speech on the subject of national finance which culminated in him proposing two resolutions to the House. William FitzWilliam, 2nd Earl FitzWilliam, offered only a partial rebuttal of Shelburne's arguments as 'it was unnecessary for him to go much into either of the resolutions, because the bill must be disposed of first, it having been ordered to be read a third time'. David Murray, 7th Viscount Stormont, also took up the procedural issue, arguing that the House 'was out of all order' for the only question properly before it was the third reading of the Loan Bill and it could not consider another question 'before they had got rid of the first'. Shelburne explained that he had allowed the order of the day to be read by accident. The House then accepted a compromise offered by Lord Chancellor Thurlow, who suggested that 'If the noble Viscount [Stormont] persisted in the form being so strictly observed, it was still in his noble friend's power, with the indulgence of the House, to recover all, by moving the Order of the Day to be adjourned for an hour.'[31] This was, perhaps, an unusually gentle intervention by Thurlow, whose domination of the House and its procedures was invariably partisan and frequently intimidatory. Yet even Thurlow did not always find it easy to dictate procedure. In May 1782 a proposal by the duke of Richmond that was designed to shorten debates over the Cricklade Disenfranchising Bill was opposed by Thurlow 'on the score of informality and injustice'. Although Thurlow was backed by Mansfield a heated argument ensued and it was some two hours before Richmond could be persuaded to withdraw his motion.[32]

As noted above, theoretically a commoner keeper of the seal was not able to address the House and this is conventionally held to have prevented them from defending or

---

[26] HMC, *Hastings*, iii, 38–9.

[27] Rees, 'Practice and Procedure', 234.

[28] Hansard, *Parl. Debs*, 1st ser., i, col. 423.

[29] Almon, *Parl. Reg.*, iv, 257.

[30] Shelburne, whose earldom was Irish, was entitled to sit in the house of lords at Westminster as he was also 2nd Baron Wycombe in the British peerage.

[31] Almon, *Parl. Reg.*, xi, 159–71.

[32] Almon, *Parl. Reg.*, viii, 278–82.

explaining chancery decrees when they came before the House on appeal. It has been said that Lord Keeper Henley's decrees were liable to reversal for this very reason and that 'He was frequently much out of temper with the proceedings in which his opinions were reversed, when he thought it impossible to maintain that they were wrong.' According to this tradition, once he became a member of the House 'this system of reversal came to an end'.[33] The assertion deserves further investigation for it is known that Lord Keeper Wright was able to explain the central issue in at least one case: an appeal brought by Charles Mordaunt, 3rd earl of Peterborough, in 1703.[34] Similarly, Cowper addressed the House against two private bills that he considered to be fraudulent early in 1706, almost a full year before he became a peer.[35]

When the Speaker was also a peer there is no doubt that he *was* able to participate in the debates of the House, although as noted above, in order to do so it was necessary for him to move away from the woolsack. His position as a crown nominee meant that his failure to do so on important issues would be interpreted by members of the House as a silent attack on the administration and its policies. Conversely, it is occasionally possible to catch glimpses of his influence on ministerial tactics within parliament. Lord Keeper Somers was deeply involved in the extra-parliamentary discussions that orchestrated the implementation of the decision to bring an act of attainder against Sir John Fenwick.[36] The decision to try the jacobite rebels in the aftermath of the rebellion of 1745 led to a series of formal motions to ensure that the necessary preparations were made. These passed as a matter of course until John Berkeley, 5th Baron Berkeley of Stratton, moved for the opinion of the House as to whether the bishops ought to be summoned. The participation of the bishops in capital cases had been a contentious issue for nearly three-quarters of a century and perhaps not surprisingly, Berkeley's intervention 'produced a private debate round my Lord Chancellor of near an hour'.[37]

4. *The Chancellor and the Crown*

As well as presiding over the day-to-day formalities of business the Speaker was, above all, the hinge between the crown and the lords, responsible for carrying messages and addresses to and from the crown. He was also the voice or mouth of the House. When, on occasion, it became necessary to reprehend the conduct of members, it was the chancellor who proclaimed judgment or reprimand. It was Lord Chancellor Cowper, for example, who reprimanded the printers, Wilkins and Anderson, on their knees at the bar of the House, for printing a protest over the Septennial Bill in 1716.[38] Similarly in March

---

[33] Horace Twiss, *The Public and Private Life of Lord Chancellor Eldon: With Selections from His Correspondence* (1844), 176.

[34] *The London Diaries of William Nicolson, Bishop of Carlisle 1702–18*, ed. Clyve Jones and Geoffrey Holmes (Oxford, 1985), 179–80.

[35] *Nicolson London Diaries*, ed. Jones and Holmes, 362, 376.

[36] Ruth Paley, 'Justice and Sir John Fenwick', *King's Law Journal*, xix (2008), 511.

[37] HMC, *Carlisle*, 201–2.

[38] *LJ*, xx, 344.

1792, it was Thurlow who delivered the sentence of the House against Richard Cooksey for his offence in breaching the privilege of George William Coventry, 6th earl of Coventry.[39]

Between 1660 and 1832 all but one chancellor (Anthony Ashley Cooper, earl of Shaftesbury who served briefly in 1672–3) were chosen from the ranks of successful lawyers, but the deciding factor in their appointments was not their legal ability alone but their political allegiance. The chancellor's relationship to the crown and his fellow ministers ensured that he was a major political figure in his own right. He was a member of the cabinet and of the privy council and thus an important member of the inner circle of policy-making ministers. Before the revolution of 1688 the lord chancellor's speech at the opening of parliament was as important, if not more important, than that of the monarch. After the revolution, when the habit of a lord chancellor's speech was lost, he nevertheless played an important part in the drafting of the monarch's speech. Indeed, as the survival of heavily amended drafts of the monarch's speech amongst the papers of lord chancellors Clarendon and Cowper, as well as stray references in correspondence, readily establishes, in the first half of the period under review the monarch's speech was actually written by the lord chancellor.[40] By the mid 18th century, when the political landscape was being reconfigured by the emergence of the office of prime minister, the lord chancellor's role in drafting the king's speech was much diminished but he was still consulted over the content at an early stage. In 1739 Walpole explained that it was his practice to draft the first version of the speech himself, he then passed it to the lord chancellor and a few others for comments and amendments, before taking it to the cabinet council. Walpole's account makes it clear that the lord chancellor could, and did, alter the draft.[41] The chancellor's services to the crown also included rather more informal gestures of political support: in 1820 Eldon bought a house in London for the express purpose of preventing its sale to Queen Caroline and consequent embarrassment to George IV. He immediately put it on the market again, specifying that potential purchasers must promise not to rent the house to the queen.[42]

Since they were appointed by the crown, there were times at which the crown's perception of political allegiance overrode those of its other ministers. A lord chancellor who enjoyed the support of the crown was, to a certain extent, free to pursue policies independent of the remainder of the administration. This was, of course, especially true in the earlier part of the period when parliament was an occasional event rather than a permanent feature of political life and when factional rather than party politics were the rule. But it remained true for much of the 18th and early 19th centuries. Lord Cowper's credit with Queen Anne meant that his refusal to continue to serve in 1710 was a major blow to Harley's attempts to construct a ministry. Thurlow survived the fall of the North ministry and remained in office under Rockingham and Shelburne. He lost office under the brief Fox-North coalition but was reappointed by Pitt the Younger. Though his relationship with his fellow ministers was often somewhat fragile, he was able to rely on

---

[39] Almon, *Parl. Reg.*, xxxiii, 372.

[40] Paul Seaward, *The Cavalier Parliament and the Reconstruction of the Old Regime, 1661–7* (Cambridge, 1988), 19; Hertfordshire ALS, DE/P/F135: speeches from the throne; HMC, *Downshire*, i, 587.

[41] Harrowby MSS Trust, vol. 430: diary of Sir Dudley Ryder 1739–41, 14 Nov. 1739.

[42] Public Record Office of Northern Ireland, Castlereagh Papers, D3030/Q2/2/pp. 232–3: Lord Castlereagh, London, to Sir Charles Stewart, 16 Sept. 1820.

the support of George III to maintain his position. Similarly Lord Eldon remained in office with only a short break in 1806–7 through successive administrations for over 20 years, because the strength of his commitment to the defence of the anglican church secured him the support of the crown and outweighed differences with ministers over other policies.

Contrariwise, Lord Somers's fall from office in 1700 was attributed to his having made 'himself so much a party in the affairs at the Council table',[43] whilst in Lord Egmont's schedule of those to be turned out of office at the accession of Prince Frederick, the then lord chancellor, Lord Hardwicke, tops the list.[44] Hardwicke was such a major political figure that early in 1740 Sir Robert Walpole tried to nominate him as the next prime minister.[45] Hardwicke did not want to be prime minister but, nevertheless, during his tenure of office he was a major political player. So, too, was Lord Chancellor Thurlow who according to one opposition sympathiser was not so much 'a public man who influences public affairs, but . . . the Dictator of the State who decides them'.[46] Hardwicke, who held the seals for nearly 20 years, exercised significant authority by virtue of his long experience and his considerable abilities. Thurlow, on the other hand, depended on his intimidatory manner to keep the peers in order, though he, too, was extremely knowledgeable about aspects of procedure.

5. *The Chancellor and Parliamentary Management*

Strange though it may initially seem, it is likely that the most important aspect of the chancellor's role as a parliamentary manager was not his ability to preside over the day-to-day business of the house of lords but his ability to exert influence over members (and membership) of the Commons. The chancellor stood at the centre of an extensive web of patronage and was thus a political (and electoral) force to be reckoned with. He handled much of the crown's ecclesiastical patronage and used it to forge alliances with supplicants who ranged from individual clients to bishops and fellow ministers of the crown. Such appointments had electoral implications: 'they think it of great concern to their Interest upon elections for Parliament' wrote Vanbrugh of a soon-to-be-vacant Gloucester prebend in 1707, in an attempt to influence the lord chancellor's decision. The proposed candidate was suitable in all respects. He was not only the uncle of one of the local MPs and 'remarkable for his good life' but also known for 'his steady zeal in all times to the honest interest'.[47]

The chancellor's electoral influence also extended to his ability to manipulate local government offices. He assisted in the ritual of pricking sheriffs. His control of the seal was central to the later 17th-century campaign against the corporations and the attack on city livery companies. The chancellor's supervision of commissions of the peace

[43] Bodl., MS Ballard 10, f. 40.

[44] BL, Add. MS 47012A, f. 81.

[45] Harrowby MSS Trust, vol. 430: diary of Sir Dudley Ryder, 16 Feb. 1740.

[46] John Almon, *Biographical, Literary and Political Anecdotes of Several of the Most Eminent Persons of the Present Age* (3 vols, 1797), iii, 18.

[47] BL, Add. MS 61353, f. 21; Hertfordshire ALS, DE/P/F56: Sunderland to Cowper, 5 Aug. 1707.

conferred similar electoral influence. Politically-motivated purges of commissions of the peace were commonplace under Charles II and James II and continued until at least the 1720s.[48] As the duties of these unpaid justices became more and more onerous and the difficulty of securing sufficient active justices grew, so the habit of purging commissions for political purposes fell into disuse, but, even so, it is clear that political considerations continued to affect the nomination of those *added* to commissions. The political partisanship of local justices was an important factor in local elections throughout the period under review, especially in the boroughs. As late as 1806 it was alleged that justices of the peace in Guildford had arrested a man on a trumped up charge in order to force him to vote for ministerial supporter, George Holme Sumner.[49] Local officeholders and other members of the electorate were also likely to be influenced by the chancellor's ability to shape the content of the charges to grand juries delivered by the judges when they rode the twice-yearly circuit of assize courts. In January 1754 the lord chancellor's speech consisted of a homily suggested by the king on the need 'to press on the country the practice of morality, religion and all kind of virtue'; but he then added, of his own volition, an entreaty that the judges should also make people sensible of the blessings of government and justice.[50]

The chancellor's influence over the judiciary went even deeper than this. As head of the judiciary he was responsible for a range of appointments in chancery and influenced the careers of barristers. Shortly after the Hanoverian succession, in the course of defending his own position at the centre of government, Lord Chancellor Cowper emphasized the importance of his parliamentary role in terms of the leadership of the lawyers in the Commons rather than as Speaker of the house of lords. He made it clear that the chancellor had an important role in the management of the Commons through his ability to hold out the promise of legal preferment.[51] Some 20 years later similar remarks were made by Hardwicke when he explained the appointment of a king's counsel with the words that 'he thought it reasonable to strengthen the hands of the government with lawyers of merit'.[52] Cowper's diary suggests that these were no idle words: in 1705 at the request of Godolphin he was prepared to use his influence over members of the Commons to secure the failure of the proposed Place Bill.[53] One of his predecessors, Somers, was credited with managing the election of the Speaker of the Commons in 1701.[54] The lord chancellor played a major role in the nomination of judges. In the earlier part of the period under review he also influenced their removal. The conventional belief that political manipulation of judicial appointments was

[48] Lionel K.J. Glassey, *Politics and the Appointment of Justices of the Peace* (Oxford, 1979), *passim*.

[49] *The Times*, 7 Nov. 1806, p. 3.

[50] Harrowby MSS Trust, vol. 430: diary of Sir Dudley Ryder, 28 Jan. 1754.

[51] Cowper's main purpose in drafting this account was to warn against Lord Townshend who was thought to be grooming Thomas Parker for the chancellorship. According to Cowper, Parker's gratitude to Townshend for the decision to grant him a peerage and an additional pension of £1,200 a year meant that Townshend would be able to 'absolutely draw to himself a superintendence of the law and the ecclesiastical preferments annexed to the lord chancellor's office' and thus secure his position within the administration in order to limit the crown's ability to choose its own ministers: Hertfordshire ALS, DE/P/F57: draft outgoing letter, c. spring 1717.

[52] Harrowby MSS Trust, vol. 430: diary of Sir Dudley Ryder, Feb. 1740.

[53] *Private Diary of William, First Earl Cowper*, 10.

[54] National Archives of Scotland, GD406/1/4791: [Gavin Mason to Hamilton], 11 Feb. 1700/1.

prevented by the Act of Settlement which required judges to be appointed during good behaviour is not entirely correct since that provision did not come into effect until Anne's death. Furthermore, even after that date it seems to have been understood that all judges' commissions lapsed on the demise of the crown. At her accession Anne removed two whiggishly-inclined judges, Sir John Turton and Sir Henry Hatsell, from office.[55] At her own death the judges were protected for a period of six months by the provisions of the Act for the Security of Her Majesty's Person[56] but George I then removed three judges, Thomas Trevor, Baron Trevor, Sir William Banister and Sir Thomas Powys. George II dismissed John Fortescue Aland in 1727 although he later reappointed him. It was only in 1761 as a result of a statute sponsored by John Stuart, 3rd earl of Bute that the tenure of judges was genuinely secured as during good behaviour.[57] That these monarchs acted without the advice or prompting of their various lord chancellors is extremely unlikely. Cowper's role in George I's removals is well known. It was Cowper who advised the king that Trevor 'went violently into all the measure' of Harley's ministry, that Banister owed his office to Harcourt, Cowper's tory predecessor, and that Powys, who had served James II loyally before the revolution of 1688, was still a jacobite at heart.[58]

The lord chancellor's role in issuing writs may also have given him a rather more prosaic influence over parliament: we know, for example, that Cowper was approached in 1708 by Lord Wharton who wanted him to delay issuing election writs for Wiltshire in order to help the whig interest there.[59] He had less ability to influence membership of the house of lords in that it had been decided in the early 17th century that the writs that summoned the peers to parliament were issued as a matter of course. The only occasion on which we know that a writ was deliberately obstructed – but technically not refused – was in 1708 when opposition groups conspired to invite the duke of Cambridge (the future George I) to take his place in the House against the wishes of Queen Anne. The ability to influence the timing of writs may also have been subject to political manipulation. Three peers were created in August 1673: Thomas Osborne as Viscount Latimer, Robert Paston as Viscount Yarmouth and Richard Butler (already earl of Arran in the Irish peerage) as Baron Butler. Each received a writ of summons on 17 October to attend the House when it reassembled after an adjournment of nearly seven months on 20 October.[60] Charles II intended the meeting to be no more than a formality at which parliament would be instantly prorogued to begin a new session a week later in order to allow time for the marriage of the duke of York to Mary of Modena to be consummated and, therefore, become legally binding. Members of the Commons were determined to use the meeting of 20 October to oppose the marriage and they were assisted by Lord Chancellor Shaftesbury in the Lords. Shaftesbury deliberately delayed the

---

[55] Turton was closely associated with the country whig Foley family whilst Hatsell was associated with Charles Montagu, the future earl of Halifax: BL, Add. MS 70209: Richard Avenant to Robert Harley, 22 July 1706; Suffolk RO (Ipswich), Gurdon MSS, M142(1) Vol. II, p. 31.

[56] 6 Anne, c. 7.

[57] 1 Geo. III, c. 23.

[58] Cowper's advice is published in John Campbell, *Lives of the Lord Chancellors* (8 vols, 1845–69), iv, 285–6. A manuscript draft is held at Hertfordshire ALS, DE/P/F147.

[59] W. Speck, *Tory and Whig* (1970), 80.

[60] J.C. Sainty, *Peerage Creations* (Parliamentary History Text and Studies 1, 2008), 11; *LJ*, xii, 586.

prorogation by insisting on a meticulous observation of the formalities relating to the introduction of the new peers, thus allowing time for York's opponents in the Commons to carry their motion.[61]

6. *The Political and Parliamentary Significance of the Chancellor*

As already mentioned, the Speaker of the Lords could, if a member of the House, participate fully in its business in his personal, rather than official, capacity. Chancellors regularly spoke in debates. They often drafted and introduced legislation of their own. Sometimes the legislation that interested them was on controversial but non-party subjects such as, in the case of Lord Hardwicke, the state of the law on marriage. They were also involved in drafting or approving legislation for more overtly political purposes. In 1749 Dudley Ryder (then attorney general) recorded his participation in a series of meetings that involved Lord Chancellor Hardwicke, the solicitor general, the two secretaries of state, the archbishops and five bishops, in order to draft a bill for the reform of the university of Oxford – a bill that had more to do with ways of dealing with a perceived infestation of jacobites than with the quality of education offered there.[62]

When lord chancellors presided over trials in the House they were scrupulous in taking the advice of the judges. Even the notoriously partisan George Jeffreys, Baron Jeffreys, was careful to do this. Nevertheless, as head of the judiciary the chancellor could, and did, sometimes manipulate the law for political purposes. In May 1708 Cowper was an accomplice to the decision of the cabinet to instruct the judges to take bail for James Hamilton, 4th duke of Hamilton, who was in custody on charges associated with a failed Franco-jacobite invasion. The decision to bail Hamilton was a political one – stemming from an agreement over the election of representative peers for Scotland in the 1708 elections.[63] Eldon was prepared to declare that it was lawful for George IV to exclude the queen from the liturgy and refused to allow her the status of queen consort at her trial.[64] Not surprisingly the formal distinction between the Speaker's private and public personas sometimes became blurred so that it is often difficult to be sure whether a punctilious regard for form stemmed from the chancellor's determination to carry out his duties as Speaker as impartially as possible or simply cloaked his personal or political prejudices. When Eldon refused to receive petitions because of minor informalities of style, did he do so because he was genuinely concerned about the correct form of words or because he objected to their content?[65]

There is a self-evident contradiction between the important but straightforward ceremonial duties carried out by the officeholder as Speaker of the House and the extensive political power that he wielded outside the House. Lord chancellors were, by the standards of the day, exceptionally busy men with a wide range of responsibilities.

[61] K.H.D. Haley, *The First Earl of Shaftesbury* (Oxford, 1968), 336.

[62] Harrowby MSS Trust, vol. 430: diary of Sir Dudley Ryder, 12 Apr. 1748.

[63] BL, Add. MS 61499, f. 2.

[64] Rose A. Melikan, *John Scott, Lord Eldon (1751–1838): The Duty of Loyalty* (Cambridge, 1999), 307.

[65] Melikan, *Eldon*, 273.

Their office was well rewarded but productive of what their contemporaries recognized as 'incessant labours'.[66] Yet despite all their other responsibilities their attendance in the house of lords to carry out what seem to be largely empty formalities was exemplary. The standing orders of the House required their Speaker to be in constant attendance and it is clear that chancellors were indeed rarely absent from the chamber unless disabled by illness.[67] It is difficult to believe that the hours that they were forced to spend in the House were not detrimental to the time available for their many other duties. It seems faintly ridiculous, for example, that on 14 August 1755, Dudley Ryder, then in the midst of presiding over the assizes at Croydon, had to rush back to London in order to prorogue parliament and then rush back to resume his place on the bench in the afternoon.[68] Nevertheless, it seems that chancellors valued the office of Speaker of the house of lords. In 1804 George III told George Rose that despite the heavy pressure of business he experienced in both offices, Eldon would not hear of separating the chancellorship from the speakership of the Lords 'as the profession (meaning the Law) would never forgive him for being the first to agree to the offices being divided' even if there were to be a complete indemnity for the profits of the speakership.[69] At a time when the house of lords was still a powerful element in the constitutional triad, the office of its Speaker was clearly of great prestige.

In order to assess the significance of the Speaker's role fully it is necessary to look behind the formal function and to attempt to uncover the informal networks that composed the 18th-century equivalent of what are now known as 'the usual channels'. Some 20 years ago Sir John Sainty wrote of the emergence in, or about, the period of the Hanoverian succession of a proto-leader of the House, usually the northern secretary of state, who organised pre-sessional meetings in order to orchestrate the address in reply to the speech from the throne.[70] The strength of the 'party of the crown' in the Lords meant that less effort was required to manage a following there than in the Commons. Nevertheless, it is clear that the chancellor, like other prominent ministers, was an active participant in the various informal groupings that characterised political life in the period between the Restoration and the Great Reform Act. Lord Chancellor Cowper's surviving papers, for example, include notes of a meeting with seven bishops to discuss the proposed repeal of the Occasional Conformity Act. The meeting was probably held in the autumn of 1717 or spring of 1718 and was aimed at securing their support or suggestions either for the bill or for some expedient to attain the same end. Early in the previous reign Lord Chancellor Somers and the other junto lords had used socio-political meetings at Newmarket and various taverns and aristocratic houses to organise their followers. Towards the end of the period Lord Eldon was responsible for mobilising support for the return of Pitt the Younger to office and the dismissal of Addington.

From the appointment of Clarendon in 1660 to that of Brougham in 1830 it was unusual for the lord chancellor not to be an active, committed and prominent politician.

---

[66] Rees, 'Practice and Procedure', 492.

[67] Rees, 'Practice and Procedure', 489–91.

[68] Lincoln's Inn, Ryder transcripts, xix, 28.

[69] Leveson Vernon Harcourt, *The Diaries and Correspondence of George Rose* (2 vols, 1860), ii, 178–9.

[70] J.C. Sainty, 'The Origin of the Leadership of the House of Lords', in *Peers Politics and Power: House of Lords 1603–1911*, ed. Clyve Jones and David Lewis Jones (1986), 207–27.

The precise level of influence that he exercised was, of course, very much dependent on the individual officeholder and his relationship to the crown and his fellow ministers. It was probably also influenced by his relationship to previous chancellors as there were times when those over whom he presided included highly experienced former holders of the office. Macclesfield was particularly unfortunate to have been appointed chancellor at a time when the House included both of his immediate predecessors. It must also have been affected by the evolution of the constitutional and organisational context within which he operated. The establishment of annual parliaments transformed the political scene after 1689. The first half of the 18th century then saw some of the power of the chancellor gravitate to the newly-developing office of prime minister and the emergence of party politics. It also saw the creation of new means of parliamentary management of the Lords including the appearance of the leader of the House, the appointment of a chairman of committees and the careful management of proxies. Just how each individual was able to respond to the complex political demands that were placed on him and how he, in turn, was able to shape the conduct of parliamentary business was as much a function of his own interpersonal skills, and his relationship to the crown and its ministers as of the formal responsibilities of his office.

Thurlow, Eldon and Lyndhurst and the Management of the House of Lords

RICHARD W. DAVIS

From 1783 to 1846 lord chancellors played an important role in managing the business of the house of lords. Not surprisingly, as the career of Lord Thurlow will illustrate, their position was not as strong as it had been before 1783 when the office of leader of the House was created. Before then a chancellor could manage the House by himself, as Thurlow did, and Eldon from 1801 to 1803 when there was no regular leader. Yet even when there was a leader, a chancellor could be a major force. Lord Grenville, the first strong leader, yearned for one who would play the role of an active second-in-command. Eldon played it, but more at the beginning than toward the end of his career. This was because of clashes with Lord Liverpool, who had been leader of the House before he became prime minister. But long since, Eldon had become a power in his own right as the revered head of the high tories. Lord Lyndhurst played the role to perfection because of his long partnership with the duke of Wellington, who trusted and admired him.

Keywords: house of lords; lord chancellor; Grenville; Thurlow; Eldon; Lyndhurst; Liverpool

On 13 May 1792 Lord Grenville, leader of the house of lords, wrote to his brother about arrangements for the dismissal of Lord Chancellor Thurlow, who had recently left his place on the woolsack to attack Pitt's cherished sinking fund. The bill passed by only six votes. The government's plan was to put the seals in commission. This concerned Grenville, as 'I do not look without some uneasiness at the increase of personal labour of all sorts that this will bring upon me'. Thurlow's removal from office was a relief to Grenville, but clearly the suspension of the office was not.[1]

Grenville's concern was not only for the more obvious advantages it afforded of advice and assistance in dealing with specialised legal questions. He had much broader views. Another letter to his brother, Lord Buckingham, this one in 1797, provides an example. Lord Moira, who had intimated that he was going into opposition, had given notice of a motion for a full-dress debate on the state of Ireland. He was to be joined by a dismissed lord lieutenant, FitzWilliam. Grenville told Buckingham that 'the Lord Chancellor will not be there, so that I shall have the whole battle, or nearly so upon my shoulders. It is not, however, the first time that this has happened to me, and most probably it will not be the last.'[2]

---

[1] Duke of Buckingham and Chandos, *Memoirs of the Court and Cabinets of George the Third, from Original Family Documents* (4 vols, 1853–5), ii, 209.

[2] Buckingham, *Court and Cabinets*, ii, 366.

The lord chancellor in question was Loughborough, whose appointment ended the short period – less than a year – that the office was in commission. He first presided over the Lords at the beginning of January 1793. In that capacity he was much praised, but unfortunately not in others. According to Lord Campbell, who was old enough to remember: 'The Chancellor seldom spoke in the House of Lords, and the brilliant reputation he enjoyed as a debater in the House of Commons had much faded.'[3] So one can understand Grenville's disappointment. Unlucky though he himself was, however, his expectations were quite clear. He wanted a lord chancellor who would share with him the burdens of debate and the trials of leadership. In this article I intend to look at three lord chancellors during the period from 1778 to 1846 who more or less fit these specifications.

Two, Lord Eldon and Lord Lyndhurst, fit them fairly well. Thurlow less well, but he is a good illustration of how a chancellor could lead the House by himself. His tenure began in 1778. He was, therefore, well entrenched before there was a leader of the House, which did not happen until 1783.[4] Even then the new leaders did not have much luck leading Thurlow. Campbell's phrase to describe him, which was also a contemporary one, was the 'organ' of the government in the Lords, which is also what Peel called Wellington in the 1840s. He was not, strictly speaking, responsible for the conduct of government business in the Lords. That was supposed to be the function of the leaders of the House. Nevertheless, Thurlow was the dominating figure and the one who kept the House firmly in line with government policy.

Thurlow had a reputation for being crude, rude, and overbearing. A striking example came soon after he became chancellor. The duke of Grafton had twitted him with not being quite to the manner born, and for the newness of his peerage. Thurlow rose from the woolsack and walked to the top of the dukes' bench, as chancellors did when they wanted to express a personal opinion not connected with their presiding role. Who had the better claim to respect? Thurlow wanted to know – 'the man who is summoned to a peerage by his Sovereign as a reward of a life passed in serving his country, or he who inherits a seat in this House which was bestowed as the wages of the prostitution of his great grandmother?' Actually we do not know precisely what Thurlow said; this comes from Campbell.[5] The *Parliamentary History of England* was too decorous to include such things.

Yet if we cannot find out much about the crudeness, there is plenty of evidence about the rudeness and the overbearing behaviour. The Contractors Bill of 1782, to bar contractors from the Commons, he described as a 'puny measure', designed to 'deceive and betray the people'. When he was reproved for calling it a small reform, he indignantly denied that he had said so. He had said that it was 'no reform at all', and that the bill was 'a jumble of contradictions'.[6] Burke's bill for reforming civil list expenditure was 'a crude, incoherent, half-formed, ill-digested, unconnected abstract of a plan'.[7] In

---

[3] Lord Campbell, *Lives of the Lord Chancellors and Keepers of the Great Seal of England, from the Earliest Times to the Reign of Queen Victoria* (new edn, 10 vols, Boston, 1874–5), viii, 461.

[4] Sir John Sainty, *Leaders and Whips in the House of Lords, 1783–1964* (House of Lords Record Office Memorandum No. 31, 1964).

[5] Campbell, *Lives*, vii, 60–1.

[6] *Cobbett's Parliamentary History*, xxii, cols 1356, 1363, 1378–9.

[7] *Cobbett's Parl. Hist.*, xxiii, col. 139.

1788, when Bishop Watson spoke on whether a Scottish representative peer accepting a British peerage could continue to sit as a representative peer, Thurlow advised him that 'he should have taken care to have read the articles of the Treaty of Union, before he ventured to let loose his opinions on the subject'.[8] The Insolvent Debtors Bill was, he said, 'Of all the productions he had ever read, the most vague, loose, and unintelligible compound of blunders and absurdities.'[9] Regarding the 1788 Slave Trade Bill, the chancellor 'presumed that the wish of their lordships was to pass some bill of regulation; but as the bill stood it was nonsense. He, therefore, concluded that some amendments would be proposed to connect the nonsense of one part of the bill, with the nonsense of the other.'[10]

The purpose of these remarks was to intimidate, and some lords were intimidated. In July 1781, Lord Abingdon attempted to move Fox's bill to amend the Marriage Act. Thurlow told him that it was quite out of the question, too late in the session. Abingdon said that 'he knew that he was not equal to a contest with the learned lord', but he would put his thoughts on paper and read them to the House on Thursday.[11] Thurlow, however, had even more effective methods for controlling the proceedings of the House. When he was taxed by the duke of Richmond in 1779 with making amendments to bills in order to make them less likely to pass, Thurlow replied that 'he never presumed to rise and controul the sense of the House, but in instances in which the form of their proceedings was about to be departed from'.[12] In fact, he began to manipulate the orders of the House in this, his first session, and never ceased. In the debate on Admiral Keppel's court martial in 1779, he called the duke of Bolton to order in the middle of his motion for going into committee, and launched into remarks of his own. Thurlow then peppered Lord Shelburne with calls to order ostensibly for departing from the subject matter of the debate – in fact, to destroy the coherence of the earl's argument.[13]

An issue which followed soon after might seem of less moment, but reflected growing frustration in the House. Opposition lords were anxious to supply a comfortable place for members of the Commons who wished to attend their debates, pointing out that strangers were already allowed in the House by connivance. Thurlow was entirely in favour of that practice, but professed himself unable to put a question prohibited by a standing order. The duke of Manchester then proposed that a gallery be built. Thurlow wouldn't have this either. Manchester complained that 'of late it was a constant practice to throw the orders of the House in the teeth of every motion that was offered to their consideration'.[14]

The next example was of much greater importance. At the end of December 1780 George III sent a message that Britain was now at war with Holland, the last tolerably friendly European power was one no longer. Naturally this put the British cause in

---

[8] *Cobbett's Parl. Hist.*, xxvi, cols 605–6.

[9] *Cobbett's Parl. Hist.*, xxvii, col. 547.

[10] *Cobbett's Parl. Hist.*, xxvii, col. 641.

[11] *Cobbett's Parl. Hist.*, xxii, cols 617–18.

[12] *Cobbett's Parl. Hist.*, xx, col. 588.

[13] *Cobbett's Parl. Hist.*, xx, cols 95–6, 102–4.

[14] *Cobbett's Parl. Hist.*, xx, cols 470–3.

North America in even more jeopardy. Not surprisingly, the opposition was anxious for a broad-ranging debate. A motion was made for an address. The duke of Richmond thereupon moved that 'this motion for an Address be postponed, in order that the House may take into consideration another motion for an Address to his Majesty' for a wide range of papers.

The chancellor then informed the House that he would put Richmond's motion as stated, but he had grave reservations. 'Whenever the Crown made any communication to Parliament, either from the throne, or by message, the speech was immediately taken into consideration, previous to the discussion of any other business.' He had looked back to the Glorious Revolution, and this was the way it had always been. Therefore he could only look upon Richmond's motion as a direct negative or a postponing of the address by a previous question. In the event of a debate, the question that he must put was: 'Whether the motion for the Address, or the motion made by the noble duke should first receive their lordships' approbation.'

A long debate ensued in which the opposition tried its best to widen the discussion, with Thurlow helpfully reminding them of the narrow question before them, and of their duty not to stray beyond it. Toward the end of the debate, Lord Camden commented on Thurlow's tactics: 'The learned lord who spoke last, with his usual dexterity in debate, had, as he said, brought the question within a narrow compass. He had indeed! He had reduced it to a mere question of order, out of which he had endeavoured entirely to exclude the substantial merits of the subject matter of debate'.[15] It was by such means that Thurlow held sway over the House.

It is not too much to say that up to 1782 Thurlow dominated the Lords. Thereafter the situation become cloudier. The king foisted him on Rockingham's government, which he then opposed from the woolsack. He also served in Shelburne's ministry, but not in the Fox-North coalition. For a while he got on well enough with Pitt, but not after his flirtation with the whigs during the first regency crisis. After that his days were numbered, especially after Grenville became leader in 1790. His opposition to the sinking fund simply provided the occasion for his removal.

Thurlow owed much to his close relationship with George III, which long sheltered him from the ire of his colleagues, and gave him an independence he would not otherwise have had. Lord Eldon's position from beginning to end was firmly based on his adamantine opposition to catholic emancipation. It was for proposing such a measure that Pitt had been forced to resign in 1801, and why the king and Henry Addington chose Eldon as the next lord chancellor.

It was not long, however, before it was evident that they had got something more than a good lawyer and a good protestant. As Addington moved toward peace with Napoleon, Grenville, seeing a national disaster in the return of almost all Britain's recent acquisitions, began to launch his thunderbolts. The first was a swingeing attack on the preliminaries of peace on 3 November 1801. It was the lord chancellor who rose to answer him. The next Grenville attack, which occupied 55 columns of *Parliamentary History*, was also answered by Eldon. His responses were shorter, but they were competent statements of the government line that peace was necessary, and the peace of Amiens

---

[15] *Cobbett's Parl. Hist.*, xxi, cols 1007–9, 1043–60.

the best they could get.[16] What is noteworthy is that it was Eldon who responded to the former foreign secretary who had held that office from 1791 to early in the same year in which they were speaking.

Eldon and Grenville continued to spar over this session and the next. In the period from 22 November 1803 to 29 March 1804, Eldon spoke 17 times, surpassed only by the new leader of the House, Hawkesbury (later Liverpool) who spoke 30 times. Only 31 other lords spoke at all.[17]

From April to August 1804, the chancellor spoke 44 times, the leader of the House, 37. The hotly-contested debates over the Volunteer Bill dominated discussion. There was also a bill to allow the Irish militia to serve in Britain, as well as an Irish Militia Augmentation Bill. In addition there was the Aylesbury Election Bill, one to deal with corruption by extending the borough's boundaries. Eldon was actively engaged in all these issues.

By this time Pitt had returned to office, on 10 May 1804. The period from then until Pitt's death and the succession of the ministry of All the Talents in 1806 was less frantic for Eldon but still active, the high point being the defeat of Grenville's catholic emancipation motion in 1805. The legislation introduced by the Talents, especially that to remove catholic and dissenting disabilities by degrees, made Eldon an aggressive opponent and a busy member of Portland's government that followed. After 1807, however, he was not as broadly active in debate as he had been earlier, but he rallied to the government's defence when it was hard pressed over the orders in council in 1808 and 1809. In the debates in late 1810 and early 1811 he, after Liverpool, was the government's most powerful spokesman against an unrestricted regency.

Eldon's next prominent intervention began on 19 March 1812, when Lord Boringdon moved that the king be addressed to appoint a ministry that would unite all classes of his subjects. Eldon made clear that the existing administration was solidly against catholic emancipation.[18] In April he successfully opposed a committee of the whole House to consider the question.[19] In July he moved the previous question to defeat Lord Wellesley's resolutions that would have committed the House to such action the following year.[20]

For several years after 1812, mainly because of differences with Liverpool, Eldon was mostly quiet on large public issues, save for emancipation questions. But in 1817, when the House was about to discuss the report of the secret committee appointed to consider the necessity of suspending *habeas corpus*, it became involved in a rancorous debate. A petitioner who claimed that the information in the report was inaccurate and damaging to innocent people asked to be allowed to submit evidence at the bar against it. The whig Lord Grosvenor had introduced the petition, and he and his party were determined that the petitioner should be heard. The government was equally determined that he should not be. Eldon decided to use the argument that Grosvenor was out of order on the technical grounds that, despite the fact that the report of the secret committee had

[16] *Cobbett's Parl. Hist.*, xxxvi, cols 171–4, 256–60.

[17] Hansard, *Parl. Debs*, [old ser.], i, Index of Names: House of Lords.

[18] Hansard, *Parl. Debs*, [old ser.], xxi, col. 69.

[19] Hansard, *Parl. Debs*, [old ser.], xxii, cols 688, 699.

[20] Hansard, *Parl. Debs*, [old ser.], xxiii, col. 833.

previously been read to the House and printed copies supplied thereafter, since they had not formally discussed it, in theory they knew nothing about it. It was not Eldon's finest hour. Lord Grey could be relied upon to provoke him into a fury, and did on this occasion. The chancellor lost track of the proceedings, arguing against the petition being received when the question had become whether it should be read. But, at least, Eldon's enthusiasm for the cause could not be doubted, and the government won the day.[21]

In November 1819, Eldon answered Grey's amendment to the address arraigning the government's policy on Peterloo and calling for an inquiry. Eldon said that a parliamentary inquiry would interfere with the regular course of justice. In any case, it was unnecessary, because it was 'his unqualified opinion that the meeting at Manchester on 16th August was, in every sense of the word, illegal'.[22]

Yet despite his good service, Eldon's colleagues had grown tired of him by this time. There had been difficulties from the moment Liverpool became prime minister in June 1812, differences over legal patronage, and over Liverpool's failure to consult the chancellor on important political questions. Yet there was no major row until 1819 when most of the cabinet were for basing the country's currency on bullion, and the chancellor strongly opposed. Bullionists, he said, were almost as dangerous as Spenceans. Liverpool threatened to resign, and Eldon drew back, but relations remained chilly.[23] However, there was a very good reason for not trying to get rid of Eldon. As the protestant champion, he had built up a substantial following. The bishops deferred to him as did the ultra protestant peers. It was an impressive array.

This raises the question of whether he retained his position because he was the head of a party, or because he was managing for the government the biggest political question of the day? The answer is some of both. In 1829, after catholic emancipation had been carried, he would have been declared by acclamation head of the new but short-lived party founded by the ultras, had it not finally been reluctantly decided that he was too old.[24] Yet Eldon was right in 1826, when having mooted retirement to Liverpool and found him strongly opposed, he thought the reason for the prime minister's reluctance was 'an unwillingness that my departure should precede what may come forward on the Catholic question'.[25] Liverpool had thought the triumph of emancipation quite possible in 1821. In 1825 he was almost sure that it would happen and was preparing to resign, and Peel with him. This was not a time when they wanted to be rid of Eldon.

During the period when he was in his ascendance on the question, no measures to repeal, or even to lessen the sting of, religious disabilities, were passed. Besides the defeat of two emancipation bills in 1821 and 1825, and of an 1822 bill to restore the rights of catholic peers, the fate of two other bills suggests the authority the chancellor wielded. In 1824 Eldon opposed a Dissenters Marriage Bill supported by the archbishop of Canterbury, which was defeated by a vote of 105 to 66. In the same year he opposed another bill supported by the prime minister to enfranchise English catholics, which was

---

[21] Hansard, *Parl. Debs*, [old ser.], xxxv, cols 478, 479, 481.

[22] Hansard, *Parl. Debs*, [old ser.], lxi, col. 38.

[23] Campbell, *Lives*, xviii, 120–1.

[24] R.W. Davis, 'The Duke of Wellington and the Ultra Peers', in *Wellington Studies III*, ed. C.M. Woolgar (Southampton, 1999), 35–55.

[25] Campbell, *Lives*, ix, 244.

also defeated by 139 to 101.[26] Eldon left office when Canning became prime minister in 1827.

It was only in Addington's, and to a lesser extent Pitt's, administration that Eldon fully realized Grenville's ideal of loyal, persisting, and broad-gauged support. Yet he continued to give powerful assistance when needed, and on the great question of the day he seemed invincible.

Lyndhurst was an expert manager, but his talents were exercised most impressively in managing whig legislation in the 1830s. In the committee on the 1835 Municipal Corporations Bill, Lyndhurst relentlessly revised it to his own specifications. On one amendment, the prime minister, Lord Melbourne, sarcastically professed himself 'unwilling to offer any factious opposition to the Bill of the noble and learned Lord', but he wished to retain a certain proviso. Lyndhurst replied: 'The noble Viscount is not quite correct in calling this my Bill; but I am quite certain that it is not his', and the proviso was struck out. In one of the last important pieces of whig legislation that Lyndhurst took charge of, the Irish Municipal Corporations Bill of 1840, he showed himself at his most brazen, even brutal. When the Commons sent up its amendments, Lyndhurst announced that as the Lords had been discussing these issues for three months, he would not discuss them further. When the amendments were moved, he would simply state whether he agreed or disagreed with them. The amendments were then read *seriatim*. Those Lyndhurst objected to were negatived without a division, the others were adopted.[27]

In 1827, Lyndhurst had become chancellor in Canning's brief government. He proposed only one measure in the short session, a Dissenters Marriage Bill. Eldon was beside himself, but the bill died for lack of time in any case.[28] Lyndhurst remained chancellor in Goderich's government, which never met a parliament, and in Wellington's. When the government decided in 1828 to give way before Lord John Russell's majority in the Commons for removing dissenting disabilities, Lyndhurst in the Lords became a tower of strength. Wellington boasted to a not amused George IV, that 'Neither Lord Eldon or Lord Redesdale could make any reply to his argument on the Test Act.'[29] The bill passed relatively easily, substituting for the sacramental test a declaration 'on the true faith of a Christian' not to use any appointment to office to weaken the Church.

When Wellington decided at the end of the summer of 1828 that catholic emancipation could be put off no longer, he asked the king and was granted permission to take counsel with two of his colleagues, and them alone. The two were the lord chancellor and Robert Peel. In the parliamentary battle the following year Wellington owed most of his debating power as well as his majority to the whigs. Fully half of Wellington's party, 112 embittered ultras, made ferocious attacks on the government which had to spend much of its time defending itself.[30] Such was the case with Lyndhurst's speech in

[26] Campbell, *Lives*, ix, 194–5; Horace Twiss, *The Public and Private Life of Lord Chancellor Eldon* (2 vols, 1846), ii, 107–8, 110–2.

[27] Hansard, *Parl. Debs*, 3rd ser., xxx, col. 481; lv, col. 1356.

[28] Dennis Lee, *Lord Lyndhurst: The Flexible Tory* (Niwot, CO, 1994), 61.

[29] Southampton University Library, Wellington Papers 1/930/34: draft Wellington to George IV, 25 Apr. 1828.

[30] Richard. W. Davis, *A Political History of the House of Lords, 1811–1846: From the Regency to Corn Law Repeal* (Stanford, CA, 2008), 154–5.

the final debate. In the course of it he alluded to the fact that catholics had been expelled from parliament relatively late, in 1678. Eldon asked whether he had known that the previous year. Lyndhurst replied that he had not, 'but he had been prosecuting his studies; I have advanced in knowledge; and in my humble opinion, even the noble and learned lord might improve himself in the same way'.[31]

This was much more like the Lyndhurst who returned to office in 1841 than the overbearing bully who had forced the Irish Corporation Bill through the previous year. Though he still forced his way, it was discreetly, with guile and bluff good humour. Lyndhurst was asked to take charge of three measures by Peel's government in the 1840s. The third, a Charitable Trusts Bill, died with the government in 1846, but two were passed, the Dissenters Chapels Act in 1844 and the Jewish Disabilities Act in 1845. The issue in the Chapels Bill was whether unitarians should have to give up most of their denominational properties to trinitarian dissenters. The latter and other enemies of the bill argued that since unitarianism had been illegal up to 1813, unitarians had no right to any property acquired before that time. The purpose of the bill was to establish such a right. The Jewish Disabilities Act opened municipal office to jews.

Peel had been determined since 1835 to wrench his party toward liberal attitudes on religion, but his brief government in that year achieved nothing. Nor had any headway been made thereafter. The Lords blocked every effort for jewish emancipation, and if there was any group their lordships found less acceptable than jews it was unitarians. The declaration 'on the true faith of a Christian' was not aimed at jews, but chosen on the mistaken assumption that it would exclude unitarians. To get these two bills by the tory lords would likely require not only someone willing to advocate them, but also someone respected by those of ultra leanings, of forceful character and presentation, and with the hide of a rhinoceros.

The chancellor introduced the Chapels Bill on 3 May 1844. The second reading had been *pro forma*, so Lyndhurst made some remarks before going into committee. He said that he had never expected when he agreed to bring it forward that this moderate measure of justice would be met by 'such clamorous opposition', with petitions in great numbers against it.

He then proceeded to explain this phenomenon away. He had examined the petitions. The greater portion of them were couched in the same language of 'surprise' and 'alarm'. They were obviously written by the same hand and came from the same source. He, therefore, dismissed them as unworthy of attention. But there were what he called 'numerous' petitions on the other side from churchmen, presbyterians (the name under which most unitarians had gone before 1813), and from other denominations of dissenters unspecified. These petitions were not couched in general terms, but pointed out specific hardships and evils and asked the Lords for a remedy.

He also noted the daunting opposition of Henry Phillpotts, the bishop of Exeter, a high churchman of the old sort, in the sense of being an ardent defender of its privileges and properties. Of the bishop, who was present, Lyndhurst said that his opposition would be formidable, but not, he thought, enough to prevail on this occasion. He also noted the new company, with the emphasis on *new*, the bishop was keeping, referring to the angry

---

[31] Hansard, *Parl. Debs*, new ser., xx, cols 203–4.

orthodox dissenters. Lyndhurst went on to acknowledge in advance the loyal support he expected to receive from his 'right reverend friends', the bishops. This was a joke, but a joke with a purpose.[32]

It was meant to make the bishops uncomfortable, and it did. Charles Blomfield, bishop of London, was clearly uneasy about differing from the chancellor, especially on a government measure. Yet he was also seething over Lyndhurst's speaking 'somewhat sarcastically of his new associates'. The gibe, of course, had been aimed at Phillpotts. Blomfield, however, was determined to make it abundantly clear that *he* had neither new friends nor associates in this matter. In short, the bishop of London did not consort with dissenters of any variety. What Lyndhurst wanted was to keep the bishops off balance – Blomfield's gratuitous display of pompous bigotry was a sign of his success. Nevertheless, though dismissing those who would benefit, the bishop took it upon himself to move the rejection of the bill. It was the unitarians he had in *his* sights.[33]

The debate, however, was not encouraging for the two bishops. The bishop of Exeter left the House, and the bishop of London decided there was no use going to a division. The third reading took place a week later. The bishop of Exeter was back, with what he thought was an insoluble conundrum. The way of deciding the doctrine of a congregation in the past in order to establish a right, was to judge by the doctrine of its minister. The bishop thought he had found a chapel in Cork that had had two ministers at the same time, one orthodox one heterodox. What did Lyndhurst make of that? Lyndhurst replied that in such a case the doctrine of the congregation could not be determined. The bishop, however, kept pushing. At last, the chancellor said that he had no intention of talking about an 'invention' (i.e., fabrication). Lord Monteagle knew the Cork congregation well, and informed him that there had never been more than one minister, a unitarian. The bishop flew into a rage and dared Monteagle to come forward and challenge him to his face. Monteagle obliged. The division on the third reading was 44 to 9. No bishops were represented on either side.[34]

The Jewish Disabilities Bill was a more sober and serious business. In introducing the second reading on 10 March 1845, Lyndhurst said that it was the object of the bill to get rid of some 'anomalies, and some inconsistencies, and I may be permitted to say absurdities' regarding the admission of jews to corporate offices. Later he said barring jews by a declaration on 'the true faith of a Christian', was 'a species of mockery'.

He then went on to give a frank explanation of the bill. The grounds were narrow, but that was deliberate. He and his colleagues were 'anxious that this measure should pass'. They did not wish, therefore, to rest 'it upon those great views of general policy (civil and religious liberty, for example) which might admit much matter of controversy, of difficulty, and of doubt; and in the consideration of which the particular measure might be forgotten and lost'.[35]

The bishop of London revealed what it was they were trying to avoid, as well as the success of the tactics employed. He had on a former occasion opposed a similar measure because he thought it likely to lead to the admission of jews into parliament. He would

---

[32] Hansard, *Parl. Debs*, 3rd ser., lxxiv, cols 579–80.

[33] Hansard, *Parl. Debs*, 3rd ser., lxxiv, cols 588–96.

[34] Hansard, *Parl. Debs*, 3rd ser., lxxiv, cols 821–6, 832.

[35] Hansard, *Parl. Debs*, 3rd ser., lxxviii, cols 515–22.

not offer any opposition to this measure. The reason was that this bill had nothing to do with parliament. It simply removed the necessity for jews to declare on the 'true faith of a Christian' to qualify for municipal office. Thus it made jews eligible for municipal office, but for none higher. For those who feared it, it would not allow jews to legislate for what many believed would then cease to be a christian nation. Nevertheless, it did give the Jewish Board of Deputies what they had requested, a request Lionel de Rothschild entrusted to his next-door neighbour, and which the duke of Wellington duly delivered to the cabinet.[36]

Thus it was that the whole discussion radiated the same spirit of warmth and goodwill which the architect of the bill had wished to inspire. There were no loud voices of conflict or dissent. Lyndhurst had presided over the whole with dignity, good feeling, and good sense. He was truly a man for all seasons.

What conclusions might we draw from the careers of the three lord chancellors discussed above regarding their importance in managing the business of the house of lords for much of the period between 1778 and 1846?

Clearly one crucial factor was the appearance of leaders of the House, initially one of the secretaries of state. Later, peers who were prime ministers, such as Grenville, Liverpool and Wellington, became leaders as a matter of course. At least potentially, these new officials posed a serious threat to the powers of lord chancellors. How dangerous that threat was depended on the leader. The first in 1783 was Earl Temple, later marquess of Buckingham. He lasted only three days, resigning in the uproar over his part in bringing down the Fox–North coalition by a vote in the house of lords. It was he who delivered George III's threat to consider as an enemy any lord who voted for the government's India Bill.[37] Lord Sydney served as leader from 1783 to 1789, the duke of Leeds from 1789 to 1790. Pitt, the prime minister, did not have a high opinion of either, and as one historian has said of the small cabinet of seven in which they sat: 'it had more blue blood than strength'.[38] He was clearly not referring to Lord Thurlow, who had no blue blood, but a great deal of strength, and nothing to fear from such leaders.

Thurlow, however, met his match in Grenville. No insult was left unanswered, no patronising tolerated. In letter after letter, Grenville with perfect but cold politeness reproved Thurlow for his language, for his tone, and for anything else he wanted to tax him with. In the House, whenever Thurlow veered from government policy, Grenville was on his feet to repudiate him. There was no doubt that Grenville was a strong leader, and though Thurlow did not go graciously, he went.

Lord Eldon's situation in the beginning was in some ways similar to Thurlow's. Eldon became chancellor in April 1801, following Pitt's and Grenville's resignations. From then until November 1803 there was no regular leader of the House.[39] Eldon reigned supreme. In November 1802, when there had been a possibility of Grenville rejoining Pitt to form a ministry, Buckingham had strongly advised his brother not to, among

---

[36] Hansard, *Parl. Debs*, 3rd ser., lxxviii, col. 524; Davis, *House of Lords*, 304.

[37] Sainty, *Leaders and Whips*, 2; R.W. Davis, 'Grenville, George Nugent-Temple, First Marquess of Buckingham', *ODNB*, xxxiii, 727–30.

[38] J. Steven Watson, *The Reign of George III, 1760–1815* (Oxford, 1960), 267.

[39] Sainty, *Leaders and Whips*, 2.

other reasons because he might suffer from jealousy, 'including perhaps the Chancellor (from House of Lords jealousy)'.[40]

Addington's appointment of Hawkesbury as leader at the beginning of the session in November 1803 cannot have been a welcome development for Eldon. On 20 March the following year the chancellor asked Pitt for a meeting, and a few days later they agreed that Eldon should act as an intermediary between Pitt and the king for the purpose of removing Addington as prime minister and bringing Pitt back into office. That happened, largely due to Eldon's influence with an ailing monarch, on 10 May. In Pitt's new government, while Eldon naturally remained lord chancellor, Hawkesbury was given a new office as home secretary at the same time retaining the leadership.[41] This was hardly a bonus for Eldon.

Whether or not the two things were connected, Eldon and Hawkesbury were almost immediately locked in conflict over a rather unusual case. The Grenvilles wished to take advantage of proven bribery in the borough of Aylesbury to secure their control there by a considerable expansion of its boundaries, thus creating a larger electorate in areas where the family was fast extending its influence.

The Grenvilles were the leading family in the opposition. They were also, however, the prime minister's cousins, and it seems to have been the latter consideration that told in this instance. The Grenville cause was vigorously pressed by the leader of the Lords. Dogged in his opposition was the lord chancellor. It was the former who prevailed on 15 June when the second reading was passed, 39 to 7.[42]

Such clashes would happen again. With the exception of the Talents' ministry of 1806–7, Hawkesbury, or Liverpool as he would become, and Eldon remained partners in government until Liverpool's stroke in 1827, but it was never an easy relationship. To determine the cause of the relative reduction of Eldon's activity in parliament after 1804 would not be easy. To a large extent it was inevitable. Like Thurlow, Eldon had started his career in the Lords without a leader. Like Grenville, Liverpool was a leader who intended to lead. Personal animosities may have speeded up the process, for certain periods or individuals.

Probably the chancellor who came closest to meeting Grenville's high standards was Lord Lyndhurst, and the secret of his success is quite simple. From 1828 onwards he enjoyed the full confidence of the duke of Wellington. Wellington genuinely admired him, for his legal knowledge, for his skill as a debater, for his oratory, and for the great respect he enjoyed in the Conservative Party. The duke relied on him heavily to manage large, complicated measures, such as the Reform Bill in 1832, the 1835 Municipal Corporations Bill, and a number of crucial Irish bills. Indeed the duke relied more heavily on his chancellor than any other leader of the House in this period. Lyndhurst's level of support might have surpassed even Grenville's expectations.

---

[40] HMC, *Fortescue MSS*, vii, 120.

[41] William Hague, *William Pitt the Younger* (2005), 525–9, 533.

[42] *Cobbett's Parliamentary Debates*, ii, cols 513–5, 516–8, 681–2, 683.

'Nothing Could Exceed the Badness of His Character Even in This Bad Age'

SIR WILLIAM McKAY

Initially the model for the speakership of the US house of representatives could not but be drawn from Westminster, though the occupants of the chair in the Commons around the time of independence were not impressive. Not however till Henry Clay's election in 1812 was the American Speaker transformed into a partisan, politically-active leader of the House. The contemporary Commons Speaker, Manners Sutton, though he failed to be re-elected to the chair on political grounds, was not a party leader. Between Clay and the civil war the intensity of party conflict obscured the role of the Speaker, and minorities flourished. Speaker Reed in the 1880s believed in the rights of the majority and used the authority of the chair to promote them. He ended the practice of members delaying business by refusing to answer a roll-call though present, and he developed special rules to accelerate the progress of bills. About the same time, Speaker Brand in the Commons, in the face of Irish obstructionism, also reasserted the rights of the majority by introducing the closure, to which guillotines were later added. Reed's authoritarianism broke in the hands of Speaker Cannon in 1909–10 as progressive members of his party rebelled. By then the Commons speakership had entered a period of complete political neutrality. Speakers O'Neill and Gingrich in the last quarter of the 20th century regained much of the power and authority which Cannon's speakership had lost.

Keywords: speakership; Henry Clay; Manners Sutton; Speaker Reed; Speaker Brand; Speaker Cannon

Horace Walpole's judgment on Speaker Sir Fletcher Norton seems to indicate that the newly-formed US Congress would have been well advised not to regard Westminster as any kind of model. He may have been right: comparative parliamentary procedure is a barren field in which few practical ideas flower.[1] In its modern guise, it was the brainchild of Gilbert Campion (later Sir Gilbert Campion GCB, clerk of the house of commons and still later Lord Campion) and a colleague, Wilfred Johnston. They made a, doubtless, agreeable tour of European legislatures one summer, collecting data. Unluckily for them, the summer they chose was 1914. After the Great War and more especially in the 1950s and 1960s, the concept was very popular. Its popularity may have waned since. Nevertheless, and leaving aside politicians' claims about a 'special relationship' between the USA and the UK, the two legislatures are close enough to allow conclusions to be

---

[1] The concept of a parallel sitting of the house of commons in Westminster Hall normally to debate matters raised by individual members, while the main chamber is sitting on other business, is an idea the origins of which lie in the federal Australian Parliament in Canberra, and may be an exception to this rule.

drawn from a comparison of procedural development. This article concentrates on the speakership of the house of commons and the US house of representatives.

1

The US constitution is typically terse on the speakership. 'The House of Representatives shall choose its Speaker' (article 1, section 2). The Constitutional Convention said nothing about what kind of Speaker the new Congress should have. Congress itself made rules which mention the Speaker in 1794, 1799 and 1811. Most refer to basic aspects of the post – keeping order, calling members, controlling the premises – which tell us little about the nature of the speakership. Even where the content of the rules goes further, it is not easy to see what is distinctive about the kind of speakership they reflect. Permitting Speaker's rulings to be appealed – which has never been permitted at Westminster and is beginning to be a real nuisance in Washington – may not reflect a new understanding of the proper powers of the chair but only a desire to curb the excesses of bullies like Fletcher Norton. The rule of 1789 that the Speaker may vote only where his vote would be decisive or in a ballot suggests that there was no desire to move too far from the British House.

Whatever the view of the founding fathers about directly following Westminster, the fact that many of them had personal experience of colonial legislatures which themselves depended to varying degrees on the British model probably allowed transatlantic influence in at one remove. It is worth noticing that Muhlenberg, the first Speaker, had presided over the Pennsylvania House.

Yet even if they had intended to follow Westminster, the Americans might have found it difficult. Sir Fletcher Norton – 'his demeanour overbearing and his manner coarse' – was Commons' Speaker as independence was being won. A man who argued that levying war against the king was treason might not have gone down too well as a model for Congress. He was a far from ideal exemplar in the chair, freely abusing members of both Houses: 'Pray, gentlemen, be orderly. You are almost as bad as the other House.' He was a tory before election to the chair, but in office it was antipathy to the court which characterised his speakership and was the cause of his failure to be re-elected in 1780. On the other hand, Fletcher Norton was an effective Speaker, and he deliberately avoided intervening in debates in committee. Had they looked for other models, the Americans would have been no further forward with the hopeless Sir John Cust who preceded Fletcher Norton, or his successor, the shy and inexperienced Sir Charles Cornwall.

Despite the legacy of Arthur Onslow, a Speaker from whom Thomas Jefferson (no less) was prepared to take lessons, the link between the chair of the Commons and ministerial office was sometimes uncomfortably close. Grenville, the Speaker after Cornwall, had been chief secretary for Ireland. Henry Addington, Grenville's successor, went straight from the chair to be prime minister. There were those who were uneasy at such developments. In the debate on the speakership election in 1802, Sheridan argued strongly against too close a connection between Speakers and ministerial office. (George Canning, by contrast, promised not to laugh at Addington's new post.) Speakers of the house of representatives, however, were clearly party men almost – not quite – from the outset. As a Federalist, Frederick Muhlenberg was not re-elected to the chair in the second Congress when his party fell out of favour. Jonathan Dayton, however, elected Speaker in 1795, came from the minority. But there bipartisanship stopped. Theodore Sedgwick, Dayton's successor, was thoroughly partisan, and though until 1839 Speakers were elected by secret ballot, no presiding officer since 1795 has come from anything but the majority party.

2

A Speaker elected as a member of a party does not necessarily make the discharge of the office partisan. Henry Clay of Kentucky did that. In 1812 the old Congress was seen as ineffective and rudderless. The new House was inexperienced, full of young men from the frontier, looking for leadership, war-hawks all of them, breathing fire against both the British and their Indian allies, and the Spaniards. President Madison they regarded as hopeless. Clay had talent, youth, ambition and speaking ability. He had experience too. He had sat in – though never elected to – the US senate and he had presided in the Kentucky house of assembly. Though still a very young man, on his first day in Congress he was elected to the chair at the first ballot, heavily defeating a former Speaker, Nathaniel Macon on the way, a feat never equalled before or since.

Clay had one even greater advantage, not of his making. The existing party system was in flux. Clay grasped the opening which that offered, and in so doing turned the Speaker into a leader and shaper of national destiny. His approach has been described as 'to govern or rule the House from the Chair and to persuade it from the floor'. Dayton had spoken in committee 15 years earlier, but Clay developed the practice. He also voted enthusiastically, though originally the Speaker was entitled only to vote (ballots apart) to make or break a tie.

He did not wholly abandon impartiality in the chair, describing the Speaker's role as 'remaining cool and unshaken amidst all the storms of debate, carefully guarding the preservation of the permanent laws and rules of the House from being sacrificed to temporary passions, prejudices or interests'. At the same time, he and his allies on the floor worked the rules to shut off inconvenient debate and deliver the results Clay – not the president – wanted.

Above all, Clay showed his successors how to construct a power base from the chair. From 1790 Speakers had been empowered to nominate to standing, select and conference committees. Clay honed the weapon. He immediately nominated war-hawks to all committees, holding back three of them to be his floor managers. He mollified those who lost status by mendaciously assuring them that they had given up nothing at all. He appropriated the right to refer bills to committees, leaving them free to ignore legislation he and they did not like. As the number of standing committees went from nine to 25 while he was Speaker, and the proportion of bills referred to them increased from under half to over 90%, his control became more complete. Most war legislation and much of the rest was shaped by him. John Quincy Adams said that Clay was the man whose influence and power, more than any other, produced the war of 1812. He may be said to have founded the whig party. Whatever the founding fathers thought a Speaker should be, this was surely not it. On the other hand, there was no other contemporary locus for political leadership in the legislature within a system of separation of powers. The position of majority floor leader was not recognized until the very end of the century.

After Clay, while the Speaker gained power to nominate chairmen and even minority members of committees, as civil war moved closer elections became very bitter. Between 1839 and 1863, there were 11 Speakers and only one served more than one term.

Clay was the longest-serving 19th-century US Speaker, but the career of his contemporary Mr Speaker Manners Sutton at Westminster was longer, though far less influential. Unlike Clay, he was said to have ridden the House on a snaffle rein and not a bit. Though he had been a tory, the whigs re-elected him to the chair in 1832 because they thought he was the best man to control the reformed House whose temper they were unsure of. When he spoke in committee he apologised. His connection with politics was not entirely severed – he was at various times thought of for the home office and once even as prime minister – but he was denied an eighth term in the chair in 1835 because he was suspected of caballing against Melbourne's government, advising on the appointments to the cabinet and recommending the dissolution for party purposes. When he was defeated in the contest for the chair – by only ten votes – the last occasion on which such a thing happened, opinion quite soon formed that Speakers should not interfere in politics but should be re-elected to the chair, whichever party was in power.

3

The second of the trio of American Speakers, Thomas B. Reed of Maine, a Republican from an old Mayflower family, became Speaker in 1889. Clay's fiery trajectory did not immediately change the character of the office. Before and after the civil war, the increase of party conflict and cohesion in Congress nurtured high levels of partisan voting. In one legislative day in 1854, there were 101 roll-call votes on the Kansas-Nebraska Bill. There was no opening for Clay's kind of speakership. The House fell victim to a culture of delay and filibuster. Reed came to the chair when it had long been the practice of the minority to move dilatory motions, that is propositions (such as a motion to adjourn) interposed into the main debate which – if agreed – would have the effect of deferring, perhaps to the Greek kalends, the main decision. Such safety valves can be useful, but they can also be obstructive nuisances. Reed asserted the rights of majorities. For him the best system of government was one in which 'one party governs and the other watches'. In Czar Reed's opinion, the rules of the House were not there to protect the minority but to promote the orderly business of the House – i.e., of the majority. When asked, 'what then is the function of the minority?', he replied: 'to make a quorum and draw its pay'.

Quorums indeed were to feature in one of Reed's most notable coups, eliminating the disappearing quorum. Ever since John Quincy Adams had used the tactic to frustrate action on a pro-slavery measure in 1832, the constitutional requirement that 'a majority of each House shall constitute a quorum to do business' had been open to abuse. Originally all members were expected to vote. Adams sat tight when a vote was called and there was no way of recording the presence of a quorum. The business could not be completed. By the end of the century, this had become an art form. Within a year of taking office, Reed dug a pit for the obstructionists and they fell in.

The house of representatives adopts its rules at the beginning of every Congress. In 1890 Reed contrived to avoid a decision by referring the rules to the rules committee for review. The Speaker's powers then depended on 'general parliamentary law' modified by House practice, which he interpreted as outlawing the disappearing quorum and entitling him to refuse to entertain dilatory motions. This lasted for three months, in the course of which the Speaker upped the ante. The House considered a contested election for West Virginia, and the Democrats – knowing they would lose – pulled the disappearing quorum lever. The votes cast just reached the necessary figure but then two of the five Democrats voting withdrew their votes. Reed, knowing the Grand Old Party would stand firm, simply directed the clerk to record as present 160-odd members who had refused to vote. When challenged by Congressman McCready, Reed replied: 'The Chair is making a statement of fact that the gentleman from Kentucky is present. Does he deny it?' There was no answer to this existential conundrum. Three days of bedlam ensued, but Reed stuck to his guns and the disappearing quorum practice itself disappeared.

There was of course much more to do. Even before he became Speaker, Reed had form. He had been a member of the rules committee since 1882 and had had a lot to do with the development of the concept of special rules, which allowed the House to make a rule governing the progress of a single bill without suspending the general rules, for which a larger majority was required. By the time Reed was elected to the chair, the practice had become commonplace, and indeed it is the tool which Speakers have used ever since to move forward the legislative programme of their party.

Reed went even wider than disappearing quorums and special rules. In 1890, the rules committee reported a package of changes which included giving the Speaker the power to rule dilatory motions out of order; the quorum in committee of the whole was reduced from a majority to 100, diminishing the possibility of lengthy points of order that a quorum was not present; and the Speaker was given the authority to refer all bills and resolutions to the appropriate committee without what was often time-wasting debate on the floor. So absolute was Reed's authority through the rules committee that when told of a prolonged debate in the senate, he remarked: 'Thank God the House of Representatives is not a deliberative body.'

Reed lost the chair later in 1890 and the Democrats reinstated the disappearing quorum rule, but when Reed as minority leader successfully used the old rule against them, they equally brazenly reintroduced his rule.

Much of this has echoes across the Atlantic, not in detail of course, but in the nearly contemporary struggle in the house of commons against prolixity and obstruction. Like Reed, Mr Speaker Brand had to resort to robust but revolutionary expedients to recover the House to majority control (though it was a majority which for decades had been reducing the time available to back benchers). The problem was hardly a new one. A series of select committees had been trying over almost as long to tweak procedure to make it more efficient. Well before the crisis came, Brand told a procedure committee that obstruction was an abuse of the privilege of freedom of debate for the purpose of defeating the will of parliament. He claimed to have no difficulty in distinguishing between legitimate opposition, however badly deployed, and wilful obstruction.

The time to make good the claim came when Charles Parnell led the Irish in the latter direction. Reed faced the Democrats on his own. By contrast, Brand had governmental backing for what he did in 1881 – the cabinet met in his library to plan the details. Beginning on 31 January the house of commons began a sitting of $41\frac{1}{2}$ hours on a motion to give priority to a bill for the defence of persons and property in Ireland.

Dilatory motions, Reed's bugbear, punctuated the debate. After talks with the parties, Brand took the chair at nine in the morning, – the deputy Speaker having presided continuously for an incredible nine-and-a-half hours – waved down the interminably prolix Joseph Biggar and with the paper shaking in his hand put the question. The Irish were taken completely by surprise. When a member asked on what authority he had acted, the Speaker said: – to prolonged cheering in all parts of the House – 'I acted on my own responsibility and from a sense of duty to the House.' It might have been Reed. The next day Irish obstreperousness revived, but (doubtless to immense personal satisfaction) Brand named, and the House duly suspended, three Irish members individually and the other 28 *en bloc*.

There followed a number of changes to the standing orders designed to remove the weapons the Irish had used and to reinforce the powers of the chair if they found others. Some innovations were peculiar to the house of commons; others had clear American parallels, as the problems were similar. Mr Speaker Brand – like Reed – was empowered to refuse to accept or otherwise blunt the effect of dilatory motions. Guillotines were introduced, and though they differ from special rules in form, their intention is exactly the same. To a lesser degree the same is true of the closure, which originally was entirely in the Speaker's hands. (In a more modern context, the elaborate business motions which flourished before the days of programme motions, though less draconian in form, were similar in purpose to special rules.)

4

In the hands of Joseph G. Cannon of Illinois, like Reed, a Republican, who became Speaker in 1903, the authority of the Speaker of the house of representatives was further developed – and then broken. Cannon was not Reed's equal in intellect. He was an arbitrary and cantankerous old man, but as an authoritarian he had few equals. He once killed a forestry bill with a snort: 'not a cent for scenery'. As chairman of the appropriations committee he had authorised the spending of $50 million on the war with Spain – without letting his committee colleagues into the secret. As Speaker, Cannon chaired the rules committee, and the other five members were chosen by him. He controlled floor recognition, named the members of committees ignoring seniority, and determined the floor agenda. It was an unparalleled collection of powers. One disgruntled member of his own party, when asked for a copy of House rules, sent a photo of Cannon.

Six years into his speakership however, progressive members of the Grand Old Party began to find his politics – not his authority – irksome. Cannon believed he was defending constitutional propriety. He was not particularly friendly with President Theodore Roosevelt, who he said had no more use for the constitution than a tom cat for a marriage licence. It was said of the president that he cultivated the rules committee as if it was a grove of oranges, but all he ever got were lemons. Calendar Wednesdays, one a month, allowed committees to bring to the floor bills for which the rules committee had granted no hearing or special rule. Cannon could not resist, but managed to frustrate much of these gains.

His opponents returned to the charge. In the 1909 session, 12 Republicans refused to vote for him as Speaker. The Democrats proposed increasing the size of the rules committee, removing the Speaker and allowing him to appoint only the committee of ways and means. Cannon blocked that, but at the cost of establishing a unanimous consent calendar when on two days a month congressmen could bring up minor bills without the Speaker's consent. He had to guarantee the minority (not just his chums) a motion to recommit, and the rules were changed to increase the number of votes needed to set aside calendar Wednesdays.

Nemesis finally arrived in 1910. Cannon tried to shut down calendar Wednesdays, and a group of Republican progressives in concert with the Democrats responded by moving as a matter of constitutional privilege to remove the Speaker from an expanded rules committee. For two days the House debated the status of the motion, and in the end Cannon ruled against its privileged status. The ruling was appealed, Cannon's view was overturned and he was removed from the rules committee.

There was no British parallel. Cannon's dictatorial position could not be matched at Westminster. The Commons speakership moved in a quite different direction. The tighter the government's control of the time of the house of commons as the 20th century progressed the more important the Speaker's neutrality in ensuring that the instruments of control were not used too oppressively. By comparison with the increasing partiality of the American speakership, there were 18 uncontested elections to the chair in the first half of the 20th century, and even after the election upheavals of 1906 and 1945 the sitting Speaker was not disturbed.

5

In Washington, Cannon was followed by 60 years of decentralisation of power to standing committees and the seniority rule. Then came the 1960s and a resurgent young Democratic caucus, keen to enact Kennedy's programmes. There was a general agreement that the relatively weak speakerships of John McCormack and Carl Albert had paralysed Democratic legislative initiative. The rules committee was enlarged and the Speaker recovered powers to select the chairman and majority members, even to the extent of denying them floor time. Power granted in 1975 to refer bills to committees sequentially or to several committees at once cut across the jurisdiction of the standing committees. Closed rules, which restricted debate on the floor, increased fourfold in the 15 years after 1975. Twenty years later closed rules were applied to 70% of all bills. Speakers became national figures. Tip O'Neill's status was enhanced because he led the Democrats in their confrontation with Ronald Reagan, as Gingrich – who had more central authority than had been seen since the days of Uncle Joe Cannon – confronted Bill Clinton. But Speakers were also more politically and personally exposed. Speaker Tom Foley lost his seat in the House – the first incumbent Speaker to do so since 1862 – because of perceived failings in the administration of Congress (and more immediately because he fell out with the National Rifle Association).

In short, whatever the speakership of the US house of representatives was intended to be, its development for the first century-and-a-quarter of independence can sustain a broad comparison with the Speaker of the house of commons. In the 20th century, the British Speaker's neutrality became one of the few means by which the iron grip of government on the legislature could be moderated. In America, the Speaker of the House emerged as a national party figure, sometimes almost a leader of the opposition.

The Role of the Speaker in the 20th Century

THE RT HON. BARONESS BOOTHROYD

Baroness Boothroyd was Speaker of the house of commons from April 1992 until October 2000. She describes her approach to the job of Speaker: how she routinely briefed herself for the business of the House, and how she approached some of the more difficult decisions required of the Speaker, including the selection of amendments, the use of the casting vote and allowing members to make personal statements. She comments on some issues concerning the management of the House's business during her time in the chair: the practice of government ministers to anticipate official statements in the media before they are made in the House; the length of ministerial answers at question time and the decision on the access of Sinn Fein members to the facilities and services of the House. She refers to the functions of the Speaker outside the chamber: chairing the house of commons commission; receiving Speakers and other public figures from other countries and representing the house of commons abroad.

Keywords: Speaker; house of commons; question time; members of parliament; parliaments

I am delighted to have been asked to participate in this most interesting conference.

Following the death of Jack Weatherill, from whom I learned so much, I suppose that I can justifiably claim to have a unique qualification to talk about the role of the Speaker in the 20th century; and I hope that I can perhaps offer you a few new insights into the operation of our parliamentary system.

I do not intend to run through all the functions that the Speaker carries out. I take it that you are all well aware of the overt responsibilities of the office. Instead I want to focus on what it is like to be Speaker, on the way in which I prepared myself for my duties, on the pressures under which I operated and on some of the functions that you may be less well aware of.

Every morning for eight-and-a-half years I woke up with a sense of the enormous privilege I had been granted in being elected Speaker, the more so because the election had been contested. I had come from the opposition benches and challenged the government candidate. I was also aware of the heavy responsibility that I bore to justify the trust the House had placed in me. Fairness and impartiality are the qualities which, above all, members expect to find in the Speaker and which will secure their support and respect. When you have been committed all your adult life to the ideals and policies of one party, impartiality is a quality that you have to work at. But if you cannot put aside partisanship you have no right to even think of becoming Speaker.

Impartiality, of course, does not operate in a vacuum. To be impartial you need to be thoroughly familiar with the issues of the day and with the attitudes taken by the political parties to those issues. You need to have your ear to the ground so that you are aware of the nuances in every situation, for example, the divergent views on particular issues *within* the parties as well as *between* them. I always took the view that political parties are coalitions within themselves and minority views need to be aired whether it suits the leadership or not.

But there is, of course, also a wider reason why the Speaker needs to be *au fait* with the issues of the day. Every sitting day he is likely to be faced with requests for urgent questions or with applications for emergency debates. On a regular basis he is required to select topical subjects for adjournment debates. On any day, points of order may be raised which are based on current events or on remarks which ministers may have made about those events outside the House.

My objective each day was to enter the chamber as fully briefed as I could be, not only about matters that I knew would come up, for example, items on the order paper, but also about those which *might* come up. How did I set about achieving this?

Equipped with a Walkman I set off through St James's park for my morning consti-tutional. I was listening to John Humphrys. I found by experience that the quickest way of getting to grips with the issues of the day was to listen to the *Today* programme. And it was, of course, on that programme that ministers were all too frequently seduced into anticipating the announcements they were due to make in the House later in the day.

On return to Speaker's House I had a long meeting with my secretary. We had by then both boned up on the order paper and we went through it in every detail, noting areas of particular interest or potential difficulty and identifying which members might have a particular contribution to make by way of a supplementary question or to the day's main debate. We would consider whether the record of the previous day's business suggested any likely point of order and we would discuss how I should react to applications for urgent questions or emergency debates arising out of overnight developments.

The next fixed point was a meeting at noon (remember that in my time the House generally sat at 2.30 until late evening). This was attended by the clerk of the House and the table clerks, the serjeant-at-arms and my three deputies. It was a crucial half-hour. It enabled the clerks to brief me and my deputies in detail on the day's business. Together we could discuss urgent questions and emergency debate applications and responses to known or possible points of order; and we would consider the previous day's events in a wash-up session and assess the mood of the House that day.

Following this briefing I would have a private meeting with my deputies in order to consider the speaking list for the day's debate. In many parliaments the party whips determine who will be called to speak. At Westminster, certainly until the 1960s, it was the practice for the whips to submit 'for the Speaker's guidance' lists of their members who wished to speak. But this obviously militated against members of an independent frame of mind and the practice now is for members to apply directly to the Speaker. I regarded it as one of my more important prerogatives – and woe betide any whip who sought to influence my choice of speakers. I would consider very carefully who should be called, taking account of their expertise, their membership of the relevant select committee, their constituency interest and their previous speaking record. I also had in mind the need to secure a properly-balanced debate. When I first became Speaker it was the practice to give priority to privy councillors: happily this was later abolished, thereby giving younger and new members a better chance of being called. I would also decide what limit to put on the length of speeches, taking account of the planned length of the debate and the number of applications to speak.

My final opportunity to be briefed for the day's business came just before I went into the chamber. I would meet with my secretary who informed me of any late developments and we would discuss, for example, who might be called at prime minister's questions for supplementaries. This was always a tricky time as events moved fast and I was anxious to call members who had not previously had the chance to question the prime minister. Some very speedy footwork went on, I can tell you, between me and my secretary during prime minister's questions.

In addition to this daily briefing process, I also took care to keep well abreast of political developments in a less formal way. I met weekly with the leader of the House, the government chief whip and the opposition chief whip. I had less frequent but regular meetings with the prime minister, the leader of the opposition and the leaders of the other parties. All of these meetings helped me to guage the mood of the parties and to understand what their concerns and priorities were. And it allowed them to make representations to me. I had some pretty frank discussions with senior politicians; sometimes they poured their hearts out to me in the knowledge that total confidence would prevail. And it was, of course, not only senior members that I received. All members knew I was available to lend them a sympathetic ear if they had a serious problem, for example, of party loyalty, and very many took advantage of this for a talk.

Looking back, the election of May 1997 was a watershed, not only for the nation but also for me as Speaker. The pressures on the government and the atmosphere in parliament were entirely different before and after that date. John Major's government had a paltry majority and rapidly diminishing public support; his party was fractured and fractious and he was beset by every sort of misfortune. There was truly a *fin de siècle* feel about it. Perhaps I might pick out a few incidents from that period that cast light on the Speaker's role.

The issue that gave John Major the greatest difficulty was our relationship with Europe. The Conservative Party was divided on the issue and the government could never be sure of getting its business through. A particular example came up in May 1993 in the context of the legislation implementing the Maastricht treaty. In the committee of the whole House, Michael Morris, as chairman of ways and means had allowed a debate on amendment 27, which was concerned with the applicability of the protocol on social policy, but decided not to allow a division to take place on it. This prompted what was effectively a motion of censure against him which was, of course, defeated. At report stage the issue for me was whether to allow a debate and vote on that amendment.

The selection of amendments is a very important function carried out by the Speaker. Usually it is a straightforward issue and my decision would rest largely on procedural advice from the clerks. On this occasion the clerk of the House observed that there were no clear guidelines to assist my decision and that it was, therefore, a matter for my broad political judgment and decision. He added, unhelpfully, that it was likely to be the most difficult decision I would have to take as Speaker.

Normally I would not allow representations to be made to me about the selection of amendments. But on this occasion I thought it best to let everyone have their say so that nobody could claim that their views had been ignored, and, of course, I was lobbied vigorously from all sides, with pressure being applied in various forms, both privately and publicly. In the event I decided to allow a debate and a vote. My reasoning was that apparent changes in the government's legal position at committee stage had not allowed a fully-informed debate to take place; that the government had only itself to blame if it could not carry a majority on such an issue; and that since the government had said that acceptance of the amendment would not prejudice its ability to ratify the treaty but would merely be untidy, there would be no harm in allowing a full debate and vote on the issue; but, naturally, I did not share these thought processes with the House. My decision was very unpopular with ministers, while the reverse decision would have been equally unpopular with the opposition. I was between a rock and a hard place. In the event the government decided not to oppose the amendment, on which they would certainly have been defeated.

In the context of the selection of amendments a short digression is worthwhile. When there is a government motion on the order paper it is the practice for the Speaker to select for debate and division an amendment in the name of the official opposition rather than an amendment from any other quarter. In November 2002, however, my successor surprised the House by selecting a Liberal Democrat amendment instead. The context was a major debate a few months before the invasion of Iraq. The official opposition amendment, though written in the form of disagreement with the government motion, really had the effect of supporting ministers. The LibDem amendment on the other hand proposed certain caveats before military action could be taken and I assume the Speaker took the view that its selection would allow the House to have a more focused debate. It was a brave decision and I have no doubt the right one; and it illustrates the importance of the Speaker's power of selection.

To return to *my* period of office, the precarious nature of John Major's majority meant that there was an ever-present risk of a casting vote being required. I found myself going into the chair almost every evening with a note of how I should cast my vote should it be needed. In practice there was only one such occasion, in July 1993, inevitably in a European context. In accordance with precedent I cast my vote against an opposition amendment to a government motion, in order not to create a majority on a policy issue where no such majority existed amongst the rest of the House. For similar reasons I would have voted against the government motion if the vote on that had been tied. Ironically it was discovered the next day that the votes had been wrongly counted and that there had, in fact, been a majority of one against the amendment. It was perhaps just as well that it was not the other way about.

Generally speaking the conventions relating to the casting vote were quite clear and I felt comfortable about the prospects of being seen to be opposing either the government or the opposition, since I could explain my action by reference to clear precedent. A more difficult issue arose in 1995 when the House debated the issue of the disclosure by members of earnings from consultancies. The Nolan Committee had recommended disclosure but the relevant select committee had, on the casting vote of the leader of the House, rejected this. Precedent indicated clearly that I should vote against an opposition motion which supported disclosure. I felt most unhappy about this; it should not, in my view, have been a party political matter and it went to the heart of the issue of public esteem for parliament, which was of great importance to me. The idea of casting my vote against disclosure went against all my instincts. The relevant section of Erskine May states that the Speaker is at liberty to vote according to his conscience but advises that in order to avoid any imputation on his impartiality he should, where practicable, vote in such a manner as to not make the decision of the House final and that he should explain his reasons. I was ready to explain my reasons even though my vote would have made the decision of the House final. But my advisors were most unhappy and it would have been a risky undertaking; so it was, perhaps, fortunate that in the event I was not required to use my vote on that occasion.

John Major's government was also beset by what came to be known as sleaze. This issue concerned me greatly as the misbehaviour of only a few individuals threatened to undermine the reputation of parliament as a whole. I made my views known to senior ministers in private and I was pleased when the Nolan Committee was set up and tough new rules were imposed, together with the establishment of the parliamentary commissioner for standards. But I was also heartened by Nolan's clear statement that the great majority of men and women in public life observed high ethical standards. Later, in October 1996, I made a public statement asking that the committee on standards and privileges undertake an urgent investigation into renewed allegations of misconduct that had appeared in the press. This led to the gratifying headline in the *Standard*: 'Sleaze – Speaker Acts'. A few months later I made a further statement drawing attention to the positive comments that Nolan had made and expressing the hope that the media would take a fairer and more balanced view of these issues. It is a sad comment on the integrity of the media that this statement was less well reported, and where it was, the reaction was unfavourable.

Another issue that was very much to the fore towards the end of the 1992 parliament was the so-called Arms-to-Iraq affair. Once the Scott inquiry was under way ministers declined to answer detailed questions on issues covered by the inquiry. This was a source of frustration to the opposition, especially when the table office, in accordance with established practice and with my approval, ruled such questions out of order. Robin Cook appealed to me on the basis that it appeared that the House authorities were protecting ministers from being seen to withhold information. I did not see why I should play the role of whipping-boy on behalf of the government so I advised Robin to table a question to the prime minister asking specifically if it was his policy to give substantive answers relating to matters within the competence of the Scott inquiry. When the answer 'No' was given, it was clear to all that such questions would not be allowed; but the row then was between opposition and government and as Speaker I was not involved in a political argument.

Later, when the Scott report was published, ministers indicated that opposition spokesmen would receive copies no more than one hour before publication. It was a huge report to digest. I thought this degree of notice was quite unreasonable and made my views known across the floor of the chamber. As a result, three hours' notice was granted and I think it was generally agreed that Robin Cook made an amazingly good fist of preparing his response in a very short time.

Another function of the Speaker is to decide whether to allow members to make personal statements and, if so, to approve their wording. Often this was to enable members to apologise for some misdemeanour or to explain the reasons for actions they had taken. It was as important for me as for them that the tone and content of their statements were appropriate and, though these were not frequent occurrences, I devoted quite a lot of effort to getting the statement factual. Different considerations applied in the case of statements explaining the reasons for a minister's resignation. These, too, required my permission but the text did not need my approval. This led to what was, undoubtedly, my most unhappy experience in the House. In June 1993 a minister sought my permission to make a resignation speech. I spoke with him in advance on the telephone and thought I had a clear understanding that he would not stray into matters that were *sub judice*. When he started doing so, to the great concern of the attorney general and the clerks, I had the invidious choice of either allowing him to complete his statement, with its implications for the House's relationship with the courts, or stopping him and appearing to block his freedom of speech. In the end I allowed him to continue, but to this day I am not sure whether I got it right.

Earlier that summer a senior treasury minister had in his resignation speech made a withering attack on the government over a major policy disagreement. Shortly afterwards yet another minister applied to make his own resignation speech. I knew full well that he had retired for personal reasons rather than resigned on a policy issue and, therefore, doubted whether it would be appropriate to allow him to make such a statement. But I was also reluctant to appear to be willing to sanction only those resignation speeches that pilloried the government. In this event his statement was the damp squib that I had expected and this strengthened my resolve to refuse permission to another recently retired minister who applied a few days later.

After May 1997 the atmosphere of the House was very different. A euphoric Labour government faced a demoralised Conservative opposition. The landslide majority that Tony Blair achieved knocked much of the stuffing out of the parliamentary process. And for me, too, the challenges were different.

There was an unprecedented number of new members – over 250 – all unfamiliar with the ways of the House and sometimes impatient with them. With the exception of a law officer, all those on the treasury bench, from the prime minister down, were new to ministerial office. The most obvious manifestation of their inexperience was in their handling of important policy announcements. In opposition they had become accustomed to using sympathetic media to get their message across. In government there was, too often, a temptation to do the same. Generally information was made available in the form of heavy briefing before a parliamentary statement, but sometimes ministers were tempted into indiscreet remarks on television or radio and there were even occasions when important announcements were simply made outside the House. Certainly ministers before 1997 had sometimes offended in this regard, but it undoubtedly became worse after that date. I took every opportunity to deplore this, making my views known in private to ministers as well as in the House. For example, in July 1997 I said:

> The practice of briefing in advance of a ministerial statement by Whitehall sources or ministerial aides has been current for quite a long time. My impression is that, over the past 20 years, it has progressively developed to the point where the rights of the House are in danger of being overlooked. The House is rightly jealous of its role in holding ministers to account. If it is to fulfil its function properly, it must be the first to learn of important developments in government policy. I deprecate most strongly any action taken that tends to undermine this important principle.

It will be sufficient to mention one specific example of ministerial transgression. In April 2000 ministers launched a new sports strategy at a press conference, with no parallel announcement in the House, and even the relevant documents were not made available to members. I commented that this was a clear breach of the conventions and was totally unacceptable, and I observed that there seemed to be a situation developing in some departments in which the interest of parliament was regarded as secondary to media presentation. The minister acknowledged that the House had been treated discourteously and apologised unreservedly.

I was, therefore, pleased when Gordon Brown indicated when he became prime minister that his ministers would respect parliament's rights in this regard. But I could not help remembering that his first major decision as chancellor, the independence of the Bank of England, was announced before the House convened after the general election. Could that not have waited a few days longer?

Throughout my time as Speaker I was concerned at the slow progress made at question time. I felt that this was unfair to other members and I regularly made efforts to speed things up. My office kept very careful records which allowed me to have an overview of how things were going in this regard. It was clear from these statistics that progress at both departmental questions and prime minister's questions slowed markedly after May 1997. Apart from my comments in the House I drew my concerns regularly to the attention of ministers, including the prime minister, but it generally seemed to be a losing battle.

A quite different, and very important, issue that required my attention after May 1997 arose from the election to the House of two Sinn Fein members who, whilst refusing to take the oath of allegiance (a requirement of all members), nevertheless wished to have access to the Commons and the use of all facilities and services. The issue was what access or facilities they should have and it was my responsibility to determine the matter. I took the view that members who would not take the oath of allegiance should not have access to the services of the House other than free stationery and postage since they were not fulfilling their democratic functions. I made this clear in a statement in May 1997 and I reaffirmed my decision in a meeting with the two Sinn Fein members held at their request. Subsequently the European Court of Human Rights upheld my decision and threw out their claims of discrimination as groundless. As the peace process in Northern Ireland gathered pace, ministers began to take the view that a modification of my decision would be a useful concession. Pressure was placed on me to this effect at the highest level. I made clear to ministers and I reaffirmed to the House that I was not going to modify my decision and that if the government wanted to go down this route it would need to place an appropriate motion before the House. It did not do so in my time as Speaker.

I have devoted most of this talk to functions which take place in, or are related to, the chamber. But the Speaker also carries out important functions outside the chamber. One of the most significant is taking the chair of the house of commons commission, the body which effectively runs the administration of the House and was responsible in my day for the £313 million spent each year and for the employment of 1,500 staff. But, of course, costs have risen in recent years, especially the cost of security. The current figures show that permanent staff have increased to 2,577 and expenditure for the Commons is £478 million annually. The commission is, in effect, the House's board of directors and

I have found chairing it a challenging task for which my previous career had given me no useful experience.

More to my liking was the representational aspect of the Speaker's role. This encompassed ceremonial occasions in Westminster Hall or the Royal Gallery such as the celebration of the 50th anniversary of the end of the Second World War or addresses to parliament by visiting heads of state (for example, Bill Clinton and Nelson Mandela); each such occasion required a speech on behalf of the Commons. But it also encompassed the more mundane business of receiving foreign and Commonwealth Speakers and other public figures who were passing through London (for example, Benazir Bhutto, a most impressive and courageous woman, the Spanish crown prince, a serious and seriously charming young man, and the Dalai Lama, who puzzled me by saying how much he liked my wig). It was also normal practice for ambassadors and high commissioners newly arrived in London to call on me. While the House was sitting, I found that meetings of this sort happened about twice a week and, of course, I needed to be well briefed for them. Then there were the more substantive formal visits by Speakers from overseas, who would be offered a two- or three-day programme including a dinner in Speaker's House, and there was a regular flow of foreign parliamentarians who came to see me under the auspices of the Commonwealth Parliamentary Association or Inter-Parliamentary Union.

I also regarded it as a most important representational duty to undertake visits to parliaments overseas on behalf of the Commons. Every summer recess I would spend up to three weeks travelling, and in total I visited 22 countries in all parts of the world. These included the USA, Russia, India and China. These visits were hard work but most rewarding. It was an opportunity not only to exchange views with foreign parliamentarians but also to propagate the importance of fully democratic systems in countries that were emerging from totalitarianism. To this end I made formal addresses to the Russian State Duma as well as the parliaments of Slovakia, Latvia and Ukraine. One of the messages that I sought to get across on these occasions was the importance of recognizing the rights of opposition parties and not running a system where the winner takes all. I found that this message went down very well with opposition parties but was not always well received by ministers. I recall, in particular, the stony faces of ministers in the parliament building in Bratislava and the hard time that I was given in a subsequent meeting with the unreconstructed ex-communist prime minister who, I assume deliberately, sat me opposite him with the bright sun shining from behind him and directly into my eyes and harangued me about the virtues of Slovakia. He is now one prime minister past his sell-by date. A happier memory was giving the Pandit Pant memorial lecture in the historic Central Hall of the Indian parliament in 1994, and three years later I was honoured to be invited to represent the house of commons, and the only foreign invitee, at the ceremony to mark the 50th anniversary of Indian independence.

When I left office I had some 25 outstanding invitations to visit parliaments overseas and I hope that future Speakers will take this part of their responsibilities as seriously as I did. I certainly felt that I was performing a useful function on behalf of the nation as well as on Westminster's behalf and after I had announced my forthcoming retirement I was touched to receive a charming personal letter from the head of the diplomatic service deploring my decision and saying how much our foreign relations had benefited from my exhaustive programmes of representational visits abroad.

To my staff in Speaker's House, headed by Sir Nicolas Bevan, I remain grateful for their support, loyalty and commitment throughout my period in office.

I am conscious that I have not been able to touch on every aspect of the Speaker's duties. For example, I have not mentioned keeping discipline in the House, including the use of appropriate language, ruling on questions of privilege, recalling parliament, certification of money bills, senior Commons appointments, the many organisations of which the Speaker is *ex officio* patron, president or trustee and so on. But I hope I have covered enough ground to give a full flavour of what it is like to be Speaker. I found it a most rewarding, as well as, at times, a frustrating experience. As I said in my valedictory statement, parliament is the chief forum of the nation and it is in parliament in the first instance that ministers must explain and justify their policies. If a Speaker can represent the interests of the House, protect its rights against the executive and help to enhance the effectiveness and the reputation of parliament at home and abroad, he will have justified his election.

Index

Abingdon, Willoughby Bertie, 4th earl of 120, 124
acts:
    5 Eliz. I, c. 18 102
    attainder of Sir John Fenwick (1697) 110
    dissenters chapels (1844) 125
    England not subordinate to France (1340) 18
    house of commons (administration) (1978) 2
    house of commons offices (1812) 2
    jewish disabilities (1845) 125
    occasional conformity (1711), repeal of 116
    the security of her majesty's person (1707) 114
    septennial (1716) 4
    settlement (1701) 114
    test (1673) 124
Adams, John Quincy, president of the USA 131,
    132
Addington, Henry, Speaker of the house of
    commons 116, 121, 124, 128, 130
Aland, John Fortescue 114
Albert, Carl, Speaker of the house of representatives
    135
Alcock, John, lord chancellor 24
Alexander, William see Stirling, earl of
Allington, William, Speaker of the house of
    commons 14, 19
Anderson, printer 110
Anglesey, Arthur Annesley, 5th earl of 105
Anne, queen 106, 111, 114
Annesley, Arthur see Anglesey, earl of
Argyll, Archibald Campbell, 8th earl [S] of 60
Arlington, Henry Bennet, 1st earl of 92, 93, 95, 95
Armagh, archbishop of see Boyle, Michael;
    Bramhall, John; Jones, Thomas
Ashe, John 88
Audley, (Sir) Thomas, Speaker of the house of
    commons, lord chancellor 23, 30, 31, 36

Bacon, Sir Nicholas, lord keeper 39
Baker, Sir John, Speaker of the house of commons
    22, 35, 37–9, 42, 44, 45, 47
Balfour of Burleigh, Robert, 4th lord [S] 55–7
Bampfylde, Thomas, Speaker of the house of
    commons 77–9, 84, 87, 89
Banister, Sir William 114
Bank of England 142
Banks, Robert see Liverpool, earl of
Barnewell, Patrick see Trimleston, baron
Barry of Santry, James, 1st baron [I] 64, 65, 68, 70,
    72–4
Bathurst, Allen, baron 106, 107
    Henry, 2nd earl 104
battles:
    Agincourt (1415) 10

Bosworth (1485) 23
Crécy (1346) 8, 15
Poitiers (1356) 8, 15
St Albans (1455) 21
Shrewsbury (1403) 17
Beaufort, Edmund see Somerset, duke of
Beauchamp, Sir Walter, Speaker of the house of
    commons 17
Bécherel 9
Bedford, Francis Russell, 2nd earl of 39
    John, duke of 18
Bell, Robert, Speaker of the house of commons 23,
    25, 31, 36, 39, 40, 44, 45
Bercow, John, Speaker of the house of commons 3
Bergavenny, George Neville, 5th lord 24
Berkeley of Stratton, John, 5th baron 110
Bertie, Willoughby see Abingdon, earl of
Berwick, James Fitzjames, duke of 100
Bevan, Sir Nicholas 144
Bhutto, Benazir 143
Biggar, Joseph 134
bills:
    amending Marriage Act (1781) 120
    Aylesbury election (1804) 122
    catholic relief (1813) 5
    chatitable trusts (1846) 125
    Cricklade disfranchising (1782) 109
    contractors (1782) 119
    dissenters chapels (1844) 125, 126
    dissenters marriage (1824) 123
        (1825) 124
    emancipation (1821) 123
        (1825) 123
    enfranchising catholics (1824) 123
    India (1783) 127
    insolvent debtors 120
    Irish militia (1804) 122
    Irish militia augmentations (1804) 122
    Irish municipal corporations (1840) 124, 125
    jewish disabilities (1845) 126
    loan (1783) 109
    monopolies (1601) 48
    municipal corporations (1835) 124, 128
    occasional conformity 99
    place (1705) 113
    private (1706) 110
    reform (1831) 104
        (1832) 128
    reforming the civil list 119
    reforming the university of Oxford (1749) 115
    renewing the charter of the bank of Ireland
        (1808) 108
    restoring the rights of catholic peers (1822) 123
    septennial (1716) 110

bills (cont.)
  sinking fund (1792) 118
  six articles (1539) 47
  slave trade 120
  volunteer (1804) 122
Blair, Tony 141
Blomfield, Charles, bishop of London 126
Bohun, Humphrey de *see* Northampton, earl of
  William de *see* Northampton, earl of
Bolton, Henry Powlett, 6th duke of 120
Bolton, Sir Richard, lord chancellor [I] 62, 65, 68, 71, 73, 74
Boringdon, John Parker, baron 122
Boyle, Michael, archbishop of Armagh, lord chancellor [I] 63–5, 68, 70–4
  Richard *see* Cork, earl of
  Roger *see* Orrery, earl of
Bramhall, John, archbishop of Armagh 62–5, 68, 70, 71, 73
Brand, Henry, Speaker of the house of commons 133, 134
Bray, (Sir) Reynold 26, 32
Bridgeman, Sir Orlando, lord keeper 103
Bristol, George Digby, 2nd earl of 106
Broke, Robert, Speaker of the house of commons 23, 28
Bromley, George 29, 30
  Sir Thomas, lord chancellor 29, 30, 32
  William, Speaker of the house of commons 99, 100
Brougham, Henry, baron, lord chancellor 104
Brown, Gordon 142
Bruges 8
Bryan, Guy, lord 9, 10, 14
Buckingham, George Villiers, 2nd duke of 93, 95
Buckinghamshire, George Hobart, 3rd earl of 118
Burghersh, Bartholomew, 2nd lord 15
Burghley, Sir William Cecil, 1st baron 26, 30, 40, 48
Burke, Edmund 119
Burnet, Gilbert 98
Burton, Thomas 79, 80
Bussy, Sir John, Speaker of the house of commons 15
Bute, John Stuart, 3rd earl of 114
Butler, James *see* Ormond, duke of
  Richard, baron 114
Byng, John, admiral 109

Calais 9, 16, 17
Cambridge, duke of *see* George II, king
Campbell, Archibald *see* Argyll, earl of
  John *see* Loudoun, earl of
  John, 1st baron 119
Campion, Gilbert 125
Canning, George 129, 130
Cannon, Joseph G., Speaker of the house of representatives 134, 135
Canterbury, archbishop of *see* Manners Sutton, Charles
Carey, Henry *see* Hunsdon, baron

Caroline, queen consort of George IV 111
Carteret, Sir George 96
  John, 2nd baron 106
Cassilis, John Kennedy, 6th earl [S] of 58
Catelin, Nathaniel, Speaker of the house of Commons [I] 62, 66, 69, 71, 73, 74
Cavendish, William, styled lord 97
Cavendish-Bentinck, William *see* Portland, duke of
Cecil, Sir Robert 26, 30, 48
  Sir Thomas 40
  Sir William *see* Burghley, baron
chancellor, lord 49, 50, 102
  attendance in house of lords 104
  management of parliament 112–15
  remuneration of 103
  significance of 115–17
  see also Alcock, John; Audley, (Sir) Thomas; Bromley, Sir Thomas; Brougham, Henry; Clarendon, earl of; Eldon, earl of; Hardwicke, earl of; Jeffreys of Wem, baron; King, baron; Loughborough, baron; Lyndhurst, baron; Macclesfield, earl of; Russell, John (d. 1494); Shaftesbury, earl of
  see also keeper, lord
Charles I, king 50, 54–7, 60, 63, 78, 79, 81, 83, 84, 87
Charles II, king 63, 64, 91, 93–6, 114
Charles VII, king of France 10, 19, 20
Charleton, Sir Thomas, Speaker of the house of commons 19, 21
Charlton, Sir Job, Speaker of the house of commons 90, 92–5
Chaucer, Thomas, Speaker of the house of commons 12, 13, 15–17, 19
Cheyne, Sir John, Speaker of the house of commons 11, 15
  Sir Thomas 26, 39
Chichester, Sir Arthur 66, 69, 70, 71
Chute, Chaloner, Speaker of the house of commons 77, 89
Clarence, Lionel, duke of 15
Clarendon, Edward Hyde, 1st earl of, lord chancellor 63, 67, 76, 78, 79, 81, 86, 102, 106, 111
Clay, Henry, Speaker of the house of representatives 131
Clifford, Thomas, 1st baron 93, 95
Clinton, Bill, president of the USA 135, 143
  Sir Henry 39
Clotworthy, Martha 72
Cobbett, William, *Parliamentary History of England* 119, 121
Cocks, Sir Robert 98
Coke, (Sir) Edward, Speaker of the house of commons 7, 23, 27, 36, 41, 42, 44, 45
commons, house of 49, 61
  Speakers of 59
    age 42–3, 77: fig. 5
    attendance 116
    attitude towards the press 82–4
    background of 3, 10–19, 76

commons, house of (cont.)
  clerks of 86
  election of 4, 11, 18, 22, 24–31, 77–9, 91–4,
    97, 98, 113
  executive power of 85–6
  experience of 42–5: figs 4, 6
  functions of 46, 48, 137–44
  innovator of procedure 94–5
  origins of 10
  presentation of 32–5
  pressures on 87–8
  remuneration of 46–7, 82
  reputation of 79–82, 84
  secretary of 137
  staff of 31, 35, 137, 142
see also Addington, Henry; Alington, William;
  Audley, (Sir) Thomas; Baker, Sir John; Bampfylde,
  Thomas; Beauchamp, Sir Walter; Bell, Robert;
  Bercow, John; Broke, Robert; Brand, Henry;
  Bromley, William; Bussy, Sir John; Charleton, Sir
  Thomas; Charlton, Sir Job; Chaucer, Thomas;
  Cheyne, Sir John; Chute, Chaloner; Coke, (Sir)
  Edward; Cordell, Sir Thomas; Cornwall, Sir
  Charles; Crewe, Sir Thomas; Croke, John; Cust,
  Sir John; de la Mare, Sir Peter; Doreward, John;
  Drury, Sir Robert; Dudley, Edmund; Dyer, James;
  Empson, Richard; Englefield, Thomas; Eure, Sir
  Sampson; Finch, Sir John; Fitzroy, Henry;
  Fitzwilliam, Sir Thomas; Flore, Roger; Foley,
  Paul; Foster, Hylton; Gargrave, Sir Thomas;
  Gildesborough, Sir John; Glanville, Sir John;
  Gregory, William; Hanmer, Sir Thomas; Hare,
  (Sir) Nicholas; Harley, Robert; Hungerford, Sir
  Thomas; Hunt, Roger; Lenthall, William; Lloyd,
  Selwyn; Long, Sir Lislebone; Lovell, (Sir) Thomas;
  Manners Sutton, Charles; Maybray King, Horace;
  Mordaunt, John; More, Sir Thomas; Morrison,
  William Shepherd; Moyle, Thomas; Neville,
  Thomas; Norton, Sir Fletcher; Oldhall, Sir
  William; Onslow, Arthur; Onslow, Richard;
  Onslow, Sir Richard; Pelham, Henry; Pollard,
  John; Popham, John; Popham, Sir John; Powle,
  Henry; Puckering, John; Redmayne, Sir Richard;
  Retford, Sir Henry; Rich, Richard; Rous,
  Francis; Savage, Sir Arnold; Sawyer, Sir Robert;
  Say, William; Seymour, (Sir) Edward; Sheffield,
  Robert; Smith, John; Snagge, Thomas; Stourton,
  William; Sturmy, Sir William; Thorpe, Thomas;
  Tiptoft, Sir John; Tresham, William; Trevor, Sir
  John; Turnor, Sir Edward; Tyrrell, John; Vernon,
  Sir Richard; Waldegrave, Sir Richard; Waweton,
  Thomas; Weatherill, John; Widdrington, Sir
  Thomas; Williams, Thomas; Wingfield, Humphrey;
  Wray, Christopher; Yelverton, Christopher
Commons Journal 29, 84, 87
Commonwealth Parliamentary Association 143
constituencies:
  Bedford 40
  Bedfordshire 40
  Bristol 37
  Cambridgeshire 38

  Carmarthen Boroughs 40
  Chippenham 39
  Colchester, MPs for 24
  Corfe Castle 74
  Devon 39
  Exeter 39
  Gatton 40
  Gloucester 38, 40
  Hertfordshire 40
  Huntingdonshire 38
  Kent 38, 39
  King's Lynn 39
  Lancashire 39
  Lancaster 37
  Lincolnshire 39, 41
  London 41
  Ludgershall 39
  Norfolk 39, 41
  Northampton 40
  Northamptonshire 40
  Oxfordshire 38, 39
  Rochester 37
  Steyning 37
  Suffolk 39
  Totnes 93
  West Looe 39
  Wiltshire 114
Cook, Robin 140
Cooper, Anthony Ashley *see* Shaftesbury, earl of
Coote, Charles *see* Mountrath, earl of
Copley, John Singleton *see* Lyndhurst, baron
Cordell, (Sir) William, Speaker of the house of
  commons 23, 45
Cork, Co. Cork 126
Cork, Richard Boyle, 1st earl [I] of 71
Cornwall, Sir Charles, Speaker of the house of
  commons 4, 130
Coventry, George William, 6th earl of 111
  Henry 92–5
Cowper, William, 1st earl, lord keeper, lord
  chancellor 102, 103, 106, 110–21, 114–16
Crawford-Lindsay, John Lindsay, earl [S] of 56, 58
Crewe, Sir Thomas, Speaker of the house of
  commons 34, 90
Croft, Sir James 25
Croke, John, Speaker of the house of commons 23,
  27, 30, 32, 35, 36, 39, 48
Cromwell, Henry 73
  Oliver 81
  Thomas 26
Curry, Anne 2, 3
Cust, Sir John, Speaker of the house of commons 130

Dalai Lama 143
Danby, Sir Thomas Osborne, earl of 92, 95–7
Darcy of Chiche, Thomas, 1st baron, lord
  chamberlain 27
Davies, Sir John, Speaker of the house of commons
  [I] 62, 65, 66, 69–71, 73, 74
  wife of 72

Davis, Richard 5

Daubeney, Giles, 1st lord, lord chamberlain 26

Dayton, Jonathan, Speaker of the house of representatives 131

Declaration of Indulgence (1672) 91, 93–6

de la Mare, Sir Peter, Speaker of the house of commons 9–11, 14–16, 21

de la Pole, William *see* Suffolk, duke of

Dennehy, Coleman 3

Dering, Sir Edward 94

D'Ewes, Sir Simonds 29, 80, 81, 86

Digby, George, *see* Bristol, earl of

Domville, Sir William 63, 64, 67, 69, 73, 74

Donaldson, George 51

Dongan, Thomas 70, 73

Donnellan, James 70, 73

Doreward, John, Speaker of the house of commons 13, 14

Drury, Sir Robert, Speaker of the house of commons 32, 45

Dublin, Co. Dublin 71

Dudley, Edmund, Speaker of the house of commons 45, 47

John *see* Northumberland, duke of

Duncombe, Sir John 92, 93, 95

Dunbar, Gavin, archbishop of Glasgow 59

Dunfermline, Alexander Seton, 1st earl [S] of, previously Lord Fyvie [S], lord chancellor [S] 53, 54

Dyer, James, Speaker of the house of commons 23, 35, 38

Edinburgh, Midlothian, castle 57

provost of 51

Edward I, king 8

Edward III, king 9

Edward V, king 46

Edward of Woodstock 9

Egmont, John Perceval, 2nd earl [I] of 112

Eldon, John Scott, 1st earl of, lord chancellor 103, 106–9, 111, 112, 115, 116, 119, 121–5, 127, 128

Eliot, Sir John 90

Elizabeth I, queen 27, 31, 35, 36, 44, 47

Elsynge, Henry 34

Empson, Richard, Speaker of the house of commons 23, 32, 36, 45

England, ambassador of 52

Englefield, Thomas, Speaker of the house of commons 22, 26, 27, 44, 45, 47

Épernon, Bernard de la Valette, duc d' 87

Ettrick, Patrick Ruthven, lord [S] 57

Eure, Sir Sampson, Speaker of the house of commons 78, 79, 89

European Court of Human Rights 142

Eustace, Sir Maurice, Speaker of the house of commons [I], lord chancellor [I] 62, 64, 65, 67–9, 71–4

Everard, Sir John 63, 64, 66, 69–71, 73, 74

Ferrers, George 47

Finch, Daniel, see Nottingham, earl of

Sir John, Speaker of the house of commons 96

Fitton, Alexander, lord chancellor [I] 63, 66, 69, 70, 73, 74

Fitzjames, James *see* Berwick, duke of

Fitzroy, Augustus Henry *see* Grafton, duke of

Henry, Speaker of the house of commons 6

Fitzwilliam, Sir Thomas, Speaker of the house of commons 23, 24, 41, 45

William, 2nd earl 109, 118

Fleetwood, William 25, 28

Flore, Roger, Speaker of the house of commons 12, 17

Foley, Paul, Speaker of the house of commons 4, 98, 100, 101

Tom, Speaker of the house of representatives 135

Fortescue, Sir John 32

Foster, Hylton, Speaker of the house of commons 6

Fox, Charles James 120

Henry *see* Holland, baron

Frederick, prince of Wales 103, 112

Frost, Walter 83

Fyvie, lord *see* Dunfermline, earl of

Galloway, Bruce 51

Gardiner, Sir Thomas 78

Gargrave, Sir Thomas, Speaker of the house of commons 23, 28, 42, 44, 45, 47

general elections:

(1701) 98

(1705) 99

(1708) 115

(1935) 6

(1964) 6

(1997) 138

George I, king 114

George II, king, previously duke of Cambridge 103, 114

George III, king 112, 120, 122, 127

George IV, king 112, 124

Gildesborough, Sir John, Speaker of the house of commons 14–16

Gingrich, Newt 135

Glanville, Sir John, Speaker of the house of commons 78, 87, 89

Glasgow, archbishop of *see* Dunbar, Gavin

Gledstanes, George, archbishop of St Andrews 54

Gloucester, Humphrey, duke of 13, 18, 20

Godolphin, Sidney, baron 106, 113

Grafton, Augustus Henry Fitzroy, 3rd duke of 119

Graham, John *see* Montrose, earl of

Graves, Michael 61

Gregory, William, Speaker of the house of commons 97

Grenville, William Wyndham, baron, previously Speaker of the house of commons 108, 118, 119, 121, 122, 124, 127, 130

Grenville, George *see* Temple, earl

Grey, Charles, 2nd earl 123
Grey of Ruthin, Edmund, 4th lord 21
Grosvenor, Robert, 2nd earl 107, 122
Guildford, Surr., jps in 113
Guildford, Sir Richard 32

Hamilton, James, 1st duke [S] of, previously
   marquess [S] of 53, 55, 60
   James, 4th duke [S] of 115
Hanmer, Sir Thomas, Speaker of the house of
   commons 99, 100
Harcourt, Sir Simon, lord keeper 105, 114
Hardwicke, Philip Yorke, 1st earl of, lord chancellor
   103, 105, 109, 112, 113, 115
Hare, (Sir) Nicholas, Speaker of the house of
   commons 37, 39, 42, 45, 47
Harfleur 17
Harley, Robert, Speaker of the house of commons
   4, 98–101, 111
Harper, George 39
Hastings, Francis, styled lord 108
   John de *see* Pembroke, earl of
Hatsell, Sir Henry 114
Hawkesbury, baron *see* Liverpool, earl of
Hawkyard, Alasdair 3
Hay, George *see* Kinnoull. earl of
Hayton, David 98
Heigham, Clement, Speaker of the house of
   commons 39, 42, 45
Heneage, Thomas 39
Henley, Robert, lord keeper 103, 110
Henry IV, king, previously Henry of Bolingbroke
   16, 17, 19
Henry V, king 10, 14, 17–19
Henry VI, king 20, 21
Henry VII, king 23, 26, 44, 47
Henry VIII, king 31
Henry of Bolingbroke *see* Henry IV, king
History of Parliament Trust 10, 14
Hobart, George *see* Buckinghamshire, earl of
Holland, Henry Fox, 3rd baron 108
Hooker, John 46
Hope of Craighall, (Sir) Thomas 55, 59–60
Hopton, Sir Arthur 39
Hoskins, Bennet 85
household, royal:
   comptroller of 3, 26, 30, 32; *see also* Knollys, Sir
      Francis
   lord chamberlain *see* Darcy of Chiche, baron;
      Daubeney, lord; Hunsdon, baron
   treasurer of 3, 12, 25, 26, 30, 32
   ushers of the chamber 29
   vice-chamberlain of 26, 29, 30
Howard, Sir Robert 93
Humphrys, John 137
Hungerford, Sir Thomas, Speaker of the house of
   commons 16–18
Hunne, Richard 47
Hunsdon, Henry Carey, 1st baron, lord chamberlain
   27

Hunt, Roger, Speaker of the house of commons
   17, 18, 28
Hussey, Sir William 23
Hyde, Edward *see* Clarendon, earl of

Ireland:
   constituencies:
      Athy 74
      County Tyrone 74
   house of commons, clerk of 63
      Speakers of, background of 64, 66–7, 69
         connections of 71–2
         election of 63–4
         religion of 70–1
         see also Catelin, Nathaniel; Davies, Sir
            John; Eustace, Sir Maurice; Mervin,
            Sir Audley; Nagle, Sir Richard
   lord chancellor 62, 63
      background of 65–8
      connections of 71–2
      election of 69
      religion of 70–1
      see also Boyle, Michael; Fitton, Alexander;
         Jones, Thomas; Loftus, Adam; Loftus, Sir
         Adam; Ryves, Sir Willliam
   parliaments:
      (1585) 74
      (1613) 62, 72
      (1634) 62, 72
      (1640) 62
      (1661) 62
      (1689) 62
   privy council 65
Inchiquin, Murrough O'Brien, 1st earl [I] of 72
International Parliamentary Union 143

James I, king 50–2; *see also* James VI, king
   of Scots
James I, king of Scots 59
James II, king, previously duke of York 73, 95, 114;
   see also James VII, king of Scots
James VI, king of Scots 50–4
James VII, king of Scots 60
Jefferson, Thomas, president of the USA 130
Jeffreys of Wem, George, 1st baron, lord chancellor
   115
Jewish Board of Deputies 127
John of Gaunt *see* Lancaster, duke of
Johnston, Wilfrid 129
Johnston of Wariston, Sir Archibald 60
Jones, Thomas, archbishop of Armagh, lord
   chancellor [I] 62, 62, 65, 67, 68, 70, 73
   Sir Thomas, Speaker of the house of commons
      91, 92

keeper, lord 102
   see also Bacon, Sir Nicholas; Bridgeman,
      Orlando; Harcourt, Sir Simon; Henley,
      Robert; North, Sir Francis; Wright, Sir
      Nathan; *see also* chancellor, lord

Kennedy, John *see* Cassilis, earl of
    Richard 70, 73
Keppel, Augustus, viscount, admiral 120
King, Peter, baron, lord chancellor 106
Kinnoull, George Hay, 1st earl [S] of 54
Knollys, Sir Francis, comptroller of the household
    25, 28, 30, 32

Lamb, William *see* Melbourne, viscount
Lambarde, William 26, 35
Lancaster, John of Gaunt, duke of 9, 13, 15, 16
La Rochelle 15
Latimer, Thomas Osborne, viscount 114
    William, 6th lord 9
Lauderdale, John Maitland, 2nd earl [S] of 58
Laundy, Philip 1, 5
Lechmere, Nicholas, baron 104
Leeds, Francis Godolphin Osborne, 5th duke of
    127
Lennox, Charles *see* Richmond, duke of
    Ludovic Stuart, 2nd duke [S] of 54
Lenthall, William, Speaker of the house of
    commons 76–89
Lewknor, Mr 31
Lilburne, John 81, 82
Lindsay, John *see* Crawford-Lindsay, earl of
Lisle, John 79
Littleton, Sir Thomas (d. 1681) 95, 96
    Sir Thomas (d. 1709) 98
Liverpool, Robert Banks, 2nd earl of, previously
    Baron Hawkesbury 122, 123, 127, 128
Llandaff, bishop of *see* Watson, Richard
Lloyd, Selwyn, Speaker of the house of
    commons 6
Loftus, Adam, archbishop of Dublin, lord chancellor
    [I] 67
    Sir Adam, lord chancellor [I] 62, 65, 68, 71, 74
London:
    city of 81
    Goldsmiths' Hall 86
    recorder of 24
    vintners' company 84
    Westminster Palace, Parliament Chamber 32
    Whitehall Palace, Waiting Chamber 32
    York Place 27
London, bishop of *see* Blomfield, Charles
Long, Sir Lislebone, Speaker of the house of
    commons 77, 89
    Sir Robert 93
lords, house of 31, 49, 55, 61
    lord chancellor in 54
Lords Journal 24
Loudoun, John Campbell, 1st earl [S] of 56
Loughborough, Alexander Wedderburn, baron, lord
    chancellor 119
Lovell, (Sir) Thomas, Speaker of the house of
    commons 23, 24, 32, 42, 45
Lummis, Edward 6
Lyndhurst, John Singleton Copley, lord chancellor
    119, 124–8

McCafferty, John 70
Macclesfield, Thomas Parker, 1st earl of, lord
    chancellor 70, 74, 104, 117
McCormack, John, Speaker of the house of
    representatives 135
McCready, congressman 133
Macdonald, Alan 2, 6
McKay, Sir William, 'a former clerk of the house of
    commons' 1, 3, 4, 7
Macon, Nathaniel 131
Madison, James, president of the USA 131
Major, John 138–40
Manchester, William Montagu, 5th duke of 120
Mandela, Nelson 143
Manners Sutton, Charles (d. 1828), archbishop of
    Canterbury 123
    Charles (d. 1845), Speaker of the house of
    commons 132
Mansfield, William Murray, 1st earl of 107, 109
March, Edward Mortimer, 3rd earl of 9, 10, 16
Marvell, Andrew 92
Mary, queen of Scots 44, 47, 50
Mary of Modena 14
Maybray King, Horace, Speaker of the house of
    commons 7
Maynard, Sir John, serjeant 93
Melbourne, William Lamb, 2nd viscount [I] 124
Meres, Sir Thomas 92–5, 97
Merula, Paul 65
Mervin, Sir Audley, Speaker of the house of
    commons [I] 62, 64, 67, 69, 70, 72–4
Milward, Robert 91, 92, 94
Mitford, John *see* Redesdale, baron
Montagu, William (d. 1706) 92
    William (d. 1843) *see* Manchester, duke of
Monteagle, Thomas Spring Rice, 1st baron 126
Montrose, John Graham, 3rd earl [S] of 53, 54
Mordaunt, Charles *see* Peterborough, earl of
    John, Speaker of the house of commons 23, 35,
    42, 45
More, (Sir) Thomas, Speaker of the house of
    commons 27, 44–7
Morison, William Shepherd, Speaker of the house
    of commons 6
Morris, Michael 138
Mortimer, Edward *see* March, earl of
Mountrath, Charles Coote, 1st earl [I] of 63, 64, 73
Moyle, (Sir) Thomas, Speaker of the house of
    commons 23, 35, 37, 42, 45, 47
Muhlenberg, Frederick, Speaker of the house of
    representative 130
Murray, David *see* Stormont, viscount
    William *see* Mansfield, earl of

Nagle, Sir Richard, Speaker of the house of
    commons [I] 62, 67, 69, 70, 73, 74
Naylor, James 80
Nedham, Marchamont 83, 86
Neville, Charles *see* Westmorland, earl of
    George *see* Bergavenny, lord

Neville, Charles (cont.)
 John, 3rd lord 9
 Thomas, Speaker of the house of commons 23,
  28, 29, 34, 42, 45, 47
Newcastle, Thomas Pelham Holles, duke of 106
newspapers:
 Mercurius Pragmaticus 86
 Standard 140
Nolan Committee 139, 140
North, Sir Francis, lord keeper 102
Northampton, Humphrey de Bohun, 2nd earl of
 14, 15
 William de Bohun, 1st earl of 15
Northumberland, John Dudley, duke of 27
Norton, Sir Fletcher, Speaker of the house of
 commons 129, 130
Nottingham, Daniel Finch, 2nd earl of 106

O'Brien, Mary 72
 Murrough *see* Inchquin, earl of
Oldhall, Sir William, Speaker of the house of
 commons 20, 21
O'Neill, Tip, Speaker of the house of representatives
 135
Onslow, Arthur, Speaker of the house of commons
 4, 5, 100, 101, 130
 Richard, Speaker of the house of commons 22,
  23, 25, 34, 37, 45, 47
 Sir Richard, Speaker of the house of commons
  99–101
Orleans 10
Orleans, Charles, duke of 20
Ormond, James Butler, 1st duke [I] of 63, 65, 69,
 71, 72
Orrery, Roger Boyle, 1st earl [I] of 63, 64, 73
Osborne, Francis Godolphin *see* Leeds, duke of
 Sir Thomas *see* Danby, earl of

Paley, Ruth 5
Parker, John *see* Boringdon, baron
Parker, Thomas *see* Macclesfield, earl of
parliaments:
 (1265) 8
 (1376), 'the Good' 8, 9, 16
 (1377), 'the Bad' 16
 (Nov. 1380) 16
 (1399) 11, 13
 (Nov. 1414) 17
 (1415) 18
 (1420) 18
 (May 1421) 18
 (1421) 14
 (1429) 19
 (1437) 12, 19
 (1439) 20
 (1447) 20
 (1449) 12, 19–21
 (1450) 20
 (1454) 12
 (1455) 21
 (1484) 23
 (1523) 27
 (1529) 30
 (1542) 35
 (Mar. 1553) 27
 (1563) 31
 (1572) 31
 (1593) 27
 (1640), 'the Short' 55
 (1640), 'the Long' 77, 82–5, 88
 (1644), 'the Oxford' 79
 (1653), 'the nominated assembly' 76
 (Jan. 1659) 77
 (1660), 'the Cavalier' 91, 95, 96
Parnell, Charles Stewart 133
Parsons, Sir William, daughters of 72
Paston, Robert *see* Yarmouth, viscount
Peel, Robert 123–5
Pelham, Henry (d. aft. 1660), Speaker of the house
 of commons 76, 79, 89
 Henry (d. 1754) 4
Pelham Holles, Thomas *see* Newcastle, duke of 106
Pembroke, John de Hastings, 2nd earl of 15
Perceval, John *see* Egmont, earl of
Peterborough, Charles Mordaunt, 3rd earl of 110
Phillpotts, Henry, bishop of Exeter 125, 126
Pitt, William, the Younger 111, 116, 118, 121, 122,
 124, 127, 128
Plymouth, Devon 80
Pollard, John, Speaker of the house of commons
 22, 23, 38–40, 44, 45, 47
Popham, John (d. 1607), Speaker of the house of
 commons 23, 23, 25, 29, 31, 34, 36, 37, 44
 Sir John (d. 1463), Speaker of the house of
  commons 12, 19, 23
Portland, William Cavendish Bentinck, 3rd duke of
 108
Powle, Henry, Speaker of the house of commons 98
Powlett, Henry *see* Bolton, duke of
Powys, Sir Thomas 114
Poynings, Sir Edward 32
privy council 27, 38, 44
Puckering, John, Speaker of the house of commons
 22, 23, 26–8, 36, 40–2, 44, 47, 48
Pym, John 76

Radcliffe, Edward 48
Rait, Robert 51–3
Redesdale, John Mitford, 1st baron 124
Redmayne, Sir Richard, Speaker of the house of
 commons 18
 Thomas 18
Reed, Thomas B., Speaker of the house of
 representatives 132–4
Retford, Sir Henry, Speaker of the house of
 commons 15, 16
Rich, Richard, Speaker of the house of commons
 23, 26, 29, 34, 45
Richard III, king 23

Richmond, Charles Lennox, 3rd duke of 109, 126
Roberts, Stephen 6
Rogers, Sir Edward 31
Roosevelt, Theodore, president of the USA 134
Roper, William 27
Rose, George 116
Roskell, J.S., professor 9, 11
Rothschild, Lionel de 127
Rous, Francis, Speaker of the house of commons
    76–8, 89
Russell, Francis *see* Bedford, earl of
    John (d. 1437) 18, 28
    John (d. 1494), bishop of Lincoln, lord
        chancellor 46
    Lord John 124
    William 97
Ruthven, Patrick *see* Ettrick, lord
Ryder, Dudley 105, 115, 116
Ryves, Sir William, lord chancellor [I] 62–5, 71, 72,
    74

Sacheverell, Henry, Dr 99
    William 96
Sadler, Sir Ralph 40
St Andrews, archbishop of *see* Gledstanes, George
St John, Henry 99
    Oliver 40
    Sir Oliver 71
St Malo 15
St Sauveur-le-Vicomte 9
Sainty, Sir John 116
Savage, Sir Arnold, Speaker of the house of
    commons 15, 16
Sawyer, Sir Robert, Speaker of the house of
    commons 97
Say, William, Speaker of the house of
    commons 89
Scotland:
    acts:
        (1584) 52
        (1641) 52
        anente the choosing of Robert Balfour, lord
            Burleigh to be president of the this court
            (1640) 55
        anente the electione of the precidente of
            parliamente (1641) 52
        authorising the election of the president 56
        subscription of any act 'in face of
            parliament' by a president sufficient in
            authorisation (1640) 57
    convention of burghs 59, 60
    convention of estates 54
    estate of nobles 60
    king's commissioner 51–4, 57
    king's secretary 53
    lord chancellor 49–52, 54–8, 60; *see also*
        Dunfermline, earl of
    lord president 50
    lord president of the college of justice 52
    lords of articles 50–2, 55, 57, 60

parliament:
    clerks of 57
    composition of 49
    president of 54, 56, 57
    'Speaker' of 59, 60
parliaments:
    (1593) 52
    (1604) 52–4
    (1612) 54, 55
    (1617) 54
    (1621) 54
    (1633) 54
    (1639) 55
    privy council 52, 54
Scott, John *see* Eldon, earl of
Scott Report 140
Sedgwick, Theodore, Speaker of the house of
    representatives 131
Seton, Alexander *see* Dunfermline, earl of
Seymour, Charles *see* Somerset, duke of
    (Sir) Edward, Speaker of the house of commons
        7, 90, 92–7, 99–101
Shaftesbury, Anthony Ashley Cooper, 1st earl of,
    lord chancellor 92–5, 111, 114
Sheffield, (Sir) Robert, Speaker of the house of
    commons 23, 26, 42, 45
Shelburne, William Petty, 3rd earl [I] of 109, 120
Sheridan, Richard Brinsley 130
Smith, David 49
    John, Speaker of the house of commons 99
Snagge, Thomas, Speaker of the house of commons
    40, 42, 44
'The Soldier in Late Medieval England', an Arts
    and Humanities Research Council project
    10, 11
Somers, John, baron, lord keeper, lord chancellor
    102, 110, 112, 113, 116
Somerset, Charles Seymour, 6th duke of 104
    Edmund Beaufort, duke of 12, 20, 21
Spain, crown prince of 143
Spottiswoode, Robert 55
Spring Rice, Thomas *see* Monteagle, baron
Stanhope, Charles, 3rd earl 106, 108
Stapleton, Sir Brian 18
statutes *see* acts
Stewart, John *see* Traquair, earl of
Stirling, William Alexander, 1st earl [S] of 55
Stormont, David Murray, 7th viscount [S] 109
Stourton, William, Speaker of the house of
    commons 11, 14
Strafford, Sir Thomas Wentworth, 1st earl of 63, 65,
    68, 71, 80
Stuart, Ludovic *see* Lennox, duke of
Sturmy, Sir William, Speaker of the house of
    commons 16
Suffolk, William de la Pole, 1st duke of 20, 21
    brother of 20
    father of 20
Sumner, George Holme 113
Sydney of Chislehurst, Thomas Townshend, 1st
    baron 108, 127

Talbot, Richard *see* Tyrconnell, earl of
Temple, George Grenville, earl 127
    Sir John 69, 71, 74
Thomas, Peter 4
Thomas of Woodstock 16
Thorpe, Thomas, Speaker of the house of commons
    19, 21
Thurland, Edward 92
Thurlow, Edward, 1st baron, lord chancellor 109,
    111, 112, 118–21, 127, 128
Tiptoft, Sir John, Speaker of the house of commons
    16–18
Townshend, Hayward 25
Tothill, Geoffrey 39
Traquair, John Stewart, 1st earl [S] of 55
treaties:
    Amiens (1802) 120
    Brétigny (1360) 8
    London (1641) 57
    Maastricht (1992) 138
    Troyes (1420) 18, 19
    Union (1707) 120
Tresham, William, Speaker of the house of
    commons 12, 20, 21
Trevor, Sir John, Speaker of the house of commons
    97
    Thomas, baron 114
Trimleston, Patrick Barnewall, 3rd baron [I] 71
Turnor, Sir Edward, Speaker of the house of
    commons 4, 91, 92
Turton, Sir John 114
Tyrconnell, Richard Talbot, earl [I] of 67, 69, 72
Tyrrell, John, Speaker of the house of commons 12,
    13, 19

United Provinces, ambassadors of 86
United States of America (USA):
    bill, Kansas-Nebraska (1854) 132
    congress 129, 130
    house of representatives 132
    Speaker of 10, 134
    see also Albert, Carl; Clay, Henry; Dayton,
        Jonathan; Foley, Tom; McCormack, John;
        O'Neill, Tip; Reed, Thomas B.

Vanbrugh, Sir John 112
Vernon, Sir Richard, Speaker of the house of
    commons 19
Villiers, George *see* Buckingham, duke of

Waldegrave, Sir Richard, Speaker of the house of
    commons 14, 17
Walker, Harold, deputy Speaker of the house of
    commons 6
Walpole, Horace 129
    Sir Robert 4, 5, 112
Watson, Richard, bishop of Llandaff 120
Waweton, Thomas, Speaker of the house of
    commons 14, 19
Weatherill, John (Jack), Speaker of the house of
    commons 136
Wedderburn, Alexander *see* Loughborough,
    baron
Wedgwood, Josiah 10
    Veronica 71
Wellesely, Richard, marquess 122
Wellington, Arthur Wellesley, 1st duke of 124, 127,
    128
Wentworth, Sir Thomas *see* Strafford, earl of
Westmorland, Charles Neville, 6th earl of 39
Wharton, Thomas, earl of 114
Whitelocke, Bulstrode 89
Widdington, Sir Thomas, Speaker of the house of
    commons 77–80, 84, 87, 89
Wilkins, printer 110
William IV, king 104
Williams, Thomas, Speaker of the house of
    commons 23, 25, 28, 30, 31, 39, 45, 47
    William 97
Williamson, Joseph 91
Windsor, Sir William 15
Wingfield, Sir Anthony 39
    Humphrey, Speaker of the house of commons
        22, 23, 26, 28–31, 36, 37, 42, 45
Wolsey, Thomas, cardinal 27, 46, 47
Wray, Christopher, Speaker of the house of
    commons 23, 28, 39, 47
Wright, Sir Nathan, lord keeper 103, 110
Wyatt, Sir Thomas 39

Yarmouth, Robert Paston, viscount 114
Yelverton, Christopher, Speaker of the house of
    commons 26, 28, 30, 32, 35, 36, 40, 42, 44
    Henry 40
York, Richard, duke of 12, 20, 21
    James, duke of *see* James II, king
Yorke, Charles 103
    Philip *see* Hardwicke, earl of